Defining Deviance

Defining Deviance

Sex, Science, and
Delinquent Girls, 1890–1960

MICHAEL A. REMBIS

UNIVERSITY OF ILLINOIS PRESS
Urbana, Chicago, and Springfield

First Illinois paperback, 2013
© 2011 by the Board of Trustees
of the University of Illinois
All rights reserved
Manufactured in the United States of America

∞ This book is printed on acid-free paper.

The Library of Congress cataloged the cloth edition as follows:
Rembis, Michael A.
Defining deviance: sex, science, and delinquent girls,
1890–1960 / Michael A. Rembis.
p. cm.
Includes bibliographical references and index.
ISBN 978-0-252-03606-4 (hardcover : alk. paper)
1. Female sex offenders—United States—History.
2. Inmates of institutions—United States—History.
I. Title.
HV6557.R46   2011
364.36082'0973—dc22   2010035387

Paperback ISBN 978-0-252-07927-6

For all of the young women
incarcerated at Geneva . . .

Contents

Acknowledgments ix

Introduction 1

1. "Segregation of Mental Defectives as a Preventive of Crime, Immorality, and Inefficiency" 13
2. "Defective Children in the Juvenile Court" 33
3. "The Relation Between Morality and Intellect" 53
4. "I Ain't Had Much Schooling" 72
5. "How a Girl of the Road Wins Rides and Influences Motorists" 94
6. "Little Savages" and "Psychopathic Deviates" 119

Epilogue. Defining Deviance in the Late Twentieth Century: The New "New Girl Problem"? 143

Appendix A. Illinois' Involuntary Commitment Law 149

Appendix B. Illinois' Model Sterilization Law 158

Notes 163

Selected Bibliography 199

Index 221

Illustrations follow page 52

Acknowledgments

A number of people influenced this project along the way. Mark Leff's dedication to undergraduate education and his amazing lectures inspired me to pursue a graduate degree in history. Maureen Fitzgerald's insight, wit, and ability to lead a discussion sustained me during grueling hours of my early work on this project. Each of them shaped the types of questions I chose to ask and the types of research I chose to pursue, and each in their own way shaped the outcome of this work. I would also like to thank Professor Karen Anderson for helping me grapple with the big questions both in this study and in my career. She and her husband Kent have remained close friends and valued mentors. I will forever appreciate Sarah Deutsch's precise editing of early drafts and her sense of professionalism, as well as her encouraging e-mails. Laura Briggs's knowledge of the secondary literature proved invaluable during the early stages of this project. My many colleagues also provided important feedback at critical moments in the writing process. Those who read all or part of the manuscript and endured my seemingly incessant ramblings strengthened this project.

A number of scholars and institutions provided support and encouragement. I could not have published this book without Susan Burch, Lauri Umansky, Alice Wexler, Simi Linton, and Paul Longmore, as well as the Society for Disability Studies and the Disability History Association. I owe a special thanks to Joan Catapano and all of the wonderful folks at the University of Illinois Press. The associate dean of the University of Arizona's Graduate College, Maria Teresa Velez, and Nancy Henkle of the university's Social and Behavioral Science Research Institute proved especially generous. The Department of History at the University of Arizona and the university's Women's Studies Advisory Council provided additional funding for research and travel to conferences. The Disability Studies Initiative and the

Disability Resource Center at the University of Arizona provided much-needed time and money, as well as a place to work on revisions. More recently, Essaka Joshua and Gail Bederman and the Department of History, the Department of American Studies, and the Disability Studies Forum at the University of Notre Dame have been overwhelmingly generous and have challenged me to think in exciting and interesting ways about disability history and disability studies. Finally, I would like to thank David Gerber, Francisco Vasquez, and all of the folks in the Department of History and the Center for Disability Studies at the University at Buffalo, and at People, Inc.

Numerous librarians and archivists helped access often obscure sources. I would especially like to thank everyone at the University of Illinois at Chicago, Special Collections; the University of Chicago, Regenstein Library; the University of Chicago, Special Collections; the Chicago Historical Society; the University of Illinois, Urbana-Champaign; the Illinois State Library and Archives, Springfield; the Northwestern University Archives; the archives at the American Philosophical Society Library, Philadelphia; the Geneva Illinois History Center; the Cook County Circuit Court Archives; the Harold Washington Public Library, Municipal Reference Collection; and the University of Arizona Libraries. Thanks also to Kent Hunter, who helped me gain access to the unprocessed Geneva records that at the time of this study were being stored at the St. Charles Illinois Youth Center, and to the volunteers at the University of Arizona's Disability Resource Center, who photocopied hundreds of journal pages.

Thanks to Jessica, Sherry, Joe, Meghan, Chris, Kim, and Casey for sustaining me spiritually, emotionally, and physically. And thanks to Jadwiga Pieper-Mooney and Liz Emens for reading various parts of the book manuscript.

This book would not exist without the love and support of my family, especially my father, Alex Rembis. His unquestioning assistance and unwavering dedication to the project provided me with the strength to complete it.

Finally, I would like to thank Rachel Gorman, who never ceases to make me think, and whose frank honesty, unique insight, and unbound energy have reaffirmed my belief that we can indeed change the world.

Defining Deviance

Introduction

> "With girls of defective mentality, among whom involvement in sex affairs is an outstanding phenomenon, the question of premature puberty with general physical over-development presents a serious problem. When this is combined with hyper-sexualism, there should be sufficient grounds to cause ... serious concern."
> —*Girls on City Streets*, 1940

Seventeen-year-old Dora Mae was incarcerated in the State Training School for Girls in Geneva, Illinois, in October 1940. Shortly thereafter, she found herself sitting in an exam room with psychologists eager to discover the cause of her delinquencies and prescribe a course of treatment. Experts noted that Dora Mae, who no doubt had become familiar with the examination process in school, in the courts, and at the Illinois Institute for Juvenile Research, "was very much at ease with the examiner." She understood the importance of the ritual of the exam, however, and she did her best to appear the well-informed test subject. Dora Mae's examiners noted that, "She had a rather superior attitude and spoke very precisely and only in complete sentences." Despite her confident and competent posture, the seventeen-year-old also exhibited signs of anxiety that never seemed far from the surface. The Geneva psychologist reported that Dora Mae "watched the scoring very closely," and if she thought things were not going well, she "would appear very stubborn and stern" until things went her way, then she "would smile easily." Dora Mae, as well as the rest of the young women incarcerated at Geneva, knew well the possible consequences of a poor performance on a mental examination—an extended stay at the training school was a likely possibility, and after July 1915, they could also be committed indefinitely to a state institution for the "feebleminded."[1]

Things did not go well for Dora Mae. Like so many of the inmates at Geneva, she was found to be mentally "defective." Psychologists classified her "as a borderline defective, very close to the high grade mental defective group." They concluded that Dora Mae's "behavior and attitude," as well as her test scores, were "typical of a defective child." Experts argued that their young test subject could not "be expected to carry heavy responsibilities" if she were paroled from Geneva, and would most likely "require very careful supervision" within the institution. Although Dora Mae "frequently asked to complete the 8th grade and go into high school," psychologists determined that this was not possible given her "mental ability." When she pressed the issue, experts countered by arguing that Dora Mae possessed no "insight into her limitations," which they cited as further evidence that she was indeed mentally "defective." Psychologists advised the Geneva staff to monitor their new inmate, and if she did not "adjust well" or showed "signs of deteriorating," they recommended that she be reexamined.[2]

Dora Mae's situation inside Geneva was tenuous at best. Staff reported that her adjustment in the institution was "fair." They claimed that she had become a "willing worker," but that she was "inclined to be quarrelsome" and did "not get along well with the other girls." Psychologists brought Dora back into the exam room to reevaluate her "in order to note whether there had been any mental deterioration." This time, Dora was not so calm. Experts described her as "very tense"; they noted that she spoke "very slowly" and that her "attention was poor." When she was unable to reply to one of their queries, she "made excuses for herself." Psychologists once again classified their young test subject as "borderline defective" and assigned her an Intelligence Quotient (IQ) of 71. The experts' final recommendation for Dora: "Consideration for placement in an institution for the feeble-minded."[3]

The administrators and staff at the state training school were able to consider placing Dora Mae in an institution for the feebleminded because of a state law passed in July 1915 commonly referred to as the involuntary commitment law. The new law, which had its roots in the eugenics movement, enabled the state to commit indefinitely to a state institution anyone found to be "feebleminded" by an expert. The initial intent of the law was to use a state-sponsored system of indefinite segregation as a eugenic measure to improve both society and the "race" by preventing young women like Dora from reproducing. According to its proponents, institutional segregation would simultaneously protect society from the unmitigated sexual advances of a specific cohort of young women, while also protecting those same young women from predatory men. The result, eugenicists argued, would be fewer "illegitimate" and "degenerate" children brought into the world, which over time would lead to an "improved" standard of living for a "better breed" of United States citizen. As Professor E. C. Hayes, of the University of Illinois, stated in reference to the new law and to the new science it served: ". . . eugenics, which holds out the hope not merely of cutting off the streams of defective protoplasm which flood us with subnormals, but also of breeding up the human herd to the blue-ribbon standard . . . depends not only on the advancement of biological science, but in the last analysis upon the application of this knowledge through the agencies of social control."[4] The 1915 commitment law received widespread support from a broad cross-section of middle-class women and men, including reformers, politicians, judges, lawyers, academics, and mental health professionals interested in applying the latest scientific knowledge and the most "progressive" means to "breed up the human herd" and "improve" society.

Illinois was not alone. The creation and implementation of a state-sponsored system of involuntary commitment in Illinois was part of a much larger, national eugenics movement. On November 7, 1915, just four months after Illinois' governor signed the commitment law, *Chicago Daily Tribune* health columnist and eugenicist, Dr. W. A. Evans, informed his readers of a nationwide eugenics program that was being "pushed" by the Eugenics Record Office (ERO) in Cold Spring Harbor, New York. The program, which was set to receive "heavy financial backing," was based on a proposal outlined in a paper presented by well-known eugenicist Harry Laughlin a year earlier at the first National Conference on Race Betterment, held in Battle Creek, Michigan. According to Evans, Laughlin's plan consisted of "cutting off the supply of defectives—by education, restriction, segregation, and sterilization." These four measures would complement one another and, over the course of seventy years, from 1915 to 1985, would "purify" the United States by eliminating the lowest 10 percent of the country's racial "stock." Evans estimated that fifteen million Americans would be sterilized; countless others would be institutionalized; so-called defectives would be barred from entering the country; and all of this would be made possible through an elaborate system of eugenic education that would extol the virtues of being well born. Evans assured his readers that "good lawyers" had informed Laughlin that the eugenics program would not violate the Fourteenth Amendment, which provides equal protection under the law for all Americans. Evans chose to title his column "Rebuilding a Nation."[5]

Rebuilding a Nation—From the Inside Out

This study focuses on one aspect of Laughlin's four-point plan to rebuild the nation. It is an analysis of segregation—often referred to as institutionalization, or indefinite commitment. Most of the evidence comes from Illinois, a national center of eugenic reform. This, however, is not an institutional history.[6] Instead, I analyze the commitment campaign and the incarceration of young women like Dora to reveal the centrality of sex, class, gender, and disability in the formation of both scientific and social reform discourse. Race too is important in this narrative, but it remains marginal. It could be said that race is present only in its absence. This is largely because explicit dichotomous articulations of racial difference (black/white) were virtually nonexistent in the utterances of the northern eugenic reformers who occupy these pages. We will encounter African American inmates incarcerated at Geneva. In fact, blacks comprised about 10 percent of Geneva's inmate population during the period under investigation. I have found no evidence, however, that indicates black girls were overrepresented among the ranks of Illinois' "feebleminded" and "mentally defective." The majority of the young women in this study were first-generation "white" ethnic Americans whose parents had migrated from various parts of Europe (primarily the north and west) and Canada in search of work in Chicago's bustling industrial and manufacturing sectors. The one thing all of the girls in this study had in common is that they were all found to be both "delinquent" and "defective."

This is a disability history. The advent of eugenics, and psychology and psychiatry, as well as broad-based efforts to rebuild a nation that appeared to many white middle-class observers to be wracked by rapid industrialization, urbanization, and immigration hinged upon a relatively recent, continually changing discourse of disablement, which in this case got materialized through popular perceptions and scientific definitions of mental and psychological "defect."[7] In the end, *Defining Deviance* is a history of the social construction of impairment itself, told through the lives of young women like Dora.[8] Though it takes a constructivist approach, this history does not seek to minimize, dismiss, or otherwise deny delinquent girls' embodiment or the material forces that produced both their delinquency and their "defect." On the contrary, it seeks to place delinquent girls and their often troubled lives at the center of an analysis of late nineteenth- and early twentieth-century reform discourse.

Defining Deviance is the story of the ways in which female adolescent "sex delinquents" became entangled in the national rebuilding project, and of their resistance to that project. It spans seventy years (ca. 1890–1960) and involves a diverse group of social actors. Numerous laypeople weave their way in and out of this narrative, but the main characters are teenage girls like Dora and the dizzying array of largely female experts who examined them. This is a story of contestation; contestation between adolescent female "sex offenders" and the women and men attempting to diagnose and treat them; and between the latter over the best possible, most effective means of diagnosing and treating a vulnerable group of young women and ultimately "improving" society.

Gender and class are key in *Defining Deviance*. Tracing the historical trajectory of eugenic segregation in Illinois has enabled me to shift the focus of the investigation away from the individuals most readily associated with eugenics onto a different set of actors, many of whom were women. Illinois has a rich history of being in the vanguard on social reform issues, and of being a place where women possessed a relatively powerful voice.[9] The experts in this study, many of whom lived and worked in Illinois, are a seemingly endless list of female physicians, judges, institution administrators, eugenic fieldworkers, social and settlement workers, and psychologists. Clubwomen and women reformers also figure prominently in this study. Unlike previous scholars, I argue that women played more than a supportive role in the formation of eugenic discourse and public policy, especially at the state and local level.[10] Middle-class white women's perceived ability to speak for "less fortunate," working-class women and children, and their status as professionals, empowered them in ways that have not been fully articulated or analyzed. By focusing on the debates that arose among female experts and reformers and their male colleagues, *Defining Deviance* makes salient the importance of gender and class in the formation of categories of impairment (feeblemindedness, mental defect) and reveals the deep-rooted connections among eugenics, disability, sexual regulation, and the emergence of a "modern," industrial urban society.

Female experts and reformers are not the only women in this story. Central to this narrative are teenage girls, like Dora. Young working-class women stood at the center of the eugenic commitment debate. Both male and female eugenicists focused their campaign to rebuild the nation on a specific group of "sexually delinquent" adolescent women whom they classified as either "feebleminded" or "mentally defective," and as the potential progenitors of large "defective" families.[11] Experts and much of the general public associated female sex delinquency with mental "defect" and argued that as a rule, "feebleminded" women had more children than their "normal-minded" counterparts. As Dr. Evans asserted in his 1915 column, "When we look into any of the well known histories of degenerate families . . . we find that the descent was from a feeble minded woman and not from a feeble minded man. . . . The feeble minded female has no mental power of resistance. Feeble-minded and idiot females are very prone to bring large families into the world. Their children are defective in one way or another."[12] Frequently eugenicists argued that the most progressive and the most effective way to prevent their delinquency and reduce the number of "defective" children born each year was to segregate young women indefinitely in a state institution.

Through the eugenic commitment campaign, impairment itself became gendered. Dominant notions of proper gender and generational roles and normative (white, middle-class) heterosexual behavior profoundly influenced both popular and social scientific understandings of eugenic fitness. Young "sex delinquents" like Dora, who violated the boundaries of "normal" female adolescent behavior, found themselves caught in a growing juvenile justice and mental health system that planted their actions firmly inside "feeble" or "defective" minds and "psychopathic" personalities. In more modern terms, they were diagnosed as having an impairment that prohibited them from functioning "normally" in society. They were disabled. Contestation arose, however, when young women like Dora, who rooted their actions not in some innate defect but rather in a growing adolescent peer culture or in a neglectful and abusive childhood, challenged the notion that they were indeed "impaired." *Defining Deviance* foregrounds and analyzes these important gender, generational, and class dynamics, which relied largely upon heteronormative notions of proper sexual activity, as they played themselves out not only in the creation of a scientific taxonomy of deviance, but also in the contestation that arose within and around the classificatory process.

Dora Mae and the other girls entangled in the burgeoning juvenile justice and mental health system were not merely the passive recipients of a subjectivity thrust upon them by a hierarchical system of oppression. To the extent possible, they actively participated in the formation of their own identity, which in turn had larger implications both for their own lived experiences and for the formation of various categories of impairment that continue to affect *psy* discourse in the twenty-first century. As Johanna Schoen and Molly Ladd-Taylor each argue in their respective studies of sterilization, we need to begin to think of the subjects of eugenic, and I would add psychological and psychiatric, discourse as being something more complex than mere victims or "heroes of their own lives."[13] By making a detailed analysis of eugenic segregation in Illinois, I move past what sociologist Nikolas Rose calls a historical "critique" of science toward a critical history of the formation of disabled identities, and a more socially complex rendering of the lives of individuals perceived to be disabled.[14]

As a critical history, *Defining Deviance* does not assume that impairment is fixed, natural, or transhistorical. In this sense, it interrogates the social construction of what generally are considered scientific "truths." Scholars have written excellent historical critiques of eugenics, psychology, psychiatry, and science generally, but they are just beginning to write a critical history of impairment. The historical critique of science has shown that human interests form all knowledge, and that the development of scientific knowledge in most patriarchal, Western, capitalist societies is intimately linked with attempts to conquer and control nature. The historical critique of science has shown, moreover, that knowledge serves power. It has unmasked what Rose describes as "servitude disguised as objectivity" and "manipulative ambition disguised as rationality." Historical critique has posed important questions regarding the relationship between knowledge and society, between truth and power, between science and subjectivity; but as Rose points out, it has done so in "a rather reductive manner." Science, when viewed through the lens of historical critique, is socially significant only in that it "serves functions, manipulates persons, enforces adaptation, legitimates status, disguises lack, provides false comforts, and the like." In other words, science becomes "a sign, symptom, exemplar, or effect of power relations." Though valuable and important, a historical critique of science leaves unexamined what Rose refers to as the "power effects" of scientific discourse.[15] Science becomes a product of power relations rather than a formative component of those relations. Historical critique leaves little room for a critical history of scientific discourse itself, one that would enable us to think differently about our current forms of scientific "truth." *Defining Deviance* contributes to an emerging critical disability history by problematizing and historicizing the very notion of mental "defect."

Rather than accept or reject the presence of defect—as previous historical critiques of eugenics have done—I think of it as a socially and historically situated state of being that was worked out both practically and discursively between subjects and experts. In thinking about the social construction of mental defect, I draw heavily upon the work of Rose, as well as Mark Rapley, Kurt Danziger, and a growing contingent of second wave disability theorists.[16] I begin with the assumption articulated by Rapley that a category of personhood or identity is not a fixed object in a static world, but rather a "status of being-in-the-world" that is actively negotiated—if not always from equal positions of power.[17] In this case, the state of being "feebleminded," "mental defective," "sexual psychopath," or "psychopathic deviate" is not an immutable essence embodied in the disabled subject; it is a product of the modes and means of the production of knowledge systems that get worked out discursively and "interactionally" between experts and their subjects. Such identities are, as Rapley notes, "essentially fluid." They are both "situationally constructed" and "contestable."[18]

Thinking of mental defect as a fluid state of being enables me to interrogate the social construction of impairment from a novel vantage point, namely that of the young women perceived as impaired, such as Dora.[19] It enables me to ask a whole series of important questions: what, for example, did it mean both ideologically and practically, vis-à-vis the dominant nondisabled culture, for adolescent "sex delinquents" to be classified as "defective" (impaired)? How did definitions of impairment change over time? Did young women accept their classification? Did they reject it? How fluid was their disabled identity? How and why and when did it manifest itself? What were the consequences of being classified as "defective" for young women? And finally, how did their subjective experiences influence the formation of scientific "truths" that continue to form the foundation of psychological, psychiatric, and eugenic knowledge at the beginning of the twenty-first century?

The point of this investigation is not to condemn late nineteenth- and early twentieth-century reformers and practitioners; nor is it to decide what is or is not impairment. Assigning twenty-first-century diagnostic labels to late nineteenth- and early twentieth-century behaviors is both futile and anachronistic. The majority of the young women in this study acted out, sometimes violently, both inside and outside the institution, most of them came from abusive and neglectful homes, and many of them became the victims of sexual assault. The majority of the girls had little, if any, formal schooling and many learned to express themselves in deviant, defiant, and in some cases, destructive ways. It can be argued (quite easily) that the diagnostic and treatment regimes developed and deployed by eugenic reformers were at once an ideological imposition of their own middle-class values and standards on working-class girls *and* an earnest attempt to explain outward manifestations (some might say "symptoms") of physiological and psychological phenomena (some might say "pathology"). The more important task before the historian of disability and eugenics is to engage simultaneously in a sustained analysis (critical history) of the formation of power/knowledge systems of "impairment" and to retrieve and recount, as much as the scant sources will allow, the lives and experiences of the young women who found themselves caught at the center of this emerging discourse.

Eugenics and Other *Psy* Discourses

We cannot begin to analyze the creation of various categories of impairment without first acknowledging their social, cultural, and historical location.[20] The social construction of a particular understanding of impairment can be linked directly to the rise of both social reform and social scientific discourse during the late nineteenth and early twentieth centuries. The period of this study (ca. 1890–1960) was one of profound global restructuring characterized by massive migration, social and economic displacement, vicious and often bloody class conflict, and ultimately by the emergence of a new modern urban, industrial, capitalist order. Chicago, the hub of the nation's transportation, manufacturing, and commercial networks, literally stood at the center of this often violent and conflicted transformation, and as a result also became a center of "progressive" reform and social science research. Though they disagreed over subtleties, an emergent group of middle-class experts and reformers, driven by their own ambition to secure a foothold in the American psyche and a positivist modernizing ethos that centered upon "bringing order to chaos" and "improving" society, used science and the state, as the historian Michael McGerr argues, "to remake society in their own image."[21] The efforts of scientists and social reformers had a lasting impact on modern articulations of impairment, the legacies of which will be traced in this study.

One historian of social science has referred to the period around the turn of the twentieth century as an "age of scientific revolution."[22] The "knowable" universe expanded with the work of individuals such as Max Planck, Albert Einstein, and Sigmund Freud, and new technologies such as the x-ray. Even more important for our discussion was the publication of Darwin's *On the Origin of Species* (1859) and *The Descent of Man* (1871), as well as the emergence of social Darwinism and the notion of the survival of the fittest made popular by British philosopher and sociologist Herbert Spencer. Darwin's work, among other things, led directly to the aristocrat statistician Sir Francis Galton's creation of the science of eugenics, which he formally named in 1883.[23] Galton's work, in turn, fueled the interests of Karl Pearson, the man most readily associated with the creation of modern statistical analysis. Galton's work also found a welcome home in the United States, where Charles Benedict Davenport and Harry Laughlin, with the help of their wealthy benefactors, were building the institutional base for an international eugenics movement. By the early twentieth century, both the material foundation and the ideological scaffolding that Dr. Evans and other leaders of the national rebuilding project would rely upon had become part of what Snyder and Mitchell have referred to as the "eugenic Atlantic."[24]

Essential to both social science research and social reform discourse were increasingly narrow definitions of normality. As scholars have shown, the *psy* discourses, with their attendant technologies of power, profoundly and perhaps permanently altered perceptions of normality.[25] Lennard Davis has argued that normality has a history, and it can be traced roughly to the mid-nineteenth century.[26] In the premodern and early modern eras, when most people living in the Western world held a profoundly religious worldview, the human condition was measured in light of a Divine ideal that no one save the reigning monarch could hope to achieve. The Enlightenment and the rise of modern biomedicine began to change perceptions of human diversity.[27] The advent of statistics, Darwinism, and eugenics during the nineteenth century produced a new conception of normality rooted not in creationism but rather the "normal distribution" of a given trait within a "controlled" subject pool, or the "standard deviation" from a socially constructed mean. Statistics, along with the experiment—within which I would include the "standardized" test—became what Rose refers to as "truth techniques" developed and deployed by social scientists in their "materialization" of scientific "truths." As other scholars have pointed out, and as this study will show, the development and acceptance of various "truth techniques" and the scientific "truths" they created were neither immediate nor uncontested.[28] This, however, did not stop eugenicists such as Evans from making claims concerning the power of science to rebuild the nation from the inside out.

By 1915, it had become common for a whole host of reformers, experts, and other advocates interested in "improving" life in America to turn to eugenics. Evans, who regularly wrote on eugenics in his column, "How to Keep Well," first introduced Chicagoans to it in 1912. On March 10, 1912, Evans pleaded with the readers of the *Tribune:* "If you have not seen the *American Magazine* for March, get it and read, 'A New Science and Its Findings,' by Nock." Excited to educate the readers of his daily health column, Evans provided a brief definition of eugenics that came straight from Galton himself. According to Evans's reading of Galton, eugenics was the science that dealt with "all influences that improve the inborn qualities of the race." For further clarification, Evans turned to Davenport, who was director of the Eugenics Record Office in 1912. "The eugenical standpoint," Davenport declared, "is that of the agriculturist who, while recognizing the value of culture, believes that permanent advance is to be made only by securing the best blood. Man is an organism—an animal—and the laws of improvement of corn and of racehorses hold true of him also. The success of a marriage from the standpoint of eugenics is measured by the number of disease resistant, cultivable offspring that come from it." According to eugenicists like Evans, campaigning for pure milk and crusading against infant mortality—both of which he did as Chicago's health commissioner—were vital reform efforts, but they attacked only part of the problem. "We have been so busy with environment," Evans asserted, "that we have forgotten team work. Race betterment is loaded in a two horse wagon, to which is hitched Improved Environment and Eugenics."[29] The message in Evans's column was clear. Here at last was a means of affecting real, lasting change, but only if reformers and the American public embraced the new science and its findings.

Although they harbored lingering reservations concerning the new science, eugenicists made bold assertions about its power to "improve" society. Evans and other eugenicists contended that insanity, alcoholism, drug addiction, cancer, consumption, neurosis, hereditary deafness, multiple sclerosis, and many other "ailments," "conditions," "diseases," and "handicaps" could all be greatly reduced or even eliminated only if society worked toward improving the quality of the gene pool as well as the swimming pool. According to eugenicists, breeding up the human herd would result in improved morals as well; adultery, prostitution, and "illegitimate" births would all be greatly reduced because teenage "sex delinquents" like Dora would be confined to institutions during their reproductive years.

Despite his enthusiasm for eugenics, Evans, like most Americans, remained wary of the new science. He held some doubts about a science that dated back only a few years. Eugenics was, as he stated in the title of one of his columns, "the baby science." It was "immature in years" and would "certainly be immature in its conclusions." Errors would creep into some of the findings; some of its principles would be abandoned; other principles would be modified, but in the end, Evans believed that the "methods and the general outlines" of eugenics would stand the test of time. When it came to implementing eugenic measures, Evans remained even more cautious. "We will all agree," he argued, "that man made laws will never supplant the laws of nature. Even the laws of custom and society will yield slowly, where they yield at all. The students of eugenics, as a general rule, think the regeneration of the race will come about more through intelligence and information than through legal enactments." According to Evans, eugenicists preferred simply to "state the known facts and the principles deducible from them, and then to leave the results to the wisdom of men."[30] This nexus that Evans articulated so clearly, this point of contestation, of formulation and formalization, the point at which scientific "facts" got created and principles became "deducible," and power got deployed by wise men—or in this case mainly women—forms the core of this analysis.

Organization

Defining Deviance is divided into six chapters. The first three chapters track the development of scientific explanations of social problems in the United States from the 1890s through the 1930s, with a specific focus on Illinois. The chapters analyze the influence that a gendered, middle-class conception of eugenic "fitness" had on both the social construction of the defective female sex delinquent and on the formation and implementation of a state-sponsored system of indefinite segregation. Central to the first three chapters is an examination of eugenics infiltration into American popular culture and the social sciences, as well as the role it played in the formation of the juvenile justice and mental health systems.

In the first chapter, I analyze the influence that an ascendant eugenic discourse had on women reformers and women professionals, who in turn played a pivotal role in the passage of Illinois' new commitment law. In chapter 2, I examine the biologization and sexualization of female delinquency through an emergent social science discourse that relied upon the authority of dominant assumptions concerning gender, class, sexuality, and generational roles. Critical to the second chapter is an analysis of how white, middle-class women who at least rhetorically dedicated their lives to protecting the welfare of "less fortunate" women and children came to focus their commitment campaign on a vulnerable group of ethnically white, working-class women. In chapter 3, I broaden the historical focus by analyzing both changes in eugenic thinking and the rise of new community efforts to prevent delinquency during the interwar period. The two developments, I argue, were very much related. Crucial to chapter 3 is a discussion of the persistence of eugenic commitment and the resilience of mental classifications of female sex delinquents despite changing attitudes and the rise of new systems of intervention. Biological explanations of social deviance and the perceived need for eugenic confinement did not disappear during the 1920s and 1930s. They merely became part of a much broader approach to the study and prevention of juvenile delinquency and "race betterment."

An analysis of the ritual of the examination, both inside and outside the exam room, is vital to chapters 4 and 5. In these chapters, I go inside the institution, focusing specifically on the interactions between experts and their subjects, in an effort to deconstruct the social and relational processes that gave rise to various classifications of mental "defect." The two chapters bring to light the contestation that occurred as experts attempted to use mental, psychological, and psychiatric evaluations to construct a seemingly "normal" (in appearance), largely white, working-class group of adolescent women as "defective" and in need of indefinite incarceration.

In chapter 6, I widen the historical lens once again by examining changes in both social attitudes and scientific theories concerning the causes and possible treatments of delinquency after the Second World War. I argue that changes in some states, like Illinois, that began before the war dominated social science and social reform discourse in the postwar period, eventually leading to the end of eugenic commitment by the 1950s. Although the circumstances under which girls were committed to Geneva had not changed much in the sixty-odd years of the institution's existence, the ways in which experts thought about the perceived impairment that supposedly caused female juvenile delinquency and the possible consequences of female juvenile delinquency had changed considerably, so that explicitly negative eugenic measures no longer figured prominently in discussions of possible prevention and treatment programs.

Eugenic institutionalization may have ended by the 1950s, but remnants of eugenic thought continue to surface in more recent scientific, legal, and popular efforts to delimit young women's sexuality and define their (mis)behavior. In the epilogue, I briefly consider the role of disability in what I call the new "new girl problem."

At its core, this book shows how prevailing notions of gender and sexuality and generational roles led to a disciplining of delinquent women through the construction of certain changing definitions of impairment not by a cadre of domineering male scientists, but by a loosely organized, often contradictory collection of maternalist reformers, women professionals, and their male colleagues. More important, it reveals the contestation that arose in the creation of systems of evaluation designed to mark, measure, and classify young women whom the dominant society perceived as a threat not only to the sexual and eugenic purity of the American race, but to the very existence of "modern" America.

1

"Segregation of Mental Defectives as a Preventive of Crime, Immorality, and Inefficiency"

> "The best minds of to-day have accepted the fact that if superior people are desired, they must be bred; and if imbeciles, criminals, paupers and otherwise unfit are undesirable citizens they must not be bred."
> —Victoria C. Woodhull Martin, 1891

> "To be of eugenic value an institution for defectives must retain its charges permanently."
> —Dr. Clara Harrison Town, 1914

On July 1, 1915, after nearly twenty years of intense lobbying and debate, Illinois became one of the first states to pass a eugenic commitment law. House Bill No. 655, which passed both the House and the Senate without a single dissenting vote, provided for the legal commitment of "feebleminded" persons.[1] Under the new law, a judge who suspected that an individual who appeared before the court was "mentally deficient" could order a commission to examine the defendant. If the commission found the defendant to be "feebleminded," then the court could deal with the individual as such, and not as a criminal.[2] *The Institution Quarterly*—a journal issued jointly by the Illinois State Board of Administration, the State Charities Commission, and the State Psychopathic Institute—explained to its readers that the new law enabled the state to commit an offender to an institution for life, "not on account of his crime or offenses, but on account of his mental deficiency."[3] Proponents of the new law touted it as one of the first comprehensive plans for "cutting off streams of defective protoplasm" and "breeding up the human herd."[4] They argued that the new system of indefinite segregation would remove a group of individuals who were "necessarily poor, underfed, unhappy—altogether wretched" from the community and place them in an institution where they would be "childishly happy." Reformers asserted, moreover, that the new system would improve both society and the race permanently by preventing "feebleminded" individuals from propagating "their kind—the defective degenerate kind."[5] The commitment law received widespread support from experts and laypersons interested in using the state and eugenics to "breed" better humans, curb delinquency, and improve Chicago's slums.

Like most reform efforts in Illinois, the campaign to enact the 1915 commitment law was waged by both middle-class women and middle-class men. The committee that drafted the commitment bill consisted of a cross section of Illinois' vibrant middle-class reform community and included medical doctors, a psychologist, a legal scholar, a judge, a social worker, and a member of the Illinois Federation of Women's Clubs (IFWC). Among the many organizations that supported the bill were the Illinois State Charities Commission, the Chicago Municipal Court, the Illinois State Medical Society, and the IFWC. Four members of the ten-member committee that drafted the original bill were women.[6] Mrs. A. E. (Lulu Treat) Walker, chairman of the Legislative Committee of the IFWC, represented her organization at committee meetings. The other three women who served on the committee were professionals. Dr. Anna Dwyer was the physician to the Morals Court, as well as a member of the Illinois State Charities Commission. Dr. Clara Harrison Town served as director of the Department of Clinical Psychology at the Lincoln State School and Colony for the Feebleminded, and later obtained a position as a psychologist at the Orthogenic Clinic at Rush Medical School in Chicago. Town also served as the IFWC's resident expert and advisor on matters concerning feeblemindedness, delinquency, and eugenics, and represented the IFWC in Springfield when House Bill no. 655 came before the Illinois General Assembly. The last woman on the committee was Minnie Low, superintendent of the Bureau of Personal Service, a prominent social work agency.[7] As this brief sketch indicates and as this chapter will show, a diverse group of white, middle-class women played a critical role in the debate over the eugenic segregation of Illinois' "defective" residents and ultimately worked closely with their male colleagues to create a state-sponsored system of eugenic commitment.[8]

Maternalist Reformers and the Eugenic Commitment Law

Women's involvement in eugenics arose, in part, out of their presumption that they possessed the power and authority to speak as "universal mothers" on behalf of impoverished women and children.[9] Throughout the nineteenth century, middle-class white women increasingly extended their role as wife and mother—a role that the dominant Anglo-American culture imbued with reformative capacities—beyond their own homes. By the end of the century, they had become highly visible, influential advocates of a number of reform efforts designed ostensibly to improve the lives of immigrant and working-class women and children. Women's historians refer to these women as maternalist reformers. Both "traditional" and "professional" maternalists worked closely with one another, and with their male colleagues, to make eugenic commitment a reality in Illinois.[10]

For traditional maternalists, such as Walker and the members of the IFWC, the eugenic commitment law represented yet another way to use science and the state to improve the lives of Illinois' less-fortunate citizens. Formed in 1894, the IFWC initially consisted of sixty clubs. In less than twenty years, the Illinois Federation became one of the largest, most active state federations in the General Federation of Women's Clubs, boasting 561 clubs and more than fifty thousand members.[11] The women of the IFWC considered themselves "women of the old type," who maintained a "motherly heart" and looked "well to the ways of their own households," as well as those of other, less fortunate women. They promoted legislation designed to improve everything from public health and working conditions for women and children to the quality of roads and public libraries.[12] They were eager, however, to employ new methods and extend the boundaries of reform, and they worked actively to create the eugenic commitment law.

In 1914, Walker recommended that the federation unite on one fundamental legislative measure designed to provide permanent custodial care for all "feebleminded" persons living in Illinois. According to Walker, the eugenic commitment law would provide "treatment and surveillance, not punishment" to a class of "feebleminded" individuals who "under suitable surroundings and environment" would be "reasonably content . . . useful citizens." Without such care, the same "feebleminded" individuals would commit society's "worst crimes" and live a life of "unhappiness, misery, and degradation."[13]

At the end of 1914, clubwomen met in what the *Chicago Daily Tribune* described as the "first women's legislative congress," where they discussed a broad range of reform initiatives. When the women closed the first day of their legislative session, they had passed six measures, two of them eugenic. The first was "a eugenics law demanding a health certificate from all persons before marriage, with severe punishment for those who violate or who assist in the violation of the law." The second measure was the eugenic commitment law. On the last day of the women's congress, amid a flurry of debate, a majority of the women present decided to reject the eugenic marriage law, but not the commitment law. In all, there were more than twenty measures endorsed during the three-day session. Illinois' lieutenant governor, who was overseeing the meetings, assured the women that their bills would be presented to the state legislature during the next session.[14]

The clubwomen left their meetings at the Congress Hotel in December 1914 certain their voice would be heard. Walker, who served on the committee that drafted the official commitment bill, must have been emboldened by the show of support. She proudly reported in December 1915 that although the Federation Board had endorsed other bills that year, they had put their greatest efforts toward the bill for the "Commitment and Care for Feeble-Minded Persons."[15] For the women of the IFWC, the commitment law represented the vanguard of progressive legislation. It was the manifestation of the cumulative efforts of scientific experts, middle-class reformers, and political leaders to use science and the state to solve long-standing social problems.

For professional maternalists, the campaign to create the commitment law grew out of their educational and practical, work-related experiences. All three women professionals who served on the committee that drafted Illinois' commitment bill fell squarely within the burgeoning ranks of "new women" who were attending college and graduate and professional school in greater numbers each year, and who focused their studies in areas that represented the forefront of the emerging mental health and social work professions.[16] Although they faced restricted access to medical and graduate school, and severely limited training and career options, middle-class women created a niche for themselves in "maternalist medicine" and public health.[17] They sought out, and in some cases created, local, state, and national agencies that would provide them with room for employment, advancement, intellectual growth, and the opportunity to work with women and children.[18] In Illinois, professional maternalists were instrumental in creating the Juvenile Court, the Juvenile Psychopathic Institute, and the Juvenile Protective Association, as well as other organizations that provided services to women and children.[19] The first female judge in the country, Judge Mary Margaret Bartelme, sat on the bench of the Cook County (Chicago) Juvenile Court, and other women professionals, such as Superintendent Low and Drs. Town, Dwyer, and Clara Hayes, held important positions in other state institutions and organizations.

Female professionals steeped in scientific training took a pragmatic approach to solving social problems and were willing to experiment with new methods of reform, including eugenic measures, which by the second decade of the twentieth century had become a significant part of both popular and scientific discourse.[20] With its emphasis on using science to improve both the race and society, eugenics appealed to a broad cross-section of Americans, including women working in the newly emerging *psy* professions and social work. As Linda Gordon put it in her now classic study of birth control, "free lovers and suffragists alike" were willing to use eugenics to achieve their reform goals.[21] Professional maternalists embraced eugenics in part because it provided seemingly simple solutions to complex social problems. Proponents presented eugenics as an overarching theory of human development with far-reaching scientific and social implications.[22]

Eugenics also fit well with dominant scientific theories that rooted modern social problems in the minds and bodies of the deviant "other"—poor people, new immigrants, anarchists, people with disabilities—and not in social, economic, or political systems.

By 1915, the year the Illinois legislature passed the commitment law, eugenics had gained widespread acceptance among the American public. As early as January 1908, the *Chicago Daily Tribune* posed the question to its readers, "Why Not Improve the Human Race?" in the form of a full-page article on eugenics. An illustration depicting a "new woman" wearing a graduation gown and mortarboard "weeding" the garden of humanity covered most of the page.[23] A few months later, the *Tribune* announced that, "Eugenics is now decidedly in the air." The article explained that it could be "fairly deduced that eugenics is a progressive social science on the banner of which might well be inscribed: Soon health is wealth; good birth is worth; that our increased and increasing knowledge of the laws that regulate the ascent and descent of man imposes on us the duty of encouraging the spread of this new science as a wholesome, moral, and necessary department of thought and learning."[24] For its proponents, eugenics represented the scientific exploration of all things relating to human reproduction and "race betterment," both of which had taken on increasing importance in the wake of Charles Darwin, Herbert Spencer, and Francis Galton.

Americans were reading almost daily of a vast array of schemes designed to improve the human race. In 1909, *Tribune* readers learned of the eugenic plan proposed by Dr. Eugene Davenport, dean and director of the College of Agriculture of the University of Illinois. Davenport apparently "created a great sensation among the several hundred doctors" attending what a *Tribune* reporter described as "one of the largest meetings of Chicago physicians in the history of the city," when he proposed that "all the 'culls' or 'scalawags' of the human race should be taken before the courts, scientifically investigated, and if found unworthy, colonized and allowed to die off."[25] In December 1912, health reformer, physician, and eugenicist Dr. W. A. Evans devoted the majority of his daily column, "How to Keep Well," to eugenics. He explained Galton's theories of "positive" and "negative" eugenics, Spencer's theory of the "survival of the fittest," and the importance of human breeding. He used well-known family studies, including those of the Jukes and the "tribe of Ishmael," to highlight the importance of good breeding.[26] Dr. A. J. Ochsner of Chicago, in an address before the Southern Surgical and Gynecological Association in Atlanta, declared that "Mankind is unmistakably drifting toward an era when health will play a most important part in marriage, and there will come a time when sentiment will be a minor factor in the formation of marriage contracts." "The doctrine of eugenics," Ochsner continued, "is rapidly coming into favor all over the world and the trend of modern thought is toward its general application."²⁷ Proponents of eugenics faced challenges, mostly from individuals who opposed the infiltration of science and the state into marriage and other affairs of the heart, but there is little doubt that the nation had become obsessed with eugenics during the decade before World War I.²⁸

Americans did more than read about eugenics in the years before the war; they actively participated in a nationwide movement. Some Americans tacitly supported eugenics, like the Wisconsin couple who became the first people to get married under the state's new eugenic marriage law. Others challenged new eugenic laws. Gustave Johnson traveled from Wisconsin to Minneapolis to get married because he did not want to wait a month to be wed in his home state. He informed reporters that he would "fight the [eugenic marriage] law to the end" if the Wisconsin authorities arrested him.²⁹ There were also those individuals and organizations who actively promoted eugenics. Frederic Robinson, president of the sociological fund committee of the *Medical Review of Reviews* in New York City, put up $500 of his own money to cosponsor a contest in 1913 to create the perfect eugenic couple. Robinson and his committee would grade all applicants and when they found the best man and the best woman, the committee would pay them $500 to get married. The couple would receive an additional $500 upon the birth of their first child.³⁰

In 1915, Robinson and the *Medical Review of Reviews* launched quite a different eugenic campaign. They sent a half-dozen men whom a *Tribune* reporter described as "decrepit, poverty stricken, poorly clad, [and] underfed" out to parade up and down Fifth Avenue, Wall Street, and other crowded New York City thoroughfares wearing signs asking all who read them if the sign-bearer was fit to become a father. "We chose the most radical means," Robinson explained, "because we believe they are the most effective. Only those with the proper physical health and economic independence have a right to bear children. If we wish to aid the cause of eugenics and to advance the human race, both positively and by the elimination of the unfit, we must take drastic steps."³¹ Though it remained contested, eugenics had become part of Americana.

When the Eugenics Education Society of Chicago announced its "Baby Week" and issued a call for applicants for its "super baby" contest, they received more than four thousand responses. In the end they selected fifty "super babies" and made them honorary members of the society. Contest organizers urged the babies' parents to become members, so they could continue to study their tiny subjects.³² In September 1915, the Illinois state board of health held what one reporter described as "a new fashioned baby show" at the state fair as yet another means of measuring the eugenic fitness of Illinois' youngest residents.³³ More than once, Evans urged his readers to send their eugenic family data to the Eugenics Record Office.³⁴ Though not all participants in the eugenics movement possessed an equal voice, its public appeal during its formative years made it more likely that a broad range of individuals would contribute to the formation of popular eugenic doctrine and, more importantly, the creation of eugenic policy.

In addition to becoming part of popular culture—Evans estimated in 1916 that a eugenics story made the front page no less than once a month—eugenics had also become part of the coursework offered at colleges and universities across the country.[35] By 1916, nearly fifty colleges and universities offered eugenic coursework, and by 1920 more than twenty thousand students annually received instruction in eugenics. The University of Chicago and Northwestern University, as well as other top colleges and universities, became the leaders of eugenic thought.[36] In summer 1911, Charles Davenport and other leading scientists traveled to the University of Chicago to deliver a series of lectures on heredity and eugenics.[37] By the end of 1914 the ERO had created an official extension department to provide its lecture services to women's clubs, churches, and any other interested organization.

Women professionals exposed to eugenics in school and popular culture often became outspoken proponents of the new science.[38] In 1912, the *Tribune* described Dr. Alice Stockham as a "Noted Woman, Physician and an American Pioneer of Eugenics." A Quaker from Ohio, Stockham moved to Chicago at the end of the nineteenth century and established the Stockham Publishing Company. During the first decade of the twentieth century, she was convicted in a federal court in Chicago and fined on a charge of misusing the mails for publishing pamphlets on eugenics, which at the time of the indictment was considered immoral.[39] Stockham was not the only woman eugenicist in Illinois. Dr. Anna Blount spoke to Chicago-area women's clubs about eugenics. She also served as chairman of the Eugenics Education Society of Chicago.[40] Dr. Lois Lindsay-Wynekoop kept herself busy speaking to women's clubs throughout Chicago and its suburbs about eugenics, and Dr. Mary McEwen spoke at least once to the Francis Juvenile Aid Club about eugenics.[41] Women professionals immersed in eugenic culture and trained to root out the biological causes of social problems frequently advocated eugenic solutions to those problems. Not all professional maternalists supported "negative" eugenic measures, such as Illinois' involuntary commitment law. They did, however, constitute some of its most vocal advocates.

Women at all levels participated in the production and spread of scientific theories that directly influenced the formation of public policy. Both traditional and professional maternalists, within which I would include eugenic fieldworkers and institution administrators, possessed a powerful voice. Professional maternalists provided the evidence and the day-to-day experience, as well as the scientific rationale that lawmakers and laypersons relied upon to make informed decisions concerning public policy.[42] Women professionals collected and interpreted valuable data and reported directly to the Illinois State Charities Commission. They regularly published their findings and recommendations in numerous professional and popular journals. Professional maternalists' dual identity—maternalist reformer and scientific expert—placed them in a unique position of power and made them integral players in the web of actors who worked diligently to enact legislation that they argued would improve society and the race. For their part, the traditional maternalists at the IFWC lent much-needed support and organization to the movement to create the commitment law. State charity boards, the general public, and male experts and lawmakers viewed maternalist reformers not as marginalized and powerless, but as individuals who were uniquely qualified to address issues concerning women, children, and the future of the race.

Science, Heredity, and Social Reform

Women who struggled to create Illinois' eugenic commitment law rooted themselves in a social reform discourse that linked social improvement with an emerging medico-scientific worldview. Toward the end of the nineteenth century, professionals in various fields increasingly sought to use their knowledge and expertise for practical ends. Mental health experts were no exception. As the status of the family and the community as centers of authority and control waned, specially trained mental health experts positioned themselves as the protectors of white, middle-class morality and the saviors of the race.[43] They distanced themselves from the asylum, and their historical role as the keepers of the "insane," and became the protectors of "normality" in hospitals and clinics.[44] Lawmakers and laypersons increasingly turned to mental health professionals who were eager to offer biological explanations for the myriad modern social problems plaguing the nation's burgeoning urban industrial centers.[45]

The rise in status of the medico-scientific model had its roots in the underlying assumption that biology and heredity determined human behavior. White middle-class reformers and experts from different backgrounds argued that criminals, paupers, sex offenders, and delinquents created the degraded environments within which they lived and, more importantly, passed their tendency to engage in antisocial behavior on to succeeding generations. For reformers and experts, and most of the reading public, severe poverty, delinquency, and nonnormative sexual behavior became the material manifestations of a hidden but highly heritable impairment.

Even professional maternalists who stressed the importance of the relationship between environmental factors and antisocial behavior, such as Sophonisba Breckinridge and Edith Abbott, argued that a "considerable number" of delinquents were "mentally deficient."[46] Although recent scholars argue that Progressives' explanations of immorality did not include "innate mental defect," and that

Progressive women reformers looked to social and environmental factors rather than inherited physical and mental traits to explain delinquency, evidence from Illinois indicates that the divide between Progressives and Eugenicists was not so salient and that women reformers did indeed look to so-called inherited physical and mental traits to explain delinquency, as well as other social problems.[47]

Initially influenced by the neo-Lamarckian notion that acquired characteristics were heritable, reformers began in the 1880s to emphasize the importance of heredity in the production of antisocial behavior. They argued that a degraded environment and a lack of "proper" moral and religious education were turning Chicago's poor into criminals and that parents were passing their "wickedness" on to their children. Numerous investigators of Chicago's "dark places" and its "cess-pools of infamy" found that vice and crime thrived in its crowded communities. They claimed that everything from intemperance and "evil" thoughts to marital rape and sexual intercourse after conception influenced the quality and character of the fetus and directly contributed to the "making of criminals."[48] As late as 1913, Mrs. John Hays Hammond, a leading member of the American Association for the Prevention of Infant Mortality and an outspoken proponent of eugenics, longed for the day when women would be made to realize that, "the defects as well as the excellencies of their husbands will be reproduced in their children; that men of intemperate and immoral habits are likely to produce defective children."[49] Ophelia Amigh, superintendent of the Illinois State Training School for Girls at Geneva, declared that there was "no worse form of degeneracy than that which is inherited from intemperate progenitors, for it reaches down at least to the third and fourth generation."[50] Amigh, who was a former Civil War nurse and in her fifties when she came to Geneva in 1895, was one of Illinois' leading experts on delinquent girls. She was also one of the most outspoken and influential proponents of the eugenic commitment law.[51]

By the second decade of the twentieth century, Mendelian theories of inheritance began to eclipse older neo-Lamarckian arguments, though the latter never completely disappeared. In 1912, Dr. Evans stepped before a crowded auditorium at Chicago's Central Y.M.C.A and declared that, "The teachings of Mendelism show heredity has more influence over the development of the child than environment." Two weeks later he informed his audience that, "It has been shown by the study of certain families that criminal traits are inherited." Evans's talks were part of a five-week series of noonday lectures on eugenics.[52] Experts in a number of fields increasingly argued that although many delinquents, criminals, and paupers appeared "normal," they possessed an inherited mental "defect," initially referred to as "feeblemindedness," which made them incapable of "normal" white, middle-class reasoning and conduct.[53] According to experts, this mental "defect" passed from one generation to the next as a "unit character" that remained largely unaffected by any type of environmental or educational reform.

Edna Jathro, a fieldworker for the Committee on Provision for the Feeble-Minded, and other women reformers, such as Wilhelmine Key of the ERO, used eugenic family studies to highlight an apparent "persistence of defect through successive generations" that compelled certain individuals to engage in antisocial behavior.[54] Jathro argued that, although most impoverished persons appeared to be "nearly normal," they showed significant mental defect when they were "put to the tests of adult life and required to exercise foresight and good judgment."[55] The *Training School Bulletin*—a journal published by the eugenicists at the Vineland School for the Feebleminded in New Jersey—explained that: "Many tramps, drunkards, prostitutes, paupers, delinquents and criminals are what they are because without proper care and control it is impossible for them to be anything else."[56] *Life and Health* editorialized that "feebleminded" individuals "certainly" played a "large part in the perpetuation of the slum," because they were physically and mentally incapable of caring for themselves.[57] By the turn of the twentieth century, poverty and social deviance had been intimately and inextricably linked to mental defect; so much so, that by the beginning of the second decade of the new century Americans found themselves reading almost daily of the modern "menace of the feebleminded."[58]

Maternalist Reformers and the Feebleminded Menace

"For Care of a Dangerous Class"; that is how the *Chicago Daily Tribune* described the 1915 commitment law. The new law was not meant to provide care for persons with severe mental disabilities, many of whom had been going "voluntarily" to institutions for decades. It was meant, in the words of one *Tribune* reporter, to protect "humanity" and "public safety" from a recently discovered "borderline" group of "feebleminded" persons, who according to Dr. Ochsner, president of the Illinois State Charities Commission, would "drift" into pauperism, vagabondism, gross sexual immorality, delinquency, and crime if they were not cared for properly.[59] The new law was meant to combat the apparent rise of the "feebleminded menace."[60] The *Tribune* explained that, "Considering the frequency of horrible offenses by members of this class of the defective and the vicious perpetuation of the class by reason of our failure to keep it under control, we do not see how the legislature can fail to act without further delay." To support its bold assertions, the *Tribune* cited cases: case 6,326—male, twenty-two years, "frequent delinquencies"; case 6,036—male, fifteen years, "nuisance to neighbors";

case 5,537—female, eighteen years, "shamefully mistreated while at home"; case 6,441—female twenty-four, years, "delinquent"; case 5,697—male, twenty-one years, "guilty of petty thievery"; case 5,532—female twenty-two years, "sold into white slavery"; case 6,703—male, seventeen years, "Juvenile Court record"; and case 6,022—female, sixteen years, "became pregnant."[61]

The notion that the commitment law would provide protection for humanity and ensure public safety by institutionalizing "feebleminded" persons indefinitely played a critical role in maternalist reformers rationalization of the "negative" eugenic measure. Many maternalists who worked with Illinois' impoverished citizens argued that the vast majority of paupers, prostitutes, and criminals were indeed "feebleminded" and in need of care and protection. Dr. Town defined "feebleminded" persons as "all those individuals who are mentally defective from birth or early infancy, whatever the amount of the mental deficiency may be, provided it be sufficient to prevent them from competing on equal terms with normal individuals and from managing their own affairs with ordinary prudence." She explained that for all practical purposes, "feebleminded" individuals could be grouped into three subcategories or classes, the now infamous subgroups of "idiots," "imbeciles," and "morons." Using the "conservative estimate" that one out of every three hundred Americans was "feebleminded," Town determined that there were 18,800 "feebleminded" persons living in Illinois, the majority of whom were "high-grade imbeciles" and "morons."[62]

It was precisely these groups, the "high-grade imbeciles" and "morons," who most concerned eugenic reformers. Although according to Town, these groups were "educable," they could not "manage their affairs with ordinary prudence," and they were "very [suggestible], easily led," and "incapable of resisting temptation."[63] Elizabeth Kite, a eugenic fieldworker who worked with Henry Goddard at the Vineland school, claimed that no one was "long deceived by an idiot or an imbecile" and that it was the "high-grade Moron type" that reformers were most eager to "discover."[64] Experts argued that "high-grade imbeciles" and "morons" aggravated or intensified almost every social problem in part because they were able to drift through life undetected and unsupervised. Dr. Town asserted that the "higher grades" did not "compel attention to the same extent" as did "idiots," and that the "higher grades" usually went unnoticed and were misunderstood by the "normal" people they encountered. The result, according to Town, was that in most cases, the "higher grades" remained "at large to suffer much themselves at the hands of the unprincipled . . . and in short to make the world a more dangerous and unhappy place than it need be."[65] Dr. Thomas Leonard, superintendent of Illinois' Lincoln State School and Colony for the Feebleminded, accused experts who educated "brighter feebleminded" individuals and then released them back into society of not "playing fair," and of making "counterfeits" of the "brighter feebleminded" by teaching them "so much that they simulate the normal and deceive the unsuspecting normal."[66] Eugenicists argued, moreover, that because "high-grade feebleminded" individuals could not control their "sex instinct," they reproduced at a much faster rate than their "normal-minded" counterparts, swelling the ranks of society's "unfit."[67] According to the experts, as long as institutionalization remained voluntary, "high-grade feebleminded" individuals would continue to "deceive the unsuspecting normal" and remain free to engage in antisocial behavior and reproduce "their kind."

In their respective investigations, Town and Amigh both found that only 1,500 of the 18,800 "mental defectives" in Illinois were confined to institutions under the voluntary system that had been in place since the mid-nineteenth century. This meant that 17,300 "mental defectives," the majority of them "high-grade imbeciles" and "morons," were drifting through life unsupervised, wreaking havoc on Illinois' social and moral fabric, and draining state relief funds.[68] Superintendent Amigh declared that she frequently received girls who were "nearly women grown who should have been in a school for feeble minded long years since."[69] Both Town and Amigh argued that without permanent custodial care, "feeble-minded" women like those at Geneva would become vagrants and the "weakling mothers of feeble-minded children."[70]

Field research, conducted primarily by women, seemed to confirm the assertion that paupers, criminals, and delinquents were inherently flawed. In fall 1916, the Illinois State Charities Commission sent Miss Annie Hinrichsen to investigate "Tin Town" and "The Commons," two settlements located in a small town on the outskirts of Chicago. In her report, Hinrichsen described Tin Town as a lane of "dilapidated shacks" that ran along the Wabash River. The crowded one-room shacks in Tin Town were "built of the pickings of junk piles." Their furnishings of "battered stoves, tattered bedding, broken tables, and old boxes" appeared to have come from the same junk piles that provided the materials for the buildings. The toilet facilities were "unspeakable." Several families used a single well, and took their water for washing from the Wabash River. Adjoining Tin Town was The Commons, where, according to Hinrichsen, the tiny huts were in the last stages of decay.[71]

Living within Tin Town and The Commons, which were part of the city of Mt. Carmel, were approximately thirty families, all of whom were either wholly or partly dependent on the county. At the time of the investigation, Mt. Carmel—the seat of Wabash County—had the highest per capita expenditure of outdoor relief of any Illinois city. In 1915, county officials expended $7,000 in outdoor relief in Mt. Carmel, a city with a population of only seven thousand people. In her report to the State Charities Commission, Hinrichsen complained that the "greater part" of the money expended by Wabash County went to support the persons living in two adjacent communities, Tin Town and The Commons.

Hinrichsen employed the powerful language of eugenics in her call for reform in Wabash County. If, Hinrichsen argued, county officials did not become more vigilant and discriminating in their administration of outdoor relief and their use of eugenic segregation, Tin Town and The Commons would continue to impose a "constantly increasing burden upon the county and the State."[72] Both settlements were, in Hinrichsen's words, "hotbed[s] for the propagation of defectives and delinquents."[73] She argued that Wabash County's charity roll and its criminal records "read as one," and that 90 percent of the police work in Mt. Carmel was conducted in Tin Town and The Commons.

Hinrichsen conducted her own family studies to make her case. She asserted that 75 percent of the sheriff's criminal work for the entire county came from dependent families who lived in "the most unspeakable conditions of physical and moral degeneracy." Three of the families whom the state supported year-round were represented at the time of the study by three generations on the charity list. Hinrichsen warned that the percentage of "defectives" in the families was high, and that a community that fostered "pauperism" invariably produced the inmates of Illinois' penal and charitable institutions. She also criticized the state for its reluctance to institutionalize "defectives" as a means of preventing "degeneracy."

Prominent among Hinrichsen's studies was the case of a single mother living in Tin Town. "A.B." lived with her six children, two of them "illegitimate," in a one-room hut. Her husband had been dead for several years. According to Hinrichsen, Wabash County officials "permitted" A.B. to rear her children in a "hovel of the lowest moral and physical filth." It was well known in the community that A.B. "lived openly, and at county expense, a life of utter moral and physical degeneracy," and that A.B. kept one regular boarder, and "maintained an open house for many others." Hinrichsen complained that, although A.B.'s "mental and physical conditions were public knowledge, and her morals were public scandal," no action was taken by the county until a representative of the Illinois Children's Home and Aid Society demanded A.B.'s removal, calling her a "community menace." A.B. and her baby were committed to Lincoln on October 4, 1916. Three of A.B.'s sons were sent to the Children's Home, and two of her daughters fled to Indiana. Hinrichsen chose to title this case study "A FEEBLE-MINDED WOMAN."[74] Like most white, middle-class reformers, Hinrichsen considered women who had no husband, who depended upon the state for subsistence, and who gave birth to "illegitimate" children a "community menace." What separated Hinrichsen and other maternalists who supported the eugenic commitment law from non-eugenic reformers was their willingness to argue that most women and men who did not live "normally" were mentally incapable of doing so.

The Eugenic Commitment Campaign

For nearly twenty years, eugenic reformers waged a rhetorical campaign similar to that deployed by Hinrichsen. Both male and female reformers relied on their power as experts and as members of the "progressive" middle class to educate the public and state politicians about the dangers of the unchecked propagation of "feebleminded" offenders. Eugenic reformers asserted that detection of the type of "feebleminded" persons who were responsible for the "greater part of the 'menace'" was not within the powers of the average citizen, and that few people actually understood the severity of the "menace" caused by "feebleminded" individuals.[75] Dr. Town argued that it was the responsibility of scientists and reformers to inform the public. She urged her colleagues to "cry it from the housetop and compel the passerby to stop and listen, so grave is the situation and so urgent is the need for action."[76] Superintendent Amigh declared that no greater "calamity" threatened Illinois than the "apathy and lack of knowledge of those in power" concerning the care and supervision of its "feebleminded" citizens.[77]

In the midst of legislative discussions concerning the commitment bill, Dr. Clara Hayes of the Peoria State Hospital offered eugenic reformers the most cogent rationalization of eugenic institutionalization. She began her assessment by praising reformers who spent "much energy, time and money . . . toward bettering the condition of the city slums, and studying the conditions which seem to produce mental defectiveness." Hayes praised urban reformers who engaged in "a noble and self-sacrificing work." That work, according to Hayes, was largely ineffectual, however, because the "class of people" who lived in the slums was not "made by environment." Hayes argued that poor people created the environment within which they lived, and that the way to "improve" the condition of the city was to "remove from society the element which [made] up the slums by diminishing the birth rate of individuals mentally below par." Eugenic reformers asserted that although efforts to improve the environment in places like Tin Town and The Commons were "noble," they were a waste of time and money. The most effective and most economical way to improve society and better the lives of "feebleminded" individuals was to remove them from their environment and place them in an institution.

For Hayes, the efficacy of eugenic segregation seemed self-evident. It was modern and scientific, and noble and progressive. It would improve living conditions; provide "protection" to society from "feebleminded" individuals; and fulfill society's "obligations" to a "class of mental defectives," who supposedly were "unable to care for and protect themselves."[78] Through its invocation of an ostensibly benevolent model of reform rooted in the biologization and individuation of social problems, turn-of-the-century reform discourse had seemingly come full circle.

Eugenic reformers used modern science to root the source of social problems in the minds and bodies of the working-class residents of city slums, all the while criticizing the efforts of those reformers who had once also claimed to be modern and scientific.

According to Hayes, eugenic commitment provided, for the first time in history, the means to improve society permanently by fundamentally altering human nature. Society, Hayes argued, would accomplish "one of the most brilliant humanitarian achievements of the ages." Like the majority of her colleagues in Illinois, Hayes argued that segregation would be even more effective than eugenic sterilization. She stated that radical surgical measures to prevent "defectives" from reproducing were much less progressive. Sterilization did not make an individual a better citizen, nor did it "prevent the crime that he [was] wont to commit." Sterilization did nothing more than make procreation impossible. Hayes argued, moreover, that sterilization "probably would never reach the types that approach the normal, and they are the ones who reproduce most." She concluded that sterilization could never be practiced extensively enough to make it effective in eliminating feeblemindedness, and that in some cases it had been declared unconstitutional. According to Hayes, eugenic institutionalization was the most effective and the most progressive way to eliminate feeblemindedness and all of its degenerative consequences.[79]

Women interested in using the most modern scientific means of ameliorating the blight they encountered almost daily in their work with impoverished women and children insisted that the state needed the power to incarcerate "feebleminded" individuals indefinitely. Dr. Town, who served as chairman of the Illinois State Conference of Charities and Correction in 1914, argued that the practice of paroling and discharging "mental defectives" who engaged in antisocial behavior was not eugenic, and that "To be of eugenic value an institution for defectives must retain its charges permanently." Town agreed wholeheartedly with the assertion made by the Illinois State Charities Commission that the need for legislation that would segregate "feebleminded" individuals indefinitely was essential.[80]

Reformers recognized that the indefinite incarceration of the nearly nineteen thousand "mental defectives" living in Illinois would be costly. They argued, however, that the long-term benefits of the program greatly outweighed the cost. Both male and female reformers envisioned the creation of a system of colonies built on large tracts of land far outside city limits in which each inmate would perform tasks of manual labor and receive a level of vocational training and formal schooling that would be suited to their "mental capacity."[81] In an interview with the *Tribune*, Chief Justice Harry Olson of the Chicago Municipal Court stated that an "immediate help" in the battle against vice, crime, and delinquency would be the construction of a "big industrial farm for the feebleminded ones," where they could be "taken care of permanently."[82] Olson suggested authorities, "Put them on a farm, let them raise daisies and pansies and vegetables. . . . Let each one have a cow named after her and have her milk it herself."[83] According to eugenic reformers, colonies of this type would actually save taxpayers money, because they would be largely self-supporting. Dr. Hayes assured readers of *The Institution Quarterly* that "Colonies of this kind . . . eventually would be a far less extravagant and expensive method of caring for this class, than is now incurred in conducting the State Penal and Charitable institution."[84] If, eugenic reformers argued, Illinois' residents and its legislature could be made to comprehend the severity of the dilemma facing them, they would support eugenic commitment.

Over the course of about twenty years, from 1895 to 1915, middle-class women and men worked diligently to inform Americans about the dangers of the so-called feebleminded menace and the necessity of eugenic commitment. Margaret Reeves, a field agent for the Russell Sage Foundation, noted in her study of training schools that "a wave of interest" in feeblemindedness had "spread over the country" during the decade before the First World War. Reeves recalled that Americans "read constantly in newspapers and magazines about the large number of feeble-minded and insane people included among criminals and delinquents."[85] Both women and men conducted investigations and published their results in journals and newspapers. They spoke before women's clubs, who ultimately came to their own conclusions about the need for "protective" legislation. Clubwomen in turn formed their own legislative sessions to draft their own eugenic measures, which were eventually passed on to lawmakers. A number of civic organizations that had joined with the courts and other "official bodies" to study feeblemindedness in Illinois concluded that "sentiment in favor of legal and permanent segregation of the feeble-minded [had] been growing rapidly."[86] It was within the midst of this groundswell of support, generated by both female and male reformers, that the committee of six men and four women came together at the LaSalle Hotel in Chicago to write the bill that the *Tribune* referred to as the most important measure introduced to the Forty-ninth General Assembly.[87] In July 1915, Governor Dunne signed House Bill No. 655, creating one of the country's first state-sponsored systems of eugenic commitment.[88]

Severe Overcrowding and Other Practical Concerns

Following the enactment of the commitment law, local newspapers declared that it had successfully enabled the state to institutionalize "feebleminded" individuals who, prior to 1915, were able to remain at large. In November 1915, amid the trial of H. J. Haiselden, the Chicago doctor who withheld treatment of the "hopelessly defective" Bollinger baby, a Lake County judge committed two "feebleminded" boys to the Lincoln State School and Colony for the Feebleminded.[89] The *Tribune* ran a brief story on what were believed to be the first two commitments under the new law. "Hopeless Situation Corrected," the headline cried. The story explained that prior to the passage of the new law "there was no place where half-wits or defectives, who were a danger to the community, but who had not committed offenses of such serious nature as to be sent to the state hospital for the criminal insane at Chester, could be sent save to the St. Charles school for boys, the Pontiac reformatory, the Geneva Home for Girls, or Joliet, where they mingled with prisoners of higher mental and moral types."[90] Eugenic institutionalization had become a reality in Illinois.

Experts praised the new law. They declared it an instant success and argued that it had produced a marked change in both the quantity and character of admissions to state institutions.[91] C. B. Caldwell, who had been associated with the Lincoln School and Colony and was serving as assistant superintendent of the Peoria State Hospital in 1917, reported that the new law affected the "character of admissions [to Lincoln] at once." The staff at Lincoln increasingly found themselves dealing with "criminal feeble-minded youths" who came to them as a result of the new law. The two types of youths sent to Lincoln were young men who had acquired "criminal and destructive habits" and young women who could not "keep out of trouble of a sexual character." Officials at Lincoln found themselves forced to accommodate unwed mothers and their babies. There were also a number of "mature adults" and even a small number of "normal" people who were sent to Lincoln under the new law. Harrison Harley, a psychologist at the Juvenile Psychopathic Institute, found that 7 percent of the individuals committed to Lincoln between 1915 and 1917 did not "classify as feebleminded." He justified the commitment of "normal" people to Lincoln by arguing that in "every instance some defect of character or of self control or some mental aberration . . . made commitment imperative."[92] Harley and other experts, as well as the *Chicago Daily Tribune*, officially declared eugenic commitment a success because it enabled the state to institutionalize "high-grade feebleminded" individuals who engaged in activities deemed antisocial by the larger society.

Despite the apparent "success" of the commitment law, proponents of eugenic institutionalization found themselves facing a number of practical challenges in the years immediately following its enactment. Foremost among the complaints issued by experts was the inability of existing state institutions to accommodate their new charges. The Lincoln State School and Colony experienced the most dramatic increase in its inmate population. The new law affected other institutions as well. Many "feebleminded" offenders were sent to correctional institutions, such as the State Training School for Girls at Geneva or the boys' facility at St. Charles, resulting in overcrowding at those institutions. Lawmakers and administrators eventually opened the state colony for epileptics in Dixon to the "uneducable feebleminded," but it did little to alleviate overcrowding in places like Lincoln,

Geneva, and St. Charles that were seeing a dramatic rise in the number of "high-grade feebleminded" inmates. Despite severe overcrowding, the state legislature was unwilling to fund construction of a new institution designed specifically for the long-term incarceration of "high-grade feebleminded" individuals.[93]

Administrators and experts eager to reap the eugenic benefits of legal commitment also complained that they were finding it difficult to maintain custody of their new charges. Harley blamed Lincoln's inability to retain its inmates on family members who "as a whole [were] not willing to submit to institutional incarceration of their defective children." According to Superintendent Amigh, there was a "sickly sentimentality abroad in the land" among Illinois' less-informed citizens that impeded the efforts of eugenic reformers to institutionalize "feebleminded" individuals indefinitely.[94] In addition to inmates' families, Harley accused judges of hindering the efforts of eugenic reformers. He explained that it was difficult for the court to sustain the argument that a committed person would continue to be or would again become a "menace to [themselves] or to society" if they were released from an institution. Rather than have their decision to commit overruled by a higher court, most judges chose to release individuals whose cases appeared to be questionable.[95]

The constitutionality of the commitment law had also become an issue among experts. When the committee that drafted the bill met at the LaSalle Hotel in March 1915, several members voiced their concern for the individuals who would be prosecuted under the new law. Chief Justice Olson, one of Chicago's most avid eugenicists, initially "strenuously" objected to certain provisions within the bill. According to Olson, the bill did not adequately protect the rights of persons alleged to be "feebleminded."[96] It also did not provide for a jury trial. The bill, moreover, permitted any "credible person" to file a petition with the court and it did not delineate sufficiently the criteria for determining who could testify as an expert witness. Olson argued that "any person who may have studied psychology for even a few months and who [was] not a physician" could qualify as an expert under the original commitment bill. He concluded that mental exams, conducted by practically anyone, in secret, without a jury, would result in the "wholesale railroading of people" into institutions.[97] Olson's critique was an important one, and one that had been a topic of debate among experts across the country.

In response to mounting challenges from both the courts and the general public, experts in Illinois and elsewhere insisted that they supported a system of indefinite incarceration that actually protected the rights of both "normal-minded" and "feebleminded" individuals. Dr. Maria Dean of Missoula, Montana, asserted that the "feebleminded" had rights that reformers and the state were "bound to consider." She contended that "feebleminded" individuals were "entitled to life, entitled to their fullest development consistent with their capacity, entitled to all the joy and zest that comes from interested activity." Dean concluded that this was "wholly possible by segregation, training, colonization."[98] If, the Illinois State Charities Commission argued, the court possessed the power to rule over cases involving institutionalization, it could prevent the "railroading of any who may not be subjects for segregation." The commission asserted, moreover, that the writ of *habeas corpus* would be made available in cases involving commitment to ensure the opportunity for a subsequent "examination of the patient by the court, should question arise as to methods adopted in commitment, or as to the possibility of mental improvement."[99] In the end, Chief Justice Olson and the rest of the committee that drafted Illinois' commitment bill revised it to reflect more clearly the desire among eugenicists to create a system of institutionalization that protected the rights of individuals who appeared before the court, which ultimately made Illinois' commitment law very difficult to enforce.[100]

Facing severe overcrowding and legal challenges from both families and judges, a number of the reformers who were instrumental in pushing the commitment bill through the Illinois legislature increasingly advocated extrainstitutional treatment for certain "feebleminded" offenders. Under section ten of the new commitment law, the court possessed the power to "commit any feeble-minded person to the guardianship of a suitable person." For reasons that will be explored more fully in the next chapter, eugenic reformers employed a gendered set of criteria when determining the most likely candidates for probation. They argued that most "feebleminded" males could be supervised adequately outside the institution and that most "feebleminded" women, especially those of childbearing age, required indefinite incarceration to live "normally."[101]

Conclusion

According to proponents of the eugenic commitment law, a specific cohort of "high-grade feebleminded" individuals—usually working-class women and men—was multiplying at a much faster rate than their "normal-minded" counterparts, swelling the ranks of society's "defectives," and exacerbating social and moral decline. Eugenicists asserted, moreover, that the most effective way to improve the condition of Chicago's slums, and the race, was to remove the individuals who created the slums by using a system of eugenic segregation to prohibit "feeble-minded" persons from reproducing.[102] Proponents of the 1915 commitment law used dominant scientific theories to construct certain working-class women and men as innately inferior, impaired individuals who required indefinite incarceration to live "normally." The result was the creation of legislation that empowered the state to commit individuals who, for a number of complex socioeconomic and, in some cases, physical or cognitive reasons, deviated from normative white, middle-class notions of responsible, respectable citizenship. The biologization of social deviance, moreover, created a lasting impression within American society of the socially "dangerous" and morally "corrupting" mentally "ill" and "feebleminded," an impression that remains with us in the twenty-first century.

Eugenics, with its emphasis on biological explanations of social problems, greatly influenced the ways in which maternalist reformers viewed the working-class citizens whom they encountered through their work with the state. Unlike their nineteenth-century predecessors who rooted their reform efforts in religion and moral suasion, the women who waged the eugenic commitment campaign relied upon science and the state to solve modern social problems. Though most female eugenicists never completely abandoned environmental explanations of social problems, they increasingly argued that feeblemindedness and mental defect played an equal, if not more important role in the degradation of city neighborhoods and the devastation of the city's poorest residents, as well as the pollution of nation's racial or genetic "stock." They asserted that the vast majority of paupers, criminals, and delinquents were innately inferior to those individuals who could maintain white, middle-class standards of conduct. For those maternalists who supported the commitment law, it represented yet another means of protecting a vulnerable group of citizens from the trials and hardships of modern urban living, while also promoting public safety and improving city slums. Their education and training and their experience working in state agencies and institutions helping poor families, as well as their willingness to experiment with new models of reform, led the women who endorsed Illinois' commitment bill to support a complex combination of eugenic and socioeconomic solutions to the problems they faced.

Although women rarely held high-ranking positions in national organizations or large research-oriented hospitals and universities, they were able to make their voices heard, and ultimately affected not only the dominant scientific discourse, but also the course of action taken by many states. Though not all maternalist reformers supported eugenic segregation, those who did had a lasting effect on the course of action taken in Illinois.

2

"Defective Children in the Juvenile Court"

> "... the feeble-minded male is little to be feared. He can easily be controlled, by proper supervision, aided by good marriage laws.... As to the female, the problem is more serious. The expert viewpoint is that the female requires very close attention, much closer probably than can be given her anywhere except in an institution."
>
> —A. L. Bowen, Executive Secretary of the Illinois State Charities Commission, 1916

> "If we could have a law in this State where the power might be given to place and keep under supervision during the child-bearing age all feeble-minded girls of this and every other school of this kind, it would help matters a great deal so far as the future good of the State is concerned and cut down the expense of caring for paupers and criminals."
>
> —Ophelia L. Amigh, Superintendent, State Training School for Girls, Geneva, Illinois, 1902

Fourteen-year-old Elsie, along with her mother, her pastor, a lawyer, and a social worker, appeared before Judge Mary Margaret Bartelme in March 1924. Elsie had come to the Cook County Juvenile Court from the Chicago Juvenile Detention Home, where she had been sent after being raped by three "boys" and one man. Elsie had been charged with being "incorrigible." This was not the first time she had appeared in the Juvenile Court, and when Judge Bartelme asked Elsie's mother if she had anything further to state to the court, Elsie's mother replied: "I would like to have Elsie promise to behave herself, but you cannot depend upon her promise. She promises me so often." "That has been the trouble, hasn't it?" Judge Bartelme replied. She then sent Elsie out of the courtroom so that she could speak privately with Elsie's mother, her lawyer, and her pastor. Mrs. Hartray, the social worker, led her charge out of the courtroom.

When she was certain they had left, Judge Bartelme said, "I want you to understand about Elsie." She handed the pastor a "psychopathic" report made by Dr. Herman Adler of the Institute for Juvenile Research.[1] Judge Bartelme asked the pastor and the lawyer to read the report; they both replied that they had already read it. Judge Bartelme then turned her attention to Elsie's mother. "You understand," she said, "it is a report by Dr. Adler that her mind does not work as it should for a girl of her age. . . . You say that Elsie does not keep her promises, expecting to keep it, but she breaks that promise just as quickly as she gives it." Judge Bartelme then explained that a "high-grade feebleminded" girl like Elsie could get into serious trouble because she was "not able to reason out whether things are going to work out all right . . . it is possible that she would come to you soon to become a mother." Girls like Elsie, Bartelme concluded, required strict supervision. "Do you understand?" Bartelme asked Elsie's mother. "Yes," she replied.

Judge Bartelme suggested that Elsie be sent to the Chicago Home for Girls, where she could be protected. Elsie's mother and her lawyer and pastor agreed. Bartelme committed Elsie under court order to the Chicago Home for Girls on March 3, 1924. The eldest of the four male defendants was released because of insufficient evidence. The three "boys" remained in custody on $5,000 bond, but Elsie's lawyer informed Judge Bartelme in private that they were willing to do anything to avoid prosecution. Elsie's attorney explained to Bartelme that he planned to take Elsie to the Criminal Court building to meet privately with the state's attorney, where she would sign a statement absolving the three young men of any wrongdoing. It was all for Elsie's own protection, her lawyer had said. No mention was made of the male defendants' mental status.[2]

Elsie's case is one of thousands processed through the Juvenile Court after its inception in 1899. It is important, however, because it vividly highlights the nexus of gender, class, sexuality, and mental "defect" that proved so critical in the creation of a eugenic commitment law in Illinois and in maternalists' support of that law. Throughout the early twentieth century both the causes and possible treatments of juvenile delinquency remained gendered. Even those young women such as Elsie, who became the victims of sexual assault, overwhelmingly had their sexual transgressions defined as delinquent acts.[3] Those delinquent acts in turn became associated in both scientific studies and the popular imagination with a perceived lack of mental capacity. For many experts, reformers, and judges, sexually delinquent young women like Elsie became the embodiment of the "feebleminded menace."

In this chapter, I focus on how reformers, especially women reformers, came to target their eugenic commitment campaign on a group of ethnically white, working-class adolescents. The answer, I argue, lay in an analysis of newly emergent *psy* and eugenic discourses that rooted girls' delinquent behavior not in an abusive or neglectful home life, or the trials of city life, but rather a "defective" or impaired mind.[4] Maternalists who supported eugenic commitment argued that unrestrained—and unguarded—female sexuality had become a threat to the race and to society. Eugenics offered the best way to eliminate the "menace" caused by female sex delinquents because it would use the latest "scientific advancements" to protect teenagers like Elsie, whom the courts and resident experts considered impaired, from both their own unrestrained sexuality and from unscrupulous men. It would also prevent them from producing "illegitimate," "feebleminded" children, a seemingly obvious social and economic benefit to all Illinois residents. For middle-class white women interested in protecting a vulnerable group of adolescent girls without jeopardizing dominant patriarchal gender relations and capitalist class relations, eugenic segregation represented an effective solution to the new "girl problem" plaguing the nation's cities.

Sex in the City: Work, Class, and Delinquent Girls

While eugenicists in other parts of the country concerned themselves with other groups whom they defined as defective—recent immigrants or the rural poor—reformers in Illinois focused their campaign for eugenic commitment on young, native-born, working-class women who actively participated in the burgeoning urban industrial culture that pervaded Chicago's public spaces.[5] Between 1880 and 1930 the female labor force in Chicago increased from 36,500 to 407,600.[6] Women of all ages worked in factories, restaurants, and department stores. For young women, waged labor outside the home provided access to an expanding urban social environment that included movie theaters, dance halls, city streets, and sex.[7] Young women used their status as wage earners to challenge the boundaries of acceptable female adolescent behavior, alarming both working-class parents and middle-class reformers. They also frequently became the victims of sexual assault, which also concerned parents and reformers. Many times, adolescent girls working and socializing outside the home came into conflict with police, truancy officers, and other agents of the state, as well as their parents. New juvenile delinquency and compulsory education laws, and the growing legal and mental health systems, empowered the state to arrest and incarcerate young women who deviated from dominant notions of normative adolescent behavior and gender roles.[8] Social science and eugenics would provide the means to "explain" their behavior.

Early employment and participation in a growing urban youth culture were characteristics shared by many of the girls who found themselves entangled in Illinois' juvenile justice and mental health systems. In 1917, while serving as superintendent of the Juvenile Detention Home in Chicago, Mrs. June Purcell-Guild made a study of the "average type" of delinquent girl.[9] She found that the average age of a female delinquent was fifteen years, six months.[10] The average offender most likely had not graduated the eighth grade, and was not attending school at the time of her incarceration. The number one reason for leaving school: "had to go to work." The average female delinquent worked outside the home; she also worked inside the home, caring for younger siblings and maintaining the household. The average female delinquent contributed any wages she earned to her family. What little money she did acquire she spent on modern forms of commercialized entertainment. Most female delinquents said they "loved to dance" or were "crazy about dancing," and many were in Purcell-Guild's words "devotees of the motion picture." Only about one-half of the delinquents in Purcell-Guild's sample claimed to read regularly.[11]

According to women reformers, early employment proved especially problematic for girls. In 1910, the women of the IFWC declared that teenage girls were being morally "ruined" by early employment and increased access to modern commercialized forms of entertainment.[12] In their study of the Juvenile Court, Breckinridge and Abbott argued that female delinquents were, even more than boys, the "helpless victims of early employment." They asserted that a "typical" case was that of a German girl who began working in a factory at age fourteen. The teenager became "corrupted" when she began going downtown in search of a new job and quickly "fell into the habit of going into department store waiting rooms for warmth and rest and to read the newspaper advertisements." When she was arrested at age sixteen, she was with several companions who "were in the habit of visiting waiting rooms with the object of meeting men and going to rooming houses for immoral purposes."[13]

In most cases, young women had their delinquency defined in moral terms. Statistics gathered in the newly created Juvenile Court showed that approximately 85 percent of the 8,845 girls who appeared before the court during its first two decades of operation (1899–1919) committed "moral offenses." The most common charges were "immorality," "incorrigibility," or "disorderly conduct," charges the court and most experts considered synonymous for women.[14] In their study of the Juvenile Court, Breckinridge and Abbott argued that, "In general, the incorrigible or disorderly girl is the one who 'has a bad reputation in the neighborhood,' one who has been going with bad company and staying away at night."[15] Juvenile Court records contain numerous stories of girls sent to Geneva because they associated with a "bad" set of boys and girls, stayed out late at night, visited houses of "ill-fame," or did not attend school.[16] Although an increasing number of Americans were breaking free of the bonds of Victorian sexual reticence, unrestrained female heterosexuality was not considered a normative developmental stage for young women.

The average female offender almost always came from a "degraded" home and a large family, consisting of more than four children. They also usually came from a "broken home" characterized by death, desertion, divorce, and separation. Lena, a fourteen-year-old girl whose father died and whose mother worked as a scrubwoman, "slept in hallways and toilet rooms."[17] In other cases, the father deserted the family, leaving his wife and children to support themselves. Many female delinquents were also abandoned or neglected by their father after their mother died. In her study of delinquent girls incarcerated at the Detention Home, Dr. Anne Burnet found that only six of 106 subjects claimed to come from "good homes."[18] Reformers and the court characterized most of the homes of delinquent girls as "overcrowded," "wretched," and "dirty" places.

In most cases, parents or other relatives of delinquent girls were also considered "defective" or incompetent. Although exact numbers were difficult to obtain, experts and reformers argued that anecdotal evidence suggested that a significant percentage of delinquents had parents who were immoral, abusive, feebleminded, insane, or alcoholic. Some young sex delinquents were themselves "illegitimate" children. Other female delinquents were abused sexually in the workplace or in the home by male relatives or boarders. Middle-class professionals recorded numerous stories similar to the one told by "B," a "beautiful child of fourteen years." According to Purcell-Guild, "B's" mother was a "prostitute and had compelled her daughter to submit to a man when she was ten years of age." After that, "B" was "forced" by boys on two separate occasions. According to Purcell-Guild, "B" became "discouraged" and "went to live over a barn with a boy a few years her senior." Eventually "B" was arrested, after which she attempted to commit suicide. In the end, authorities sent "B" to the State Training School for Girls in Geneva.[19]

In many cases, the average female delinquent was attempting to escape the type of abusive situation encountered by "B." One example of such a case is that of Emily. Emily was sixteen when her mother approached the court because she was concerned about her daughter's "waywardness." According to a Hull House worker, Emily would not stay at home—she worked in a factory and boarded away from home—and when she was at home, she stayed out "all hours of the night." Emily was also dismissed from a job for stealing. Upon investigation, a social worker determined that although Emily's mother was a "respectable, well-meaning widow," she had a temper that forced her to do "extreme things." The caseworker reported that on one occasion, when Emily had been away for weeks, her mother found her and "whipped her severely on the street in the presence of young companions." The caseworker further stated that when Emily was eleven years old, she was "raped by a married man next door with whose child she was playing." And that Emily "did not tell her mother but continued to go to him until it was discovered by others." Law enforcement officials determined that the man had "ruined four dozen little girls, one of whom was pregnant," but when they attempted to prosecute the man he "ran away." The social worker told Emily's mother that she had no "satisfactory evidence" that Emily was "doing wrong" at the time of her investigation. Hull House's connection with this case ended when Emily's mother contacted a social worker in court and said that she "had decided not to send Emily to Geneva and wished nothing done."[20]

Unlike most girls, Emily avoided incarceration. Her story, however, remains similar to those of young women who ended up in one of Illinois' reform institutions. Minnie, for example, was arrested on a warrant obtained by her mother, who was divorced from Minnie's father and who was "known as a bad woman." Although Minnie's mother obtained the warrant in an effort to control her daughter, who allegedly used "bad language" and was "bold with men," it was she who found herself under the scrutiny of social workers and court officials. During Minnie's trial, it was revealed that her mother beat her, and that she was a "degenerate" who was "unfit to have a child." Minnie allegedly tried to kill herself during her trial and was eventually sent to Geneva.[21]

Many families struggling to piece together lives shattered by death, divorce, desertion, and crushing poverty found their situation further complicated by seemingly impenetrable language and cultural barriers. Although delinquents were overwhelmingly native-born, white Americans, many were raised in diverse social and cultural settings, where English was a second language.[22] Breckinridge and Abbott found that approximately 67 percent of the parents of young women who appeared before the court were immigrants from various parts of Europe and Canada.[23] Mary's parents, for example, called on Hull House workers when they received an anonymous letter stating that their fifteen-year-old daughter, who had been away from home for several months, was living in a "house of ill-repute." Mary's mother could not speak English and her father refused to take action on his own to retrieve his daughter. A Hull House worker promised to retrieve Mary, but was unsuccessful. Eventually a police officer went to the address mentioned in the letter and arrested Mary for prostitution. She was fined $100 by the Juvenile Court and sent to Geneva.

In yet another case, Jane was taken out of a lodging house when she was fifteen, on a warrant obtained by her father, whom a Hull House worker described as a "Bohemian who speaks no English." Jane's mother was dead and her stepmother had been away from home for two or three months. Jane started working in a laundry when she was thirteen, and shortly thereafter began staying out late at night at saloon dance halls. When she was taken out of the lodging house, Jane had been away from home for ten months and was allegedly being "kept" by a married man. She was fined $75 and sent to the House of the Good Shepherd.

Oftentimes, an unexpected pregnancy brought young women into contact with reformers and the court. In October 1897, a social worker visited sixteen-year-old Kattie at her older sister's residence. Kattie's mother, who worked in the Marshall Field's cloak factory, had gone to Hull House and asked that they "take charge" of her pregnant daughter. The Hull House worker who visited Kattie reported that, "By her own story [Kattie] was with four young men in one month," and that Kattie was a "thoroughly bad girl." Kattie was placed in the Erring Women's Refuge, where she agreed to stay until her baby was one year old. Approximately one year after Kattie first encountered the workers at Hull House, her fourteen-year-old sister Sarah was sent to the industrial school in Evanston because she had been "running the streets . . . in bad company" while her mother was at work. The women at Hull House learned of Sarah's incarceration when her mother came to them again and requested their assistance in getting her daughter released from the institution, which they did in 1899. In another case, a police officer arrested Dora on a complaint that was brought by her parents. Dora's parents claimed that although their daughter was only fifteen years old, she was a "confirmed street walker and pregnant." Dora was fined fifty dollars and committed to Geneva. The workers at Hull House attempted to get Dora released on probation but were unsuccessful because of her "continued bad behavior" in the institution.[24]

Many delinquent girls were indeed sexually active at the time of their arrest and incarceration. Approximately 50 percent of the inmates at Geneva in 1898 had some form of venereal disease. The percentage of inmates at Geneva with VD increased to 62 percent by 1908. By 1916, the medical department at Geneva had treated more than 4,515 cases of venereal disease. The number of cases of VD increased to 18,852 by 1930. Throughout the 1940s, the medical staff at Geneva treated between one hundred and two hundred cases of VD annually among a resident inmate population that ranged from three hundred to four hundred.[25] Geneva's 1908 annual report listed only twenty-five of its approximately four hundred inmates as virgins; fifteen girls had come to the institution pregnant, seventeen other girls had given birth before coming to Geneva, and five young women had had abortions.[26] The number of pregnant women and new mothers at Geneva rose steadily between 1920 and 1950. Geneva's medical staff provided prenatal care to approximately fifty to sixty pregnant inmates and cared for approximately thirty to sixty newborns in the institution's nursery each year during those three decades.[27]

Some young women who became pregnant actually sought out various state services and institutions in their effort to cope with the heavy burden that accompanied an "illegitimate" birth. Margaret, for example, wrote Geneva's managing officer a letter in which she begged to enter the institution until her pregnancy was over. "I hardly know how to begin a letter of this sort," Margaret wrote. "I am a girl almost 18 years of age. I have no home to go to—and am in trouble. I am in the 'family way' and have no one to go to and nowhere to turn. I have a job at the present—but cannot work much longer. My employer does not know of my predicament, and [I] do not wish to tell them until I can work no longer—else I may lose my job before enough money is saved to come to you." "I am pleading," Margaret continued, "that I may enter your institution until my 'trial' is over. If I am forced to stay until I am 21—it is O.K. with me as I have no home—no place to go in my condition. I have led a wild life—but am paying for it heavily—but I know I deserve it [and] will bear my pain [and] regret as bravely as possible. Trusting you will answer *at once* and let me know if I may come when I can work no longer. Very humbly, Margaret."[28] Geneva's managing officer replied to Margaret's desperate plea, informing her that she could not come to Geneva, "unless committed by some Court." The managing officer referred Margaret to the Florence Crittendon Home and the Salvation Army Home, which were institutions that, in her words, could take Margaret in, and "shield and protect" her and help her to get a job after the delivery of her baby.[29]

For some working-class girls, reformers' focus on the "new girl problem" meant increased surveillance of their social and sexual lives and frequent incarceration. Rebecca was a sixteen-year-old girl who was brought into court after an officer found her with a man in a coal yard on Halsted Street at two o'clock in the morning. Rebecca's mother explained to the social worker who recorded Rebecca's case that her daughter "[ran] the streets with men all night" and that Rebecca had been in the industrial school in Evanston. Rebecca was fined fifty dollars and committed to Geneva. In April 1899, Annie (fourteen years old), Maggie (fourteen years old), and Francis (fifteen years old) were brought into the Juvenile Court from Maxwell Street. The social worker handling the case reported that the three girls "Stayed away from home for weeks running to all night dances, and [were] consorting with young men." The social worker went on to state that Annie had also "collected $9.45 in a church book and used it," but that Maggie was "the worst in the group of three, as she found lodging houses for all and led to the dances." Maggie also "picked pockets in down-town stores, and taught children to do the same." According to the caseworker, Francis was the "best of the three girls and might have been paroled." Since, however, Francis "confessed, herself, that she 'ran with men,'" and because she had an older sister "on the street," she, along with Annie and Maggie, was sent to the House of the Good Shepherd.[30]

Proportionately, young working-class women who were arrested for moral offenses were more likely than young men to endure incarceration in one of Illinois' reform institutions.[31] Breckinridge and Abbott found that 21 percent of the 11,641 boys who appeared before the Juvenile Court were sentenced to institutions, versus 51 percent of the 2,770 girls who appeared before the court. Experts asserted that the disparity between the percentage of girls who were incarcerated and the percentage of boys who were incarcerated existed, in part, because adolescent boys' crimes were not as serious as those committed by teenage girls. Boys' crimes were primarily against property, and did not pose a sexual or eugenic threat to the individual offender or to society. Unlike young women, boys' sexual conduct was rarely criminalized, even in the case of rape. Breckinridge and Abbott found that 51 percent of the boys who appeared before the Juvenile Court violated property rights, versus only 15 percent of girls. In comparison, they found that only 2 percent of boys were arrested for "actual immorality." Experts and reformers viewed boys' crimes against property as a natural consequence of development and argued that young men would eventually mature and outgrow their delinquent stage. According to experts, most male delinquents did not require incarceration. Young women, on the other hand, were incarcerated in large part because experts considered sexual immorality to be detrimental not only to young women, but also to the community and the race.[32]

Although the percentage of young women (and men) committed to institutions changed over time, the gendered difference in the nature of the offenses committed by girls and boys remained unchanged.[33] In fact, during the juvenile court's second decade of operation, the percentage of males who were arrested and appeared before the court for "actual immorality" declined to .02 percent, while the percentage of young women charged with moral offenses remained high, at 85 percent.[34] Although incarceration rates also fluctuated, the percentage of adolescent girls who found themselves at Geneva for a "moral offense" remained high. Drs. Louise Morrow and Olga Bridgman, physicians at Geneva, reported in 1912 that 84 percent of the five hundred most recent admissions to that institution were incarcerated for "immorality" and "incorrigibility."[35] In an era of rapid social and economic change, young, native-born, working-class women had become the embodiment of a "civilization" that appeared to many middle-class reformers, and some working-class parents, to be drifting perilously toward its own destruction.

Social Deviance Becomes Mental Deviance

Once in an institution, working-class teenagers encountered school administrators, teachers, and other experts determined to discover the cause of their delinquency. As Augusta Bronner argued in 1914, the "question of the delinquent girl" was one that had "aroused much interest." Delinquent girls were being "studied from every possible viewpoint—mental and physical, as well as environmental and social." There was, however, a single theory that seemed to ring true among most Americans. Bronner found that many scientists and social workers, and "many of the general public" who had expressed their views on female delinquency, had "stated it as their opinion" that delinquency was "due very largely to the fact that the offenders [were] not sufficiently intelligent to care for themselves without running into difficulties." Bronner declared that popular opinion held that the "large majority" of delinquent girls were "sub-normal or feeble minded."[36]

Experts and much of the general public used emergent eugenic and *psy* discourses to confirm the popularly held assumption that a group of young semi-autonomous women who in some cases became the victims of sexual assault and rape, or who engaged in waged labor and socialized outside "traditional" forms of supervision and control, were "naturally" inferior to their nondelinquent counterparts. Experts, interested readers, and social reformers alike linked a perceived lack of intelligence to sexual delinquency and argued that "feebleminded" women were more apt than their "normal-minded" counterparts to commit moral offenses. Not all experts engaging in research in institutions espoused biological explanations of social problems. Those individuals who supported the eugenic commitment of "feebleminded" delinquents did, however, use scientific studies of incarcerated populations to legitimize their claims.

The introduction of the Binet intelligence tests to Geneva during the 1910s supplied experts, administrators, and the general public with the "evidence," or what one might call the technologies of power, to materialize their culturally freighted assertion that young women committed to state institutions were overwhelmingly "feebleminded."[37] Geneva's superintendent, Ophelia Amigh, declared that one of the most "alarming discoveries" of the early twentieth century was the high number of so-called feebleminded women incarcerated in Illinois' reform institutions.[38] In 1912, she asserted that if the Illinois legislature created a separate institution for "women and girls of defective intellect," there would be "almost no call for the school at Geneva" because the percentage of girls who would be "designated as morons" was "so large" at that institution.[41] Also in 1912, Drs. Morrow and Bridgman published the results of a study in which they administered the Binet tests to sixty girls living at Geneva. They found that only six girls tested within the "normal" range, while forty-nine girls scored within the "high-grade imbecile" to "high-grade moron" range (seven to twelve years). Five girls possessed a "mental age" below seven years.[40] In a separate study published in 1913, Dr. Bridgman reported that 95 percent of 118 Geneva inmates scored within the "feebleminded" (at least three years' "retardation") to "backward" (one to two years' "retardation") range on the Binet tests.[41] Louise Ordahl and George Ordahl obtained similar results when they administered intelligence tests at Geneva in 1915. They argued that 95 percent of the women whom they tested exhibited varying degrees of "feeblemindedness."[42]

Eugenic reformers in Illinois were not alone in their argument that a significant percentage of female delinquents were indeed "feebleminded." The Honorable George Addams, judge of the Juvenile Court of Cleveland, Ohio, argued that to a large extent the Juvenile Court dealt with the "weak and inefficient." According to Addams, individuals who worked with juvenile delinquents had known for some time that "feeble-mindedness was a tremendous burden to the race." It was not until the introduction of the Binet tests, however, that school administrators, judges, and other experts who worked closely with juvenile delinquents began to become alarmed.[43] Following a "careful and elaborate" study of the Girls' Reformatory of Ohio, Miss Emile Renz found a "startlingly high percentage of mental defectives"; 79 percent of the inmates whom she tested exhibited more than three years' "retardation." Renz concluded that the girls' delinquency was "one of mental incapacity," not a degraded environment or social and economic inequity.[44] Following a "careful study of conditions" in the Juvenile Court of Newark, New Jersey, Mrs. E. Garfield Gifford and Henry Goddard of the Vineland School for the Feebleminded found that only *one* out of one hundred subjects chosen "entirely at random" tested within the "normal" range on intelligence tests.[45]

Even more alarming to experts and reformers were scientific studies that revealed what appeared to be a definite correlation between feeblemindedness and immorality. In their study of Geneva, the Ordahls argued that at least 58 percent of the "immorality" committed by incarcerated women was attributable to "low grade intelligence."[46] Dr. Bridgman found that 104 of the 118 girls committed to Geneva during the period of her investigation were "sex delinquents," and that 97 percent of the 104 "sex delinquents" were "feebleminded." She argued that her evidence seemed to prove that "mental deficiency" played an important causative role in sexual "immorality."[47] The Ordahls explained that Geneva's "feebleminded" inmates were those young women who sought Chicago's public spaces for entertainment and company, or who had been forced, out of economic necessity, to work in factories, department stores, and restaurants. The Ordahls further explained that in practically every case, the young women had become infatuated with some young man, and "not possessing adequate intelligence for controlling otherwise legitimate impulses, their instinctive desire for male companionship [had] led to immoral conduct."[48]

According to maternalist reformers who supported eugenic commitment, a discernible group of young "feebleminded" women engaged in sexually delinquent activities that ultimately led to their arrest and incarceration in places like Geneva. Eugenics and intelligence tests enabled reformers and experts to mark, classify, and quantify female offenders' transgressions, and in turn attribute causation. Although they recognized the social and economic causes of female juvenile delinquency, and like Judge Bartelme, often empathized with young girls' plight, experts and reformers interested in using what they considered the most modern and scientific, and ultimately humane and progressive means of social reform, relied upon eugenics and psychology to incarcerate a vulnerable group of adolescent women in state institutions indefinitely.[49]

Gender and Eugenic Commitment

Most male eugenic reformers explicitly stated their desire to focus their campaign on young women. As Dr. William Healy of the Juvenile Psychopathic Institute stated in March 1915, Illinois' "first duty" was the creation of a "colony for the segregation of girls and women of child bearing age who [were] mental defectives."[50] Although Illinois' commitment law remained gender-neutral in its language, male experts agreed that "feebleminded" women posed a more serious threat to society and the race than their male counterparts. Dr. Thomas Leonard, superintendent of the Lincoln State School and Colony, argued that a "feebleminded" woman was three times as great a "menace" to society as her male counterpart.[51] A. L. Bowen, executive secretary of the Illinois State Charities Commission, asserted that "the feeble-minded male is little to be feared. He can easily be controlled, by proper supervision, aided by good marriage laws. . . . As to the female, the problem is more serious. The expert viewpoint is that the female requires very close attention, much closer probably than can be given her anywhere except in an institution."[52] According to Leonard, there were a number of women at Lincoln who might have become "quite useful members of society" if they could have controlled their "sex faculties." He declared that if all "feebleminded" women of childbearing age could be committed for the duration of their reproductive years, more than one-half of the "feebleminded problem" would be solved, because predatory "feebleminded" women would be protected from their own unrestrained sexuality.[53]

The arguments made by male scientists in Illinois reflected a larger national trend. In his presidential address to the National Conference of Charities and Corrections, Dr. Amos Butler asserted that "The debasing and demoralizing influence of an unrestrained feeble-minded woman in a community [was] beyond the comprehension of the uninformed." He argued that "feeblemindedness" was, to a "very large extent," inherited, and that it was associated with a "vast train of woes." Butler concluded his address by stating that he was grateful to those states that possessed enough "wisdom" to establish "custodial institutions for the detention and care of feebleminded women during the reproductive period." Such institutions, Butler asserted, were a "great blessing to humanity and in the end a source of public economy."[54] Throughout the country, male experts deployed moralizing diagnostic regimes cloaked in the objectifying, quantifying language of science to create a new class of sexual predator: the ubiquitous wanton "feebleminded" female. In the nineteenth century, with the emergence of "age of consent" and other campaigns, public concern had focused largely on predatory men.[55] This changed in the early twentieth century, in part because of the dramatic rise in popularity of eugenics.

If we examine only the utterances of male eugenicists, the enactment of the eugenic commitment law seems like merely another case of middle-class white men using science and the state to control women's sexuality.[56] Although this may be accurate, this argument does not fully explain women's active role in the campaign to create a state-sponsored system of eugenic commitment in Illinois, nor does it explain their focus on segregating sexually delinquent "feebleminded" women. Female eugenicists tended to use gender-neutral language in their call for the incarceration of "mental defectives." They referred to the institutionalization of "feebleminded persons" and to the "segregation [of] mental defectives, as a class." Yet they too focused their eugenic campaign on young women whom they defined as mentally "defective."[57]

Unlike their male counterparts, however, maternalists emphasized young women's vulnerability and their sexual victimization. Middle-class women did not deny that mentally "defective" adolescent women could be sexual predators. They merely offered a more complex, nuanced portrait of the "feebleminded menace" that included young women incapable of warding off the advances of predatory men. By emphasizing adolescent women's vulnerability as well as their sexual agency, maternalists modified and updated an older discourse of protection that had its roots in nineteenth-century efforts to save the nation's young women from "moral ruin." In the twentieth century, women reformers were saving and protecting not only a group of vulnerable girls, but also the future of the race itself.

The critical difference between the nineteenth-century "fallen woman" and the delinquent daughter of the early twentieth century rested not necessarily in a rearticulation of young women's heterosexual agency, but rather in a new conceptualization of the mental impairment that supposedly lay at the root of their misconduct.[58] By classifying female delinquents as inherently flawed, women reformers simultaneously highlighted their vulnerability and the potentially biologically hazardous implications of their actions.

An investigation conducted in Boston by prominent feminists Elizabeth Evans and Mary "Molly" Dewson reveals the gendered nature of eugenic reform. In their article, "Feeble-Mindedness and Juvenile Delinquency: A Study from Experience," Evans and Dewson criticized society for not taking heed when boys committed "sexual faults." Yet they asserted that the sexual double standard alone could not explain the gendered discrepancy in incarceration rates. Instead, they argued that fewer "feebleminded" boys found themselves in institutions because an "unenterprising" or "dull" boy was less likely to commit offenses against property, the most common types of offenses committed by boys. As boys got older their need to work "kept [them] under some sort of discipline," which in most cases kept them out of institutions. "Feebleminded" girls, on the other hand, could become the "prey" of "bad men," they could also support themselves by their "vices," which made them a much greater threat, both to themselves and to the community. Evans and Dewson asserted that "feebleminded" boys satisfied their sexual desires by "self-abuse" (masturbation), which did not pose any danger to the community, while similar practices in girls only served to "whet desire." They concluded that "the feeble-minded problem may almost be disregarded in connection with a boys' reform school, while in connection with a girls' reform school it takes on very large proportions." Evans and Dewson supported a system of indefinite incarceration for "feebleminded" girls, while they argued that it was "improbable that custodial care will ever prevail to any considerable extent for mentally defective . . . boys."[59]

A similar study of "mentally defective" children in Chicago conducted by the Juvenile Protective Association (JPA) further reveals the role of gender in eugenic reform.[60] In 1913, the women at the JPA, who focused much of their work on improving the social and environmental conditions of Chicago's most impoverished neighborhoods, decided within the midst of rising concern over the "feebleminded menace" to conduct a study of the living conditions of Chicago's "mentally defective" children.[61]

After nearly two years of investigation, the JPA concluded that the crisis of the "mentally defective" was serious and far-reaching. Although they acknowledged that it would have been impossible to ascertain the exact number of "feebleminded" persons living in Chicago, they estimated that it was very high, probably greater than six thousand individuals. The JPA also argued that their study confirmed the assertion that feeblemindedness played an important role in the perpetuation of vice, crime, poverty, and other social problems.

In the end, the JPA recommended a eugenic solution to the problems facing Chicagoans. They concluded that a state-sponsored system of eugenic commitment was necessary to eliminate the deleterious effects of feeblemindedness.[62] The association argued that without indefinite segregation, "mentally defective people" and their grown children would fill the city's courts and become a "menace" to the morals of Chicago's young people. The JPA declared that efforts aimed at providing more adequate care for Illinois' "feebleminded" people deserved the support of all "public spirited" citizens.[63]

Although they used gender-neutral language, the JPA supported a system of eugenic institutionalization that focused on young women. According to the JPA, the "question of permanent custodial care for sub-normal women [was] perhaps the most important of all in connection with the mentally defective." The JPA asserted that "defective" women required indefinite incarceration because they were "absolutely incapable of reform or of self-support." According to the JPA, "mentally defective" women were also "continually in danger of being victimized by vicious men." The reformers at the JPA characterized the ubiquitous "feebleminded" woman not only as a sexual agent, but also a potential victim of male sexual aggression. They argued that the "same defects" that made a "feebleminded" woman a "passionate and uncontrolled seducer of others" also made her easy prey.[64]

To clarify the ease with which young women could move between sexual agency and victimization, the JPA cited the case of a Bohemian girl named Helena. According to the JPA, Helena had "little intelligence." She was also "sexually precocious and perverted." Helena "practiced masturbation" and talked about "sexual matters to both boys and girls." When she was thirteen, a teacher and a school nurse discovered that Helena had been having "sexual relations" with boys. Helena was eventually forced to leave school because she was "too great a menace to the other children." For four years Helena lived at home; she spent her time working occasionally and socializing away from home with friends. In 1913, Helena appeared before the Juvenile Court and "told a terrible story of rape by a group of boys to whom she had been taken by a boy she knew." Upon investigation, the court determined Helena's story to be true. Four of the boys were placed under indictment and Helena was institutionalized. The JPA used Helena's case to illustrate what they considered the ease with which a young woman could vacillate between victimization and agency. They stated that, in telling Helena's story, "one [did] not know which element to lay most stress upon, her helplessness to defend herself from evil-minded men or the potentialities for evil within herself."[65] Regardless of whether eugenic reformers constructed "feebleminded" girls as sexual agents, or victims, or both, and regardless of whether they used gender-neutral language, they agreed that a "mentally defective" girl left unsupervised inevitably became a community "menace." Experts and reformers used women's "natural" weaknesses, which had become intimately bound up with a perceived lack of mental capacity, to justify control, or protection, through incarceration.

The women at the JPA, like other eugenic reformers, did not view "feebleminded" men in the same way that they viewed "feebleminded" women. In their study of "mentally defective" children in Chicago, the JPA argued that one "seldom" found "widespread demoralization" in the wake of a "mentally defective" male. They went on to argue that "feebleminded" men could work "if they had the right sort of work and the right sort of supervision." According to the JPA, some "mentally defective" men were even "capable with training of becoming self-supporting." Employment, the JPA claimed, would minimize young men's tendency toward delinquency, because their delinquency was not interpreted in sexual terms. The JPA asserted that the state needed a farm colony where "feebleminded" men could be sent "for a long enough period to fit them for self-support," but that most "mentally defective" men did not require indefinite incarceration.[66]

In December 1914, the *Tribune* published the JPA's official recommendations. Included among them were the following eugenic measures: a state institution for defective delinquents; a state institution for "feeble minded" women of childbearing age; "Laws giving the judge of the Juvenile court authority to commit to an institution the feeble minded children brought before him and giving judges similar powers relating to adult defectives"; and finally, "A commitment law and institutions to which to commit mental defectives whose presence in the community is in any way a menace or danger."[67]

Despite their explicit desire to institutionalize all "feebleminded" individuals, the JPA articulated their support for the eugenic commitment law in a manner rooted in scientific theories and social values that linked immorality, delinquency, and mental "defect" with dominant white middle-class notions of sexual propriety. The result was the creation of a system of eugenic segregation that focused almost exclusively on monitoring the behavior of women who deviated from those roles. According to most middle-class experts, as long as young men were capable of being gainfully employed in some form of waged labor, minor offenses against society could be dismissed as part of the maturation process. Young women, on the other hand, had the much more important and, for some, difficult task of remaining sexually chaste until marriage. White, native-born women's status as the moral standard-bearer of a burgeoning urban, industrial culture and the potential mothers of eugenically "fit" children placed them at the center of a eugenic debate that relied upon a newly ascendant social scientific definition of "normality."

Beginning around the turn of the twentieth century, the surveillance of female sexuality increasingly relied upon a discourse of disablement, which in turn contributed at least in part to the entrenchment of an individualized, medicalized model of social deviance and social reform. Though it never fully eclipsed other explanations, this new modern, scientific means of measuring social competence and social adjustment became dominant in the twentieth century and continues to have a powerful effect on medical, social scientific, and social reform discourse in the twenty-first century.

Challenges

Some experts, including professional maternalists, challenged the idea that female offenders were overwhelmingly "feebleminded." The writers at *The Institution Quarterly* argued that although there may have been some relationship between feeblemindedness and immorality, "how close or extensive" the relationship was, or whether a relationship existed at all, could not be determined by contemporary research. The *Quarterly* asserted that experts conducting mental exams failed to create a normative standard of intelligence for "moral" women whose socioeconomic standing was comparable to that of the "immoral" women incarcerated at Geneva. The writers at *The Institution Quarterly* expressed a lack of confidence in the tests themselves and argued that individuals conducting tests on incarcerated women were too quick to label their subjects "feebleminded."[68] In short, the staff at the *Quarterly* wanted to distinguish class from immorality and better understand the relationship between intelligence and moral capacity—as they defined it—before they came to any definite conclusions concerning the pervasiveness of feeblemindedness among female delinquents.

Augusta Bronner substantiated the assertions made in *The Institution Quarterly*. In her comparative study of the intelligence of delinquent girls, Bronner claimed that although social workers and the general public supported the assertion that most offenders were "subnormal" or "feebleminded," delinquency was caused by "something other than the intellectual status alone."[69] In a separate study conducted after she arrived at the Juvenile Psychopathic Institute in Chicago, Bronner stated that the studies conducted in places like Geneva could "hardly be accepted as giving accurate or reliable information," in part because the Binet tests were "unsatisfactory for measuring the grade of intelligence of those with a mental age above ten years"—the so-called high-grade feebleminded or moron.

According to Bronner, many factors influenced test scores. The attitude of both the person studied and the examiner affected the results of most studies. Mental exams could also be affected by certain external factors like defective vision or hearing, or mental dullness that resulted from physical ill health or the "pernicious effects of bad habits." Bronner concluded that "most of the discussion one hears so commonly now-a-days about the 'mental age' of adolescent and adult offenders is veritable nonsense." She based her conclusion on a study of boys and girls incarcerated at the Cook County Juvenile Detention Home, in which she administered Binet tests as well as other psychological examinations that she and her boss, and future husband, William Healy, had been developing. Bronner found that approximately 93 percent of boys and 89 percent of girls were "*normal*" in mental ability.[70]

In 1916, the *Tribune* ran a story on Bronner and Healy's work. In an article entitled "Juvenile Crimes Not by Morons," a reporter declared that "The majority of juvenile law breakers are not as has been generally thought, feebleminded." According to the *Tribune*, Bronner and Healy's work showed clearly that "feeblemindedness as a cause of juvenile crime has been overemphasized and that the future field for crime prevention is the home and the neighborhood." The percentages were slightly smaller than those obtained in previous studies—Healy and Bronner found 75 percent of delinquents to be "normal mentally"—but the message was clear. The *Tribune* article quoted Healy as stating that "Our data seems to have shown the common idea that feeblemindedness is the main contributing cause of delinquency to be in great part nonsense."

In his statement to the *Tribune,* Healy offered one critically important caveat, however. Though he recognized that the importance of mental "deficiency" in juvenile crime was vastly overstated, he did not dismiss intellect completely.[71] The notion that even a small percentage of juvenile offenders were definitely "feebleminded"—in this case 25 percent, which was only small by comparison with other findings, was enough for eugenic reformers. The argument that many more juvenile delinquents could possibly be mentally "deficient" only served to bolster eugenicists' claims that the state needed the power to incarcerate feebleminded offenders indefinitely.

Dr. Anna Dwyer, who served on the Illinois State Charities Commission (ISCC) and on the committee that drafted the 1915 commitment bill, was well aware of the shortcomings of modern intelligence tests. That knowledge, however, did not stop her from supporting eugenic institutionalization. Dwyer and the ISCC urged experts and lawmakers to be careful and to not get "carried away by the present day demands for radical action in treating those whose mentality falls below certain prevalent notions of what should be a mental standard."[72] Despite their cautious tone, Dwyer and the ISCC maintained their support for eugenic commitment. In a report issued in 1913, the ISCC asserted that they were "not unmindful of the prevalence of mental defectiveness" in the general population, and that they did not "underestimate its dangers, if unchecked, in the pollution of the racial stock." The commission went on to argue that, in general, they supported the segregation of "feebleminded" individuals during the "period of their productiveness," but that the state needed to "proceed cautiously in dealing with the so-called border-line classes."[73]

By fall 1916—after nearly a year of living with the commitment law—Dwyer and the ISCC remained convinced that eugenic commitment was a vital social reform measure. In addition to her other duties, Dwyer served as a physician to the Morals Court of Chicago, where she encountered the complexities of feeblemindedness and eugenics daily. Dwyer frequently examined women who were "penniless, homeless, hungry, [and] unable to compete against efficient, trained workers in the struggle for employment." She urged the state and private businesses and charities to make provisions within the community for the care, training, and employment of impoverished women. She asserted, however, that "not less" than 60 percent of the three thousand women who she examined in the Morals Court were "too defective to be safe in the outside world." She claimed that they were "mentally, morally, and sometimes physically incompetent to care for themselves." Many of them had been incarcerated in juvenile institutions. According to Dwyer, the "feebleminded" women who came through the Morals

Court were a "menace" to society and "the most flagrant carriers of [disease] and immorality."[74] Though she recognized the importance of economic and social programs, Dwyer held firm to her conclusion that the state also needed the legal means to incarcerate "feebleminded" offenders indefinitely.

Despite serious challenges, maternalist reformers' faith in the diagnostic powers of modern science had not faltered. In 1918 Geneva's managing officer, Dr. Clara Hayes, reported that she received many girls of "low mental grade." Hayes asserted that the commitment of "feebleminded" girls to Geneva was unfortunate both for themselves and for society, in part because many inmates served short sentences, usually only one year, and because inmates could not be detained at Geneva beyond their twenty-first birthday. Geneva was a training school for juvenile delinquents, not a custodial institution for "feebleminded" persons. Despite mounting opposition to eugenic commitment, Hayes maintained the argument that provisions had to be made for the maintenance and care of "feebleminded" women during their entire lives.[75] Only within an institution would young women receive the care and protection they supposedly required.

In an effort to clarify further maternalists' conviction to eugenic commitment, we must return to our opening vignette and the courtroom of Judge Mary Margaret Bartelme. According to *Current Opinion*, Judge Bartelme of the Cook County Juvenile Court treated the girls who appeared before her with "never-failing high-mindedness."[76] She always tried to impress upon her girls that she was their friend, not their enemy. "In nine out of ten cases," Bartelme observed, "these young girls are more sinned against than sinning." The girls were not "criminal." They were "as a rule, poor deluded creatures too young to have an adequate conception of the tragedy upon which they have stumbled." Bartelme maintained that a lack of "right care," as well as a lack of "right living and thinking," among the parents was an important cause of juvenile delinquency.[77] Knowing, as she did, that delinquent girls had been "misled through their ignorance of life," Bartelme made it a point never to incarcerate first-time offenders, unless they seemed "hopelessly incorrigible." She asserted, however, that, "Subnormal, weak-willed, and mentally deficient girls" required "to be dealt with in a different way." "Often they are a menace to society," Bartelme declared, "and I deem it best to send them to institutions where they will have the benefit of protection and proper direction."[78] Judge Bartelme, like many of her colleagues, believed that every juvenile delinquent needed to be examined by the Institute for Juvenile Research, and that the state needed to make special provision for the indefinite care of "borderline mentally defective delinquents."[79] By no means was Judge Bartelme alone in her decision to incarcerate indefinitely those adolescent girls such as Elsie, whom society—and perhaps more importantly, science—deemed inherently incapable of caring for themselves.

Conclusion

By linking sexual activity that occurred outside the bounds of socially sanctioned gender roles with feeblemindedness, eugenic reformers constructed sexually dubious women as "naturally" deviant (feebleminded). Gendered assumptions about "normal" and "abnormal" sex roles and power relations motivated reformers to argue that it would be more effective to incarcerate women indefinitely than it would be to incarcerate men indefinitely. Both maternalists and male experts who supported eugenic commitment agreed that "feebleminded" women of childbearing age represented the greatest social and eugenic threat. Both groups repeatedly argued that Binet tests revealed that young women incarcerated in Illinois' reform institutions were overwhelmingly "feebleminded," and that feeblemindedness and sexual "deviance" shared a reciprocal relationship. Eugenics and the Binet intelligence tests enabled experts to portray young women arrested for moral offenses as "feebleminded" individuals who were unable to control their own "sex instinct" and incapable of warding off predatory men. Unlike their male counterparts, maternalists recognized the ease with which girls could vacillate between victimization and agency, and emphasized the argument that "feebleminded" delinquent girls were vulnerable and in need of protection and care, not only from themselves, but also from men. Eugenic reformers ultimately concluded that the most effective way to eliminate "feeblemindedness" and improve society was to incarcerate "feebleminded" women offenders indefinitely. Only then would they receive the care and guidance they required, and only then would real, lasting change occur.

A typical turn-of-the-century Geneva classroom. Courtesy Geneva History Center.

Inmates reading in an early twentieth-century Geneva classroom. Courtesy Geneva History Center.

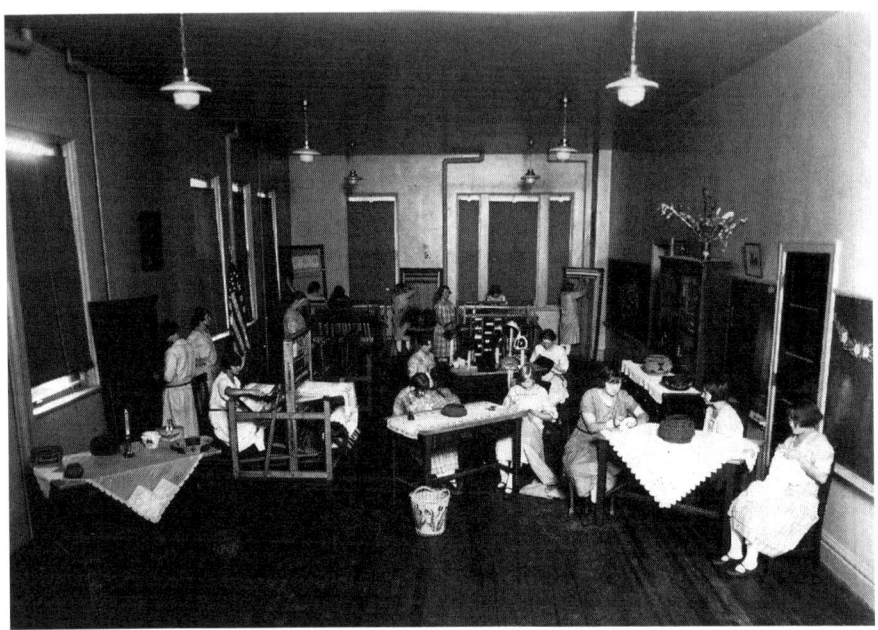
Inmates working in one of Geneva's "industrial rooms." Courtesy Geneva History Center.

Inmates engaging in physical activity on the Geneva grounds. Courtesy Geneva History Center.

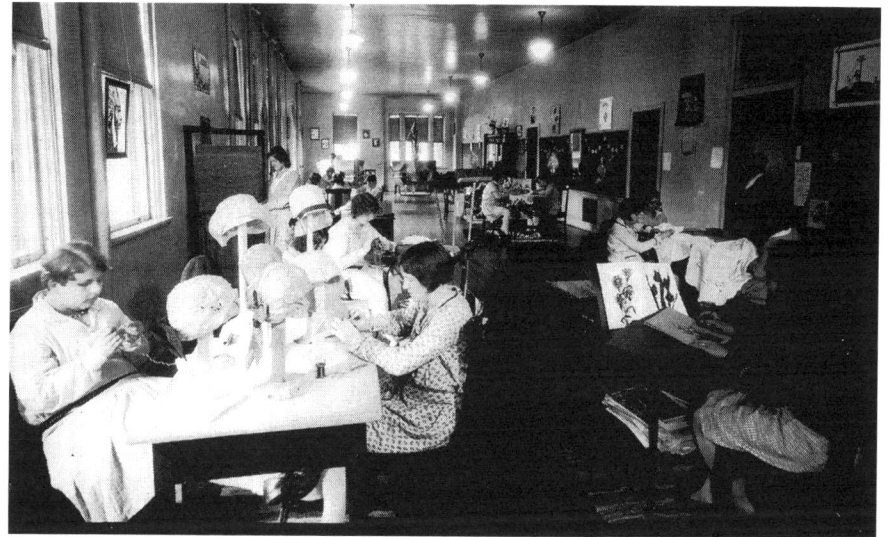

Inmates engaging in "fancy sewing" in one of Geneva's "industrial rooms." Courtesy Geneva History Center.

A typical interviewing room in the new Institute for Juvenile Research (ca. 1917). Unprocessed collection of Geneva documents.

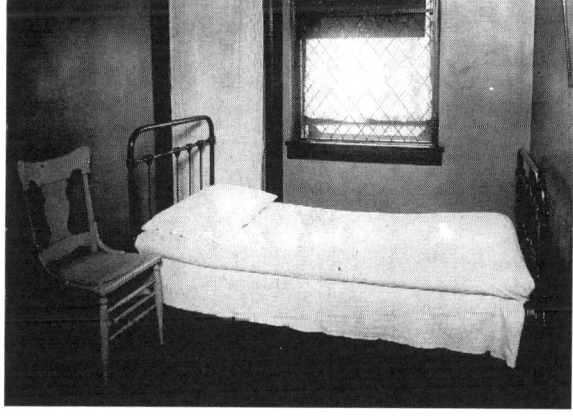

A typical turn-of-the-century bedroom at Geneva. Courtesy Geneva History Center.

Fabian Cottage, State Training School for Girls, Geneva, Illinois. Courtesy Geneva History Center.

A postcard showing the lush grounds of the State Training School at Geneva, Illinois. Courtesy Geneva History Center.

3

"The Relation Between Morality and Intellect"

> "The mere fact that a girl has engaged in illicit sex relationships does not justify the assumption that of necessity there need be any pathological mental situation involved."
>
> —Dr. Marion E. Kenworthy,
> New York School of Social Work, 1921

In 1935, Dr. Clara Chassell published *The Relation Between Morality and Intellect,* in which she analyzed the relationship between feeblemindedness and delinquency.[1] In many ways, Chassell's study reaffirmed critiques that began to emerge before the First World War.[2] Chassell argued that her research showed that feeblemindedness and delinquency shared a strong positive correlation, which appeared stronger for delinquents and female sex offenders, but that statistical data alone remained limited in its usefulness.[3] The correlation between feeblemindedness and delinquency, Chassell argued, could not be used to determine causality, nor could it be used to determine the power of biology or environment in the making of a delinquent. For these reasons, Chassell considered her statistical data to be "scarcely sufficient for predictive purposes."[4] As Lewis Terman had argued a decade earlier, few things seemed more certain than the correlation between intellect and conduct, but that correlation did not provide much of a basis for predicting whether or not a "mentally inferior" individual would become delinquent.[5]

By the early 1920s, the confluence of prominent trends in the mental health professions and the study of juvenile delinquency, as well as changing social-sexual mores, caused many Americans to rethink both the relationship between morality and intellect, and the need for eugenic segregation. Indefinite commitment remained in place after the First World War, and reformers continued to use it. Yet there were also experts, reformers, and institution administrators who chose to emphasize alternative methods of reform.[6] The results of the army mental tests, which were performed on male recruits to the U.S. Army during World War I, and changing sexual attitudes among much of the middle class compelled most experts and reformers to begin to disentangle feeblemindedness from delinquency and rethink the necessity of institutionalizing all of those individuals deemed unfit by modern science.

The postwar shift in focus did not, however, signal an end to eugenics in Illinois or elsewhere. Both eugenic commitment and the science of eugenics had never been completely accepted by the public or by experts. The interwar period marked another stage in an ongoing process. Both "negative" and "positive" eugenic measures spread throughout the country during the 1920s and 1930s. Yet the debate over eugenics became more sharply divided.[7] Some Americans sought to use eugenic segregation unabated after the war, while others argued that laws like the one in Illinois were callous and ineffective, and in need of serious reform.[8] There were also those individuals who used eugenic institutionalization infrequently, and only in cases they considered severe or problematic.[9] This last group, which comprised a majority in Illinois, argued that eugenic commitment represented merely one option in a much broader approach to preventing sex delinquency among adolescent women.

In this chapter, I analyze the shifting terrain of the eugenic commitment debate during the interwar period as a means of making salient both the persistence of eugenic segregation and the resilience of mental classifications that were at once flexible and dynamic and historically contingent. Though reformers in Illinois began to shift their focus toward "community care" during the interwar period, both eugenic commitment and the pathologization of female juvenile delinquency continued.

Community Care

Following the First World War, experts across the country increasingly advocated community care for certain "mentally defective" delinquents, as well as their "normal-minded" counterparts. As early as 1919, Dr. Clara Hayes, who had served on the staff of the Peoria State Hospital and later became the managing officer at Geneva, was beginning to have second thoughts about the wholesale incarceration of feebleminded individuals. Though she never completely abandoned eugenic segregation, Hayes appeared eager to employ a broad range of theories and methods in her effort to reform both the individual delinquent and society. She asserted that the community played an equal if not more important role than biology in the creation of juvenile delinquents. Hayes argued that although a eugenic system of institutionalization for "mentally defective" children was important, the state and the community needed to take greater responsibility in the prevention of delinquency among girls paroled from Geneva. The state needed to hire more social workers to watch over parolees, and the community needed to "assume its duty . . . to guide the lives and assist the endeavors" of its young women.[10]

Although eugenic commitment continued during the interwar period, experts throughout the country increasingly advocated the type of community care articulated by Hayes.[11] The secretary of the New York State Probation Commission declared that juvenile delinquency, "in its causes, its consequences, and its treatment," was a social or community problem, and that it could not be "cured or prevented without efficient community organization."[12] The chairman of the Senate Subcommittee on Delinquent Children asserted that juvenile delinquency was "a national, as well as state and local problem," and that it required the coordination of state, local, and county efforts to "cure and prevent delinquency."[13] Maude Miner, secretary of the New York Probation and Protective Association, agreed, and explained that the complexity of the factors contributing to delinquency necessitated a "varied and comprehensive program for protecting youth" through community efforts. Only then would "considerable progress be made in lessening the power of demoralizing influences and in attaining for each individual a larger fullness of life."[14] Elizabeth Dutcher of the Charity Organization Society of New York added that as long as "moron" women were not "markedly promiscuous sexually," they too could be given "extra-institutional treatment."[15]

Experts, reformers, and administrators increasingly characterized training schools as places where delinquents would learn to function "normally" within society. Katharine Lenroot of the U.S. Department of Labor's Children's Bureau found that much of the work being done during the 1920s was directed toward "securing socially desired conduct by positive instead of negative means." "Instead of segregation in institutions," she argued, "we are trying to adjust asocial individuals to life in the community." Scientific study was expanding the possibility of noninstitutional treatment of delinquency. Experiments with the probation and parole of "feebleminded offenders" were showing that, in Lenroot's words, the "old hypothesis that every female defective is likely to become sexually delinquent is not universally applicable." Lenroot concluded that:

> In the treatment of the delinquent girl and particularly of the unmarried mother, it is important to keep in mind always the desirability of plans which involve the maximum of normal adjustment and the minimum of differentiation from modes of living and associations which the community regards as customary . . . it should be the endeavor of the social agency not to treat such a girl as belonging to a class apart from all others, but as having normal human needs and instincts and desires which must be met, as nearly as possible, in a normal way.[16]

For the most part, women who associated themselves with the treatment of female juvenile delinquents during the interwar period moved beyond the notion that the majority of girls they encountered were innately inferior and required indefinite institutionalization to live "normally." Instead, they argued that the fundamental purpose of a training school was to "readjust and re-educate" youthful offenders, and to prepare them for a "normal" life within the community, which ironically was Geneva's original mission when it opened in 1893.[17]

By the early 1920s, administrators, teachers, and medical staff at institutions throughout the nation had begun implementing new approaches in the treatment of "defective" delinquents. When C. B. Caldwell became the managing officer at the Lincoln State School and Colony in Illinois in 1920, he began paroling "high grade feebleminded" women to work in hospitals and private homes under close supervision. Parolees lived with friends or relatives, or in the homes of their employers. Caldwell kept all of the money they earned in an institution trust fund.[18]

According to Caldwell, severe overcrowding and a countrywide labor shortage had forced him to implement a parole system at Lincoln, but his motivations for reform ran much deeper than mere practical concerns. Caldwell rooted the change in policy at Lincoln in the new postwar scientific and social reform discourse. He argued that an effective parole system at Lincoln was imperative because the institution could only accommodate approximately one-tenth of Illinois' "feebleminded" population. Caldwell further explained that he had created the parole system at Lincoln because he thought that the 1915 commitment law was too "cold blooded" and formal, and needed to be "thoroughly revised." He asserted that Illinois needed more "special education" classrooms and teachers, and that Lincoln needed to change its original mission, which was to "cure" individuals who came under its purview. Instead, Caldwell argued, administrators and teachers needed to focus on attaining the highest level of mental improvement for each inmate and on increasing the use of vocational training, with the goal of returning a greater number of inmates to the community and the workforce.[19] Clearly, Caldwell and his associates at Lincoln attempted to implement the latest scientific techniques in their treatment of "feebleminded" individuals.

Illinois' health commissioner had similar plans. He longed to have a school where "defectives might be given compulsory vocational training and taught self-control; and with proper care, would be made a real social and economic asset instead of a danger." He and the Health Department neurologist worked diligently during the early 1920s to make Illinois residents and the state legislature aware of the "urgent need" for a special school for "adolescent mental defectives."[20]

The effects of social and scientific changes were not limited to institutional care. Throughout the 1920s and 1930s, reformers in Illinois created a number of community-based programs and organizations designed to prevent juvenile delinquency and improve the lives of young people and their families. The most prominent and influential programs were those that operated in and around Chicago and dealt primarily in the lives of "normal-minded" white Protestant youth. In particular, the Service Council for Girls, the Big Brothers and Big Sisters Association of Illinois, the Division for Delinquency Prevention, and the Chicago Area Project took an active role in the lives of Illinois' young people.

The Chicago Woman's Club formed the Service Council for Girls at a meeting held on January 31, 1925. Speaking before a group of representatives from women's clubs and auxiliaries, church organizations, and service leagues, Judge Bartelme of the Juvenile Court explained that reformers needed to do more to address the needs of Cook County's white Protestant girls. Chicago's Jewish community had formed a similar organization in 1915, and Catholics in 1917, and it was time for white Protestant women to form their own service organization. The service council would provide homes, employment, clothes, and social services to a seemingly rapidly growing segment of the juvenile delinquent population, namely "girls of average intelligence."[21]

Bartelme claimed that her years on the bench convinced her of the need for the service council, as well as the Big Sister program. According to a Big Sister training manual, Bartelme "saw a pressing need for Volunteer help in the reclaiming of innocent young lives." The manual claimed that Big Sister volunteers provided "helpful friendship for underprivileged girls," in part because each volunteer confined her efforts to the development of one girl. The Big Sister program was not a "probationary system to supervise ill-adjusted girls; but a power for good in girls' lives to prevent their becoming delinquent."

Although they did not provide service to Jews, Catholics, and African Americans, the volunteer "big sisters" and the Service Council for Girls at least nominally respected homes with "foreign standards." They worked together with working-class parents and families to serve white Protestant girls of "average" intelligence, who passed through the Juvenile Court and who did not receive services from other organizations.[22]

The big sister program, along with the Big Brothers Association, quickly expanded its operations to include an increasing number of children who had not appeared in court. In one year alone, a total of approximately 2,500 men and women volunteered both time and money, as state sociologist Samuel R. Ryerson put it, to provide "the right environment" and "save the youth of the State from delinquent careers." In that same year, the Big Brothers and Big Sisters Association provided services directly to more than two thousand children. They also sponsored community-based recreational centers, workshops, and playgrounds that provided educational and recreational programs to tens of thousands of children each month, an accomplishment that did not go unnoticed by contemporary observers. Illinois received commendation from the National Probation Association and J. Edgar Hoover for its combination of community organization, prevention programs, and supervision of juvenile delinquents.[23]

Experts and politicians considered the new programs so successful that they incorporated them into the Department of Public Welfare in 1937 under the newly created Division for Delinquency Prevention. Ryerson became the superintendent of the division and the Big Brothers and Big Sisters Association became its advisory council. The Division for Delinquency Prevention adopted as its motto: "Understanding for All Youth, Prevention Instead of Incarceration."[24]

In 1932, in the midst of the Great Depression, and emboldened by the transition to a Democratic-controlled government, the Institute for Juvenile Research created its own community-based program, which it named the Chicago Area Project. According to the program's director, the institute had created the Chicago Area Project in an effort to provide aid for the development of programs that focused on the treatment and prevention of delinquency in low-income neighborhoods, where the rates of delinquency had been relatively high for many years. Three basic principles guided the experts who worked on the project: (1) delinquency was a consequence of the conditions in which children were raised, (2) previous attempts to alter both conditions and children had failed, and (3) programs to curb delinquency needed to be rooted in neighborhood life. The Chicago Area Project highlighted the importance of social experiences in childhood and adolescence in the development of attitudes and habits involved in delinquent behavior, as well as the failure of incarceration as a method of treatment of juvenile delinquency. Through educational, social, recreational, and other "character-building" programs, the leaders of the Chicago Area Project sought to prevent delinquency in areas that they described as the "deteriorated and underprivileged districts" of Chicago.[25]

Throughout the interwar period, experts, reformers, and community leaders interested in preventing delinquency and improving living conditions in some of Chicago's most blighted neighborhoods shifted their focus away from the institution and away from eugenics and "mental defect." Yet the idea that morality and intellect shared a strong positive correlation did not disappear completely after the First World War; neither did the notion that certain "defective delinquents" required indefinite incarceration to live "normally." It seems clear from evidence in Illinois and elsewhere, however, that the latter, though desirable, was becoming increasingly untenable after the war. This change, though recognized as significant by historians of eugenics, remains understudied as a pivotal moment in disability history. The interwar period marked a moment in which a fundamental shift occurred in the understanding of the impairment that supposedly lay at the heart of most antisocial behavior, a shift made readily apparent by American participation in World War I.

Redefining Feeblemindedness: The Army Mental Tests

American intervention into the First World War permanently altered the ways in which experts viewed feeblemindedness and its relationship to delinquency. In April 1917, a group of psychologists led by Robert Yerkes submitted the "Plan for the Psychological Examination of Recruits to Eliminate the Mentally Unfit."[26] Yerkes, Terman, Goddard, and other mental testers, who had been seeking a solid footing in the social sciences and additional research funds, sought to use the wartime experience to create an ostensibly standardized testing system that they could administer to a broad range of Americans. Unlike the previous decade's research, which was conducted largely by women and tended to focus on institutionalized and otherwise marginalized populations, the army mental tests would be administered to 1.75 million men entering the United States Army.[27]

The results were startling. Army mental testers "discovered" that native-born, white recruits possessed an average mental age of 13.08 years, just one year above a "high-grade moron." The average mental age of recruits with European backgrounds was 11.0 years. African Americans occupied the bottom end of the scale, with an average mental age of 10.41 years.[28] In 1920, J. E. Wallace Wallin, director of the St. Louis Psycho-Educational Clinic and Special Schools and an outspoken critic of intelligence tests, explained that the results of the army tests justified the presumption that "50,000,000 of our white citizens only reach, or will eventually only reach, approximately the intelligence level of the 'high grade morons.'" Wallin argued that evidence provided by the army tests had forced experts to reevaluate the assertion that an intelligence quotient below 70 always indicated "definite feeblemindedness," because millions of American *men* who had no records of arrest or crime, who were native-born, and who possessed intelligence levels of only eight or nine years were comfortably supporting themselves, and sometimes families as well.[29]

The importance of gender, race, and disability in this scientific revelation could not be clearer. The presumption that fifty million Americans, many of whom were male, native-born, and white, possessed some degree of mental defect made the notion that "feebleminded" individuals required eugenic segregation to live "normally" unthinkable. It also made it nearly impossible for social scientists and social reformers to continue to substantiate a direct causal link between feeblemindedness and delinquency.

Rather than abandon the testing process and the impairment it supposedly revealed, experts increasingly claimed that tests merely provided a "fair sample" of an individual's "mental ability," and argued that tests could not accurately predict an individual's propensity to engage in antisocial behavior. Dr. Herman Adler, Illinois' state criminologist and director of the state's Division of the Criminologist for nearly twenty years, explained that "Feeble-mindedness, which at one time was believed to be the major cause [of delinquency and crime], is now recognized as only one of the accessory factors and operative in only a portion of the cases."[30] Adler based his conclusions on a number of studies conducted by the division during his tenure as its director, including a study showing that male prisoners in Illinois rated higher on intelligence tests than the draft army during World War I.[31] The popularization of "knowledge" gained during the war provided what Adler referred to as an "enormous impetus" to the mental health movement by expanding Americans' understanding of feeblemindedness and its relationship to crime.[32]

The effects of the army tests could be seen almost immediately. In 1921, Healy argued that although experts had set the so-called normal mental age of adults at sixteen years, they "knew from the army experience that the average adult does not range anything like as high as that."[33] Elizabeth Dutcher declared that the popularization of psychological tests, which was "partly brought about through the war, together with the published results of the army tests," had forced experts and reformers into a "different attitude." Dutcher explained that it had become "routine" for Americans to test their families, and that experts and laypersons alike increasingly realized that "what the army tests had shown for the country at large was true for [their] own communities—that a surprising proportion of [their] families contained subnormal persons."[34]

The realization that Americans were supposedly not as smart as they had once assumed led some experts to begin to delineate between "good" and "bad" feebleminded persons.[35] As Dutcher explained, "subnormal clients differed as much among themselves as so-called normal people."[36] Edith Spaulding, of the Smith College School of Psychiatry, argued in a paper presented at the International Conference of Women Physicians that feeblemindedness was not synonymous with "badness," and that if a "feebleminded" individual was fostered in a "suitable" environment, they could express "good citizenship" and "useful occupation." Spaulding concluded that although most experts continued to recognize the "folly" of allowing "feebleminded" individuals to reproduce, the "danger" in the propagation of the "feebleminded" was not as great as Americans had been led to expect, primarily because of the important influence of environmental factors on human development. Spaulding argued that a "judicious and hygienic upbringing" of the children of "feebleminded" parents would offset any risks posed by inherited "defect."[37]

In most cases the divide between "good" and "bad" "feebleminded" individuals got articulated in gendered terms that fell neatly in line with prevailing sexual norms. George Wallace, superintendent of the Wrentham State School in Massachusetts, argued that it "Would be quite possible to indicate classes of the feebleminded that we think would safely get along in the community, such as young children, the lower grade cases if provided with physical comfort and care, the male, perhaps, more safely than the female, the girl who is not the possessor of physical beauty, the child who has a good home."[38] As Wallace indicated, the "bad feebleminded," those individuals who were most likely to face indefinite incarceration, were in most cases physically attractive female sex delinquents.

The duality of adolescent girls' existence was not lost on institution administrators and reformers, who increasingly recognized the complex causes of delinquency. Dr. Rachel Yarros, supervisor of the education of women in the Division of Social Hygiene at the Illinois State Department of Public Health, argued that between 30 and 50 percent of the "unfortunates" that she encountered were "mentally subnormal or disordered," and the "victims" of the conditions within which they lived. Yarros described the young women as "physically attractive and sexually rather over-developed," and argued that they possessed a "mental state" that made them "ready to fall prey to vicious men who are always at hand." Yarros grounded the hardships that accompanied a working-class existence in young women's desire for "treating," which frequently led to their being coerced by "lustful" males.[39] Once a young woman had her first sexual experience, she found it difficult to go back to the "dull life."[40] For Yarros and other experts, female delinquents' physical attractiveness and sexual overdevelopment stood in stark contrast to their underdeveloped mental state and deleterious environment. Female delinquents were at once physically superior and mentally inferior. They were the victims of bad breeding, bad environment, and bad men, but they were also social and sexual agents, a threat to both society and the race.

From the "Feebleminded Menace" to the "Khaki Mad Girl"

American participation in World War I altered popular perceptions of female sex delinquents in at least one other critically important way. The campaign to regulate sexual activity in and around army training camps during World War I made teen sex a national issue.[41] The federal program to make men "fit to fight" helped hasten already changing sexual mores that separated sex from reproduction and—rather reluctantly and haltingly—acknowledged female heterosexuality. It also catapulted the dilemma posed by adolescent sex delinquents into the national spotlight.

The so-called sexual revolution of the early twentieth century had its ideological roots in the rise of the "new psychology."[42] The popularization of studies conducted by Havelock Ellis, Sigmund Freud, and G. Stanley Hall contributed to the development of a new scientific discourse on human variation that weakened the link between sexual activity and procreation that had dominated much of nineteenth-century American culture. As John D'Emilio and Estelle Freedman have shown, Victorian reticence declined and sexual "expression" and "fulfillment" became "watchwords."[43] A well-known St. Louis editor announced in 1913 that it had struck "sex o'clock" in America. Much of the public entertainment that working-class youth participated in since the late nineteenth century was becoming mainstream, and increased access to movie theaters, dance halls, and automobiles was changing courtship and dating rituals.[44] Although he argued that "back in the cow pastures of the Republic the old view of sex" still prevailed, one writer for the *American Mercury* declared that "wherever lights are brighter and there are paving stones and so much as a single street-car, wherever a band, however bad, plays on Saturday nights, there you will find a change in the old [sexual] order."[45] It was apparent on the eve of World War I that an increasing number of Americans were adopting different sexual standards and openly acknowledging, if not entirely encouraging, women's heterosexuality.[46]

American participation in the First World War further entrenched already changing sexual mores. According to Jane Deeter Rippin, who was serving as the director of the Section on Women and Girls in the Law Enforcement Division of the War Department Commission on Training Camp Activities, "the conspiracy of silence" surrounding sex was broken by American involvement in the war. Rippin found that a "thoughtful and deliberate effort" was being made to educate "all classes and types of individuals" with regard to sex and sex hygiene. There existed among many Americans a newfound openness concerning sex that had been brought about by the "single necessity of making men 'fit to fight,' which [had] swept away all the age-old cautions surrounding the teaching of sex hygiene." Of chief concern to Rippin and the Section on Women and Girls was the "charity girl," women between the ages of fifteen and twenty-five who socialized with military men. According to Rippin, charity girls were women who became "promiscuous in sex relations through the influence of the contagious excitement" that surrounded mobilization camps and created an atmosphere of "romantic [glamour] around the man in uniform."[47]

Initially, Rippin and her colleagues viewed charity girls as innocent victims of men in uniform. When the Commission on Training Camp Activities was formed in September 1917, a special Committee on Protective Work for Girls was also formed. As its name implies, the committee was created under the assumption that women who socialized in and around mobilization areas were becoming the hapless victims of sexually promiscuous soldiers. The committee soon realized, however, that many charity girls were not innocent victims, and that most of them actively pursued men in uniform. Six months' work in and around military camps demonstrated that sexually delinquent or "khaki mad" girls so far outnumbered "good" charity girls that the committee was forced to reorganize its mission.[48]

Despite their newfound "openness," the committee on protective work remained reluctant to accept fully the sexual activity of young single women. Instead, they labeled khaki mad girls "delinquent" and sought more explicitly punitive measures. In April 1918, just six months after the creation of the committee, the War Department created the Section on Women and Girls and authorized it to deal with female sex offenders, marking the first attempt by the state to deal with any type of delinquency on a national level. The dramatic change in scope of the movement to treat female sex offenders brought about by wartime mobilization permanently altered the range of possible solutions to the "girl problem," which by 1918 had clearly become a national issue.

The eugenic institutionalization of all female sex delinquents no longer seemed viable. The Section on Women and Girls sought, instead, to increase the extent of public knowledge and understanding of sex delinquency and the nature and treatment of venereal diseases. They also hoped to demonstrate to local governments and other civic organizations the "waste" of allowing repeat offenders to be released after receiving only a fine or a short term in jail. The Section on Women and Girls in turn encouraged communities to provide hospitals with venereal disease clinics, to build detention houses, and to create probation systems, but they did not advocate eugenic (or indefinite) incarceration.[49]

Maternalists' work in Illinois mirrored that of their colleagues at the federal level. Illinois reformers stressed the argument that although mental "defect" certainly played a role in girls' delinquency, their actions stemmed from a number of factors and required diverse forms of treatment. Purcell-Guild found in her study of delinquent khaki mad girls held at the Juvenile Detention Home in Chicago that "the uniform tended rather to strengthen the potential sex delinquency of many girls than to have been its sole cause." She used one "very interesting" case of a white middle-class girl to illustrate her point. When examiners asked this particular sex delinquent to explain her "rather sudden, complete moral degeneration," she replied "with flippant sophistication: 'It was the lure of the uniform!'" Upon careful analysis, however, caseworkers revealed that the young woman was "always erratic and hysterical." They found, moreover, that she displayed an "amazingly indifferent attitude concerning the effects of her acts on herself and her parents." Researchers found that the girl had been brought up by "over-indulgent" middle-class parents, and that she was an "ardent 'movie fan'" who went to the theater almost daily. Her parents had permitted her to read everything, including magazines that dealt with "lurid sex problems." Researchers found that the girl's mother was a "gentle, ineffective sort of person," who had permitted her daughter to be picked up by uniformed men, with whom the girl had had her first "sexual relations." Purcell-Guild explained that in this particular case, "the girl had relations with a married soldier, ran away from her home, became entangled with pimps and thieves, was guilty of larceny and regular street-walking for pay, was arrested, tried, and sent to a correctional institution all in a few weeks. At no time did she show any positive regret, shame, or sorrow." "Can it be doubted," Purcell-Guild asked her readers, "that such a girl has carried within her make-up and in her own environment the causes for moral disintegration, and that her first misstep merely happened to be with a man in uniform?"[50]

Before the war, experts and reformers would have described this young woman as a "feebleminded menace" in need of institutionalization to live "normally," but after the war that was increasingly difficult. Changing social mores and a shifting taxonomy of both mental "defect" and juvenile delinquency did not, however, signal the demise of eugenics or of the pathologization of female sex delinquents. It increasingly meant that only those individuals whom experts considered beyond reform or rehabilitation would require eugenic segregation.

Dr. Marion Kenworthy of the New York School of Social Work was one expert during the interwar period who argued that recent transformations in diagnosis and treatment made it possible to single out only those individuals who most needed indefinite commitment. Kenworthy asserted that: "The mere fact that a girl has engaged in illicit sex relationships does not justify the assumption that of necessity there need be any pathological mental situation involved," and that it was "nonsense" to tell a young woman that she could not think about sex. Using modern psychiatric terms, Kenworthy asserted that any existence of mental defect among unmarried mothers and other "sex offenders" was largely a problem of maladjustment, and that experts needed to look for a "social-environmental situation in which special safeguards may be thrown about such individuals." Most delinquent women simply needed to learn to "manage their urges in a manner that respects social dictates."[51] Kenworthy argued that only the most "degraded" female "sex offenders" required indefinite commitment.

Eugenic Commitment Continues

Though they recognized important social and scientific changes, experts, like Kenworthy, continued to espouse eugenic solutions to the social problems they faced, especially if those problems involved women or teenage girls. Dr. Yarros of the Illinois State Department of Public Health argued that many of the girls she encountered through the Division of Social Hygiene required "permanent care." Yarros urged lawmakers to establish training schools and state farms so that "mentally subnormal or disordered" delinquents might become "self-supporting" during their incarceration.[52] Emma Lundberg of the Federal Children's Bureau argued that data secured in her study of 320 women under the age of eighteen who became mothers supported the argument that the need for "adequate provision for diagnosis and care of mentally subnormal" delinquents was imperative.[53] Carrie Weaver Smith, superintendent of the Girls' Training School in Gainesville, Texas, asserted that "feebleminded colonies" were essential, but only when the need for such care was "definitely indicated."[54] According to Elizabeth Dutcher, it went "without saying that the feebleminded woman who is markedly promiscuous sexually cannot be given successful extra-institutional treatment." "Better state provision for segregation," Dutcher urged, "must remain the only satisfactory solution for the difficulties presented by many of these people."[55] Frances Maxfield, director of the Bureau of Special Education in the Pennsylvania State Department of Public Instruction, concluded that, "Segregation may be for life, or during a period of training, or during the child-bearing period in the case of women."[56]

Illinois' most ardent eugenicists during the interwar period were Chief Justice Harry Olson of the Chicago Municipal Court and the director of the Municipal Court's Psychopathic Laboratory, Dr. William Hickson. Throughout his twenty-four years on the bench, Olson remained a strong proponent of eugenics.[57] He served on the committee that drafted the 1915 commitment bill and as the president of the Eugenics Research Association.[58] Early in his career, Olson adopted the theory that most delinquents and criminals suffered from "feeblemindedness" or some "structural brain defect" that made them either morally or mentally "insane." According to Olson, a nationwide eugenics program would prevent crime by "weeding out" the "defective stocks."[59] Dr. Hickson joined Olson in his eugenics crusade in 1914, when the state created the Municipal Court's Psychopathic Laboratory. Together Hickson and his wife, who was a trained psychologist, examined more than forty thousand delinquents and criminals from 1914 until his resignation in 1929.[60]

Throughout his tenure at the Psychopathic Laboratory, Hickson remained steadfast in his conviction to eugenics and to the pathologization of antisocial behavior. In 1917, he argued that the majority of the women he encountered were "too feeble-minded or psychopathic to make a living legitimately." He asserted that they were great "prevaricators," and that they usually began their delinquent careers during their juvenile years. Hickson concluded that imprisonment, fines, reformatories, probation, parole, religion, and the big-sister movement all failed in their attempts to eliminate antisocial behavior. This was because the only way to get at the root of the problem of delinquency and crime and ultimately offer any type of "cure" was through "scientific means and methods." "The final solution," Hickson declared, required a thorough study of the individual offender, as well as cooperation between experts, reformers, and politicians in creating and implementing a sound eugenics program. Interestingly, an independent study of the Psychopathic Laboratory conducted in 1925 found no evidence to support Hickson's claims.

Unfazed by the criticism, Hickson argued that the majority of his cases were "so deficient mentally" that it became apparent to the judge during the courtroom proceedings, and that he saw no need to conduct even a routine examination of many of the cases.[61] Just before his resignation, which one newspaper reported was shrouded in "bitter controversy," Hickson made one final attempt to make his voice heard.[62] In 1928, he argued in the *Journal of Social Hygiene* that criminals were "constitutionally defective" and that it was "impossible to reform them." "Human society," Hickson argued, was "definitely menaced by the ascendancy of the unfit." According to Hickson, science had two "recommendations" to make to those individuals who wished to end crime and save society from the "dominance of the unfit." The first recommendation was to segregate "congenital defectives" before they had an opportunity to commit crimes, and the second recommendation was to make it "impossible for defectives to reproduce their kind."[63]

Together, Hickson and Olson devised some interesting and inventive eugenic schemes that they proposed to the public on speaking tours, in journals, and through the nation's largest newspapers. In January 1928, Hickson, Olson, and the doctor, *Tribune* columnist, and avid eugenicist W. A. Evans attended the Race Betterment Conference in Battle Creek, Michigan, where Hickson passionately advocated intelligence tests for voters. "One of the most urgently necessary steps is to restore the balance of political power to where it belongs—to the better endowed mentally," Hickson declared.[64] At a meeting of the Chicago Association of Detective Sergeants, Olson advocated the use of "mind-cards" that would show an individual's intelligence and be stamped with the official state seal, for authenticity. The cards could be used as a form of identification and as a measure of qualification, primarily for employment.[65] At the annual meeting of the American Automobile Association, Olson urged his audience to "clear up the blood stream of the race" by controlling marriages. According to the reporter covering the event, Olson explained that too often "defectives" got behind the wheel of a car and ran down people on the highways. This unfortunate occurrence could have been avoided altogether through the judicious use of eugenics.[66]

Hickson and Olson always made a point of telling their audiences that they based their eugenic recommendations on their experiences in Chicago's Municipal Court, where they encountered cases like that of Tillie and Nellie, who had been indicted by a grand jury on charges of murder and conspiracy to commit murder. The two women were accused of poisoning Tillie's fourth husband, who was in a hospital suffering from arsenic poisoning at the time of the indictment. They were also charged jointly with the murder of Nellie's former husband and Tillie's third husband. During the indictment process, Olson made public a report submitted to him by Hickson that stated that both of the accused women suffered from "dementia praecox" and were "subnormal mentally." According to the report, neither woman possessed an intellect higher than that of an eleven-year-old child. The report also revealed that one of Nellie's three sons was examined by Hickson and found to be of "feeble mind." Another son had been brought before the Juvenile Court three times. The third son was on probation from the Pontiac reformatory when he appeared as a witness before the grand jury. "If," Judge Olson lamented, "we had a field worker, an eugenics expert, to check up on the history of this whole family at the time one moron was discovered, then the police might have been warned to watch this woman and so might possibly have prevented some of these crimes."[67]

As this case reveals, eugenicists increasingly relied upon both intelligence tests and psychoanalytic theory after World War I. They attributed antisocial behavior not only to "feeblemindedness," or mental "defect," but also to certain personality "maladjustments" and character "deviations." Experts argued that many delinquents who scored within the "normal" range on intelligence tests possessed "psychopathic" personalities. In most cases, they argued that delinquents and criminals who were not "feebleminded," but were "psychopathic," required indefinite segregation to live "normally," and that the incarceration of "psychopathic" individuals would benefit both the race and society.[68]

Eugenicists' increased reliance upon psychopathology can be seen in studies conducted on inmates at Geneva during the interwar period. Rather than focus on feeblemindedness, Dr. Esther Stone claimed that the "so-called normal subjects" caused the greatest amount of problems and difficulties for reformers. She argued that "normal" women possessed "just enough mentality and superficial education and ability to be a continued source of annoyance to themselves and the community." Stone declared that the "time honored classification of imbecile, moron, etc. does not adequately classify our population with reference to usefulness." She asserted, moreover, that "normal" delinquents were the "greatest failures" in life because they were "constitutionally inferior." Stone argued that "normal" delinquents were highly unstable emotionally and could not be trusted, and she asserted that many girls who were released back into the community resumed their antisocial behavior.[69]

Although she did not explicitly acknowledge it, Stone espoused a eugenic solution to the problems she experienced during her two-year investigation of inmates at Geneva. Upon the completion of her study, Stone concluded that the reformation of the girls at Geneva was difficult and often failed because by the time they entered the school (the average age was 15.6 years), they were beyond the "formative" period. The solution, according to Stone, was commitment to an institution at a young age. She asserted that it was imperative that the Boards of Education and public schools in Illinois staff a trained psychologist, so that once a child exhibited signs of "criminality" or "immorality" they could be called in to make a thorough examination of the case. If it did not appear likely that the child would outgrow their "handicap," then they could be transferred to a special school, without a court order or their parents' consent. Transferring to the new school "should be as simple as passing from one grade to the next," Stone declared. According to Stone, the school for the "psychopath" would be most successful in treating "defective" children if it was a permanent home or boarding school. She argued that the state needed to make provision to retain a person until they were twenty-five years old, at which time it could be decided, by experts, if they were ready to "mingle" unsupervised in society. If they could not, then the individual would be sent to a "community of his kind." Stone argued that sex segregation was vital in both the school and the colony, and that "by no means should marriage or sexual relations be permitted." Segregation, Stone declared, would eliminate "defectives" from the general population and improve society.[70]

Stone was not alone in her arguments. By the mid-1920s, the idea of the "defective" delinquent had gained considerable currency among the nation's leading experts. In January 1925, individuals from a number of fields met in Chicago to commemorate the twenty-fifth anniversary of the Cook County Juvenile Court and the fifteenth anniversary of the Juvenile Psychopathic Institute. Foremost among the concerns of conference participants were, in the words of famed Hull House founder and conference chair, Jane Addams, a "determination to understand the growing child and a sincere effort to find ways for securing his orderly development in normal society." Addams explained that the conference provided a "cross-section of the present widespread study of youthful behavior under a great variety of social stimuli and of its biological and cultural sources."[71] Conference attendees included Franz Boas, Grace Abbott, Miriam Van Waters, Julia Lathrop, Ben Lindsey, Julian Mack, Ernest R. Groves, Marion Kenworthy, Herman Adler, Augusta Bronner, and William Healy, as well as other lesser known scholars and reformers. Chief Justice Olson's name had been placed on the program, but it was removed when Abbott and Lathrop protested, saying that he was too "unscientific."[72]

Among the numerous topics of discussion at the conference was the relationship of psychology and psychiatry to the diagnosis and treatment of juvenile delinquents. Experts and reformers acknowledged new theories and approaches and attempted to integrate them into a more comprehensive system that focused on the prevention of delinquency. As Bronner argued, "multiplicity" was the rule; causes varied "extraordinarily" from case to case. Experts and reformers had to employ the "principle of integration" when diagnosing and treating juvenile delinquents.[73] Feeblemindedness theory, or as Healy put it, "the famous theory of degeneracy," which he argued had grown to "unreasonable proportions" before the war, no longer reigned as the dominant causal factor in most cases.[74] The army mental tests had proven, among other things, that there were "good" as well as "bad" feebleminded persons. As Adler rather bluntly stated: "It is no crime to be stupid."[75]

According to Bronner, the relationship between biology and delinquency had changed during the decade between 1915 and 1925. "There is now," Bronner argued, "quite general acceptance of the minimized role which mental defect plays in the genesis of misconduct and of the correlated fact that the feebleminded vary much in personality traits." There was, however, an equally pervasive assumption that "defective delinquents" existed, and that they, as Bronner stated, "required a special mode of treatment." Experts and reformers agreed that "defective delinquents" required indefinite incarceration in a state institution. According to Bronner, science had shown the necessity of constructing, "at once," institutions of adequate size and number to care for "defective delinquents." Bronner went on to argue that "mentally diseased" delinquents also required segregation. She concluded that "defective" and "mentally diseased" delinquents required "such constant supervision that they frequently cannot remain in the community."[76] Though the taxonomy of mental "defect" had changed, and its relationship to delinquency had become more complicated, it is clear that eugenic or indefinite commitment persisted well into the twentieth century. A glance at incarceration rates for the period seems to bear this out.

The Numbers

There is no doubt that the number of Illinois residents admitted to institutions rose steadily during the interwar period and continued to rise in the immediate post–World War II period. In 1919, the director of the Department of Public Welfare found the state's only institution dedicated solely to the care of feebleminded inmates at Lincoln "utterly inadequate to accommodate the streams flowing in upon it from every county in the state for admission." At the time there were 2,400 inmates at Lincoln, which was designed to accommodate 1,600 persons.[77] In 1920, Illinois had a total of ten institutions dedicated to the care of approximately 19,000 mentally ill, handicapped, dependent, and delinquent inmates. Although the number of custodial institutions in Illinois remained largely unchanged during the 1920s and 1930s, the inmate population continued to rise. By 1930, there were approximately 27,000 institutionalized persons living in Illinois. An additional 12,000 individuals were institutionalized during the 1930s, bringing the total to approximately 39,000 persons by 1940.[78] A 1940 report estimated that Illinois' institutionalized population rose by an average of 1,500 persons per year between 1933 and 1940.[79]

The Great Depression figured prominently in the expansion of the welfare state during the 1930s, but it alone cannot explain Illinois' burgeoning inmate population. The advent of an increasingly medicalized eugenic model of individual impairment made possible by the widespread use of psychological testing and the increasing stature of psychiatry played a vital role in the rise of institutionalization in Illinois. The state's evaluative apparatus expanded tremendously during the interwar years. The Department of Public Welfare itself increased fourfold in size during the 1930s and had an annual budget of nearly $50 million between 1933 and 1940. Composed of twenty-seven institutions and divisions, it employed ten thousand men and women and had a Department of Public Welfare in every county in Illinois by 1940. Legislators also created the State Neuropsychiatric Institute and Hospital during the 1930s, which was designed specifically to make intensive study of nervous and mental diseases in men and women.[80] In 1947, the director of the Department of Public Welfare reported that a new farm colony designed to accommodate 1,200 patients had been constructed at Lincoln during the 1930s largely because of the "upsurge of modern psychiatry," as well as increased demand for social services brought on by the Depression.[81]

Statistics show that institutionalization rates rose during prosperous times as well. In his study of the Chicago Municipal Court, historian Michael Willrich found that judges committed approximately one thousand people each year between 1914 and 1930 "to sexually segregated state institutions for the insane and feebleminded—regardless of whether the court found them guilty of breaking any law."[82] Science had enabled the state to commit society's "unfit" citizens to institutions indefinitely. Dr. Hickson confessed to committing "as high as ten cases a day" from the Municipal Court to institutions for the feebleminded. "The only practical solution we see at present for the treatment of these cases after they are recognized," Hickson argued, "is farm and industrial colonies, as extensive as possible, built on the order of detention camps." Hickson asserted that for the majority of cases, incarceration would be "for life."[83]

Economic recovery during World War II did not bring an end to involuntary commitment in Illinois; neither did the revelation of Nazi atrocities. The need for workers and soldiers caused the rate of increase per year of Illinois' institutionalized population to decrease somewhat during World War II, but the overall incarceration rate continued to expand. By 1945 there were approximately 42,000 institutionalized persons in Illinois. Following the war, the rate of institutionalization increased dramatically. Beginning in 1946, approximately eight hundred to one thousand individuals were being institutionalized each *month* in Illinois. By 1947, the Department of Public Welfare had grown to include twenty-five institutions and twenty-two divisions, with eleven institutions dedicated specifically to the care of Illinois' mentally ill, handicapped, dependent, and delinquent residents.[84]

Young women remained especially vulnerable to commitment. In their study of delinquents in Chicago and Boston published in 1926, Healy and Bronner found that the ratio of girls seen in the court in Chicago was sometimes four times as great as the ratio in Boston, and that 67 percent of girls who appeared in court were committed to juvenile correctional institutions.[85] In 1940, the Institute for Juvenile Research estimated that approximately 10–15 percent of girls who appeared before the Juvenile Court were committed directly to institutions for the feebleminded.[86] An analysis of case files and other records from the State Training School at Geneva indicates that administrators committed an additional 5–10 percent of delinquent girls each year from that institution to one of the state's two institutions for the feebleminded, located in Lincoln and Dixon.[87]

Conclusion

It is somewhat ironic that by the time Illinois enacted its eugenic commitment law in July 1915, popular perceptions of both eugenics and intelligence testing were beginning to experience significant transformations that would affect dominant understandings of feeblemindedness and the treatment of female sex delinquents during the interwar period. There is no doubt that local concerns with overcrowding and the "proper" treatment of juvenile delinquents played a critical role in the change in policy at the Lincoln State School and Colony, and the state training school at Geneva. There were, however, larger social and scientific changes taking place that had an equal, if not more important influence on social scientists and social reformers. The army mental tests and the discovery of the delinquent khaki mad girl greatly affected the ways in which both experts and laypersons articulated their understanding not only of what it meant to be eugenically "fit," but also what constituted appropriate and effective eugenic measures.

Despite these changes, eugenic commitment endured, often under the thinly veiled guise of an ill-defined but socially and eugenically significant "mental defect." In the next two chapters, we will go inside the Illinois State Training School for Girls in Geneva to explore the social creation of the impairment that supposedly lay at the root of certain young women's wrongdoing.

4

"I Ain't Had Much Schooling"

> "The emotional conditions surrounding the giving of tests must be taken into account. These are notoriously present in connection with court work, and make the latter, if undertaken by cursory methods, scientifically dangerous. There is still much room for the application of common sense in estimation of mental defect."
> —William Healy, director of the Psychopathic Institute of Chicago, 1915

> "Evelyn was neat and clean and gave the appearance of being alert and brighter than previous test results would indicate. She was self-conscious and was very anxious to do well on the tests. She was aware of her own limitations and when she became aware of her first failure she remarked, 'Something is wrong with my brain.' In her desire to do well she became overly anxious and nervous, so that her fingers trembled and she was unable to draw a straight line. Responses were given slowly."
> —Geneva Psychologist Report, 1930s

Fifteen-year-old Della was incarcerated in the State Training School for Girls in Geneva, Illinois, in 1937. Like all of the girls at Geneva, Della was forced to endure a series of mental and physical examinations upon her arrival, at which time the staff determined she was a "high grade mental defective." Della was paroled after serving nine months, despite the fact that she was "committable [to the Lincoln State School and Colony] as far as her intelligence [was] concerned." A parole violation in 1939 forced Della to return to Geneva, at which time the staff administered yet another series of examinations and found that her intelligence rating was in "fair agreement with the former Stanford Binet rating." Although she gave the "impression of being brighter" than test results indicated, the Geneva staff ultimately decided to commit Della to Lincoln indefinitely.[1]

In many ways, Della's experience is representative of the thousands of cases processed through Illinois' reform institutions during the first half of the twentieth century. Certainly not all inmates were committed to Lincoln. Yet Della's experience at Geneva is characteristic of the experience of other inmates who were forced to endure physical and mental examinations upon their arrival at an institution. In most cases, female medical staff and psychologists subjected girls to a number of different examinations during their first two weeks of incarceration. School administrators and staff would then use data obtained during testing to make a number of important decisions, including living arrangements, the type and level of training an inmate would receive while at Geneva, and ultimately whether or not an inmate was "defective" and in need of indefinite incarceration in one of the state's custodial facilities. Mental evaluations played a critical role in shaping not only the reform process, but also the ways in which reformers viewed the objects of reform.

Della's experience and others like it are important because they offer glimpses into the complex, contested evaluative process that experts used to construct a group of vulnerable young women as "defective." New scientific instruments, most notably intelligence tests, enabled experts to diagnose teenage girls like Della as impaired. That diagnosis rarely went unchallenged, however. Inmates rarely accepted experts' diagnosis or their prescribed course of treatment unquestioningly. They consistently sought to make sense of their "impairment" and their incarceration on their own terms and in their own ways. Their success was measured. Yet they rarely found themselves completely defeated.

In this chapter, I use case files and other records from the state training school at Geneva, as well as published studies of female juvenile delinquents, to analyze the psychological evaluation of inmates from the perspective of both female experts and their female subjects.[2] Throughout the first half of the twentieth century, experts conducting research at Geneva consistently argued that an overwhelmingly high percentage of its inmates were "feebleminded" or "mentally defective." Although percentages, which initially were between 85 and 95 percent, declined after 1920, they still remained high. Between 1920 and 1950, mental testers claimed that approximately 50 to 60 percent of Geneva's inmate population exhibited varying degrees of "feeblemindedness."[3] Proponents of eugenic commitment and the creation of a special institution for "mentally defective" female delinquents cited the results of studies conducted at Geneva more than those from any other institution in Illinois.

Analyzing the testing that occurred at Geneva reveals not only the importance of eugenics and other *psy* discourses in the construction of mental "defect," but also the contestation, negotiation, and redefinition that undergirded the formation of historically contingent definitions of impairment. Scholars have analyzed the ways in which various actors utilized apparent physical differences to create what Jennifer Terry and Jacqueline Urla refer to as "embodied deviance."[4] This chapter builds on that scholarship by showing that the clinician's gaze extended well beyond readily identifiable external manifestations of difference. In defining embodied deviance, Terry and Urla argue that it is "the historically and culturally specific belief that deviant social behavior (however that is defined) manifests in the materiality of the body, as a cause or an effect, or perhaps as merely a suggestive trace." Tracing the history of the idea of embodied deviance, they found that "classificatory practices at the heart of this notion [of embodied deviance] depended theoretically and pragmatically on making deviance visible." Terry and Urla assert, moreover, that experts' search for signs of deviance privileged sight above all other senses, and favored empirical observation and measurement over other methodologies.[5] Della's case and others like it illustrate that experts were not nearly so limited in their quest to "discover" embodied deviance. This chapter builds upon the literature that explores the "somatic territorializing of deviance" by making systematic study of the ways in which experts used mental evaluations of inmates to render the seemingly invisible visible and by analyzing the contestation that occurred during the evaluative process.

The Rise of Human Testing

Science, primarily eugenics, psychology, and psychiatry, enabled experts to cast sexually delinquent girls as "defective." Early twentieth-century experts and reformers argued that they could accurately "detect" inherent, embodied differences that had gone undetected in the past. For centuries, healers, scientists, social reformers, and other experts sought a reliable and accurate means of measuring one's mental and moral capacity. In the United States, two early areas of study devoted to "measuring minds" were physiognomy, which read an individual's character and temperament in his or her face, and phrenology.[6] Phrenology, which grew out of physiognomy, emerged by the 1840s as a popular technique for reading an individual's psychological strengths and weaknesses, or mental "power," through the shape of their head. The new "science" became especially popular with Americans, who valued its self-help style of reform.

After the Civil War, Americans who increasingly turned to institutions and the state to solve society's ills began to lose faith in phrenology, which seemed to lack scientific rigor and focused too heavily on individual improvement.[7] Beginning about the middle of the nineteenth century, the advent of the *psy* discourses, with their various technologies of power, profoundly altered perceptions of normality.[8] The rise of statistics, Darwinism, and eugenics, also during the second half of the nineteenth century, further altered conceptions of "normality," which were increasingly rooted not in an individual's character or temperament but rather in the "normal distribution" of a given trait within a "controlled" subject pool, or the "standard deviation" from a socially constructed mean. Statistics, along with the experiment—within which I would include "standardized" tests—became what sociologist Nikolas Rose refers to as "truth techniques" developed and deployed by social scientists in their "materialization" of scientific "truths."[9] Unlike psychological testing, both physiognomy and phrenology emphasized visual observation and relied heavily on the intuitive powers of the expert to "read" an individual, which by the end of the nineteenth century was no longer considered scientific.

During the 1890s, a growing group of psychologists considered the emergent field of anthropometric mental testing more scientific than earlier methods of measuring mental ability.[10] The popularity of anthropometric testing peaked in 1895 when, under James McKeen Cattell's leadership, the American Psychological Association created a committee to "consider the feasibility of cooperation among the various psychological laboratories in the collection of mental and physical characteristics [of college students.]"[11] Although mental anthropometry, which measured strength of squeeze, rate of movement, sensation areas, reaction time for sound, and other mental and physical processes, seemed much more scientific than earlier approaches to measuring mental ability, even its proponents admitted that they had no larger purpose in mind for the data they obtained. Early in his research, Cattell admitted that, "what the individual variation may be, and what influences may be drawn from it, cannot be foreseen."[12] For several reasons, not the least of which was the fact that anthropometric mental testing "lacked any theoretical superstructure" and could not yield data with any readily apparent statistical value, mental anthropometry all but disappeared by the beginning of the twentieth century.[13]

Henry Goddard's introduction of the Binet intelligence tests to the United States in 1908 seemed to provide mental testers with the scientific means that had eluded them throughout the nineteenth century. Dr. Clara Harrison Town, director of the Department of Clinical Psychology at Lincoln, argued that psychologists using Binet tests had "come forward with a thoroughly reliable and at the same time practical method of diagnosing the various grades of mental deficiency in the young."[14] Walter Clarke, a field secretary for the American Social Hygiene Association, argued that psychologists, by means of a "subtler science," were able to "secure more accurate knowledge of the functioning of the mind than [could] be obtained by examining the promontories and depressions of the skull."[15] No longer would scientists interested in examining human variation need to rely solely on visible markers of embodied difference. Intelligence tests and other psychological and psychiatric evaluations enabled scientists to incorporate the inner workings of the human mind into their purview, vastly expanding the parameters and possibilities of their research.[16]

Nowhere was the influence of intelligence testing and eugenics on dominant notions of embodied difference more evident than in the study of "defective" delinquents. Unlike the subjects of other American eugenic campaigns, most delinquents did not bear readily visible markers of their "deviance." They were not new immigrants. Most delinquents were native-born and white, and the majority bore no outward signs of physical or cognitive impairment. Yet their antisocial behavior signified to eugenic reformers the presence of some inherent "defect." Psychology and eugenics enabled experts and reformers who worked with delinquents—and who sought eugenic explanations for social problems—to codify and quantify that "defect." Experts used new evaluative regimes to construct a group of individuals who appeared "normal," but who for a number of complex socioeconomic reasons did not live "normally," as eugenically "unfit."

Psychological testing became the means through which eugenicists would make salient and "visible" previously undetectable makers of "defect." As psychologist Kurt Danziger argues, psychology underwent a fundamental change in the United States at the end of the nineteenth century, when its practitioners became "decisively committed" to statistical psychological studies that isolated specific human traits. Scientists in a number of disciplines, including psychology, were becoming increasingly interested in statistical studies because they enabled them to form aggregates based on test results, which in turn provided for the individuation of social problems.

Statistical studies became especially popular in the United States, where they enabled experts and social reformers to focus their efforts on using science and the state to reform groups of individuals rather than the overall social or economic structure. The quantification of psychological phenomena that resulted from statistical studies also lent an air of scientific credibility to psychologists who were eager to prove their practical worth in an American society that was increasingly turning to experts in an effort to solve social problems. As psychologist William Tucker argues, turn-of-the-century psychologists had entered into an "essentially Faustian bargain" when they failed to make a distinction between what he calls an "objective attempt to understand behavior" and the "creation of ideological support for a social order informed by eugenicist and other elitist principles." Psychologists, according to Tucker, had sold their "scientific soul" in exchange for "recognition, influence, and prestige."[17]

Statistical psychological studies figured prominently in this bargain. They were critical in the efforts of psychologists to be taken seriously. They also, as Danziger argues, "greatly facilitated the artificial creation of new groups whose defining characteristic was based on performance on some psychological instrument, most commonly an intelligence test." "A score on a mental test," according to Danziger, "conferred membership in an abstract collectivity created for the purpose of psychological research."[18] In Illinois and elsewhere, individuals conducting research in reform institutions used a number of newly created mental examinations to substantiate preconceived notions concerning not only the existence, but also the measurability of innate difference within a seemingly homogeneous white population.

By far the most important tool used by experts was the Binet intelligence test. The Binet scale consisted of a series of sixty-four tests that were graduated in order of increasing difficulty. Experts who administered the exams sought to obtain three main results. Their primary goal was to objectify their subject's perceived intellectual level, or "mental age," by assigning it a numerical value. They also sought to quantify important "practical" data, such as an individual's ability to "read, write, draw, use language, use numbers, use money, do errands, imitate, etc." Finally, experts used the Binet test to classify certain observable characteristics, for example, an individual's "attitude, his emotional condition, his speech and movements, and various other characteristics of his response and conduct." Mental testers considered individuals who showed more than three years of retardation in intelligence, functioning, or development to be "feebleminded."[19] According to Elizabeth Kite, the woman who translated the Binet test for Goddard, even though experts' "[s]ubjective appreciation of mental states" entered into the diagnosis of "most cases," they could be certain that "Binet's line of definite demarcation" insured that their diagnoses rested upon a "comparatively solid basis of fact."[20] Armed with the Binet intelligence test and their own "subjective appreciation of mental states," a diverse array of experts boldly entered places such as Tin Town, The Commons, and the state training school at Geneva ready to "discover" mental defect.

In 1910, American scientists added another critical weapon to their arsenal. In May of that year, the Lincoln State School and Colony hosted the annual meeting of the American Association for the Study of the Feeble-Minded, where mental health experts officially adopted a revised classification scheme. In an attempt to avoid confusion and further clarify their definition of feeblemindedness, and simultaneously enhance their own power and authority, the association divided feeblemindedness into three subcategories or classes: "idiots," "imbeciles," and "morons." The association arbitrarily set the upper limit of feeblemindedness at twelve years of mental development because most experts agreed that individuals with a "mental age" above twelve years were able to live on their own, and usually insisted on doing so. In an effort to establish an even more reliable "means of bringing order into chaos," experts created increasingly subtler degrees of classification that went well beyond the three primary categories of feeblemindedness.[21] The categories "idiot," "imbecile," and "moron" were further subdivided into high, medium, and low grades. Scientists also used the terms "backward," "dull," and "unstable" to codify the perceived mental capacity of those individuals who occupied the "borderland" between feeblemindedness and "normality." In later years, when the term "feebleminded" became socially unacceptable, experts substituted the term "mental defective."[22] Science, it seemed, had provided eugenic reformers with an accurate and reliable means of rendering otherwise invisible traits visible.

Experts' efforts to create a scientifically accurate and objective testing system exacerbated the likelihood that they would "discover" that an alarming number of their subjects were indeed "mental defectives." Scientists' training and their desire to legitimize their own methodological assumptions led them to highlight what they perceived as innate deficiencies in their subjects. That they focused their efforts on individuals who occupied the "borderland" between feeblemindedness and "normality" only served to strengthen experts' ability to delineate the terms of the discourse and create entirely new systems of classification. Whether conducting mental evaluations in institutions or in the field, experts carried with them the tools and, perhaps more important, the inclination to construct individuals who, for a number of complex reasons, did not live "normally" as inherently flawed.

The complex, dynamic nature of the classificatory process and the elasticity with which experts applied their methods is evident in observations concerning the prevalence of "feeblemindedness" in different communities throughout Illinois. Upon his examination of the work of mental testers in St. Clair and Peoria Counties, Harrison Harley, a psychologist at the Juvenile Psychopathic Institute, found that the number of "feebleminded" individuals that were "discovered" in each county was directly proportional to the "sensitiveness of the social conscience of the community concerned." The number of "feebleminded" persons "discovered" in Peoria County, where the "social effort" was highly organized, was higher than that of St. Clair County, where the "social effort" was not very well organized.[23] As Danziger argues, the creation of statistical psychological studies, most of which centered upon the measurement of intelligence, "opened up untold vistas" for researchers, because they enabled scientists to create "abstract collectivity" seemingly without end.[24] By the early twentieth century, mental evaluations, however fraught, had become an important and powerful means of defining embodied deviance.

"Defective Delinquents" and "Brain Touchers"

Thirty years have passed since Foucault first asked historians to write a history of the process of the examination; not a history of tests or experiments or studies, but of the examination itself, with all of "its rituals, its methods, its characters and their roles, its play of questions and answers, its systems of marking and classification." For Foucault, the highly ritualized process of the examination "combined the ceremony of power and the form of the experiment, the deployment of force and the establishment of truth." By holding its subjects in a "mechanism of objectification," the examination "transformed the economy of visibility into the exercise of power." It manifested the subjection of individuals who were perceived as objects and made possible the "objectification of those who [were] subjected." The exam established over individuals a visibility through which the examiner differentiated them and judged them; and through its "documentary techniques," the exam transformed the individual into a "case."[25]

Foucault believed that the "superimposition" of the power relations and knowledge relations produced in the exam afforded the examination "all its visible brilliance" and in the end made it possible to "qualify, to classify and to punish." But was the exam, with its techniques of "observing hierarchy" and of "normalizing judgment," a unidirectional process? Foucault seems to think it was; the examination, he argues, fixed at once ritual and "scientific" understandings of individual difference. The "pinning down of each individual in his own particularity," Foucault argues, "clearly indicates the appearance of a new modality of power in which each individual receives as his status his own individuality, and in which he is linked by his status to the features, the measurements, the gaps, the 'marks' that characterize him and make him a 'case.'"[26]

The ritual of modern psychological examination was a critical new modality of power that greatly affected the lives of its subjects; the examiner observed, measured, recorded, defined, and treated, all through a process in which power relations between scientist and subject were far from equal, but the ritual of the exam did afford its subjects some room for negotiation and redefinition. Geneva's inmates actively participated in the examination and in the formation of their own individuality, and in some cases affected not only their own lived experience, but also dominant perceptions of "mental defect" and eugenic commitment.

Case records from Illinois are full of evidence of young women using the ritual of the examination to assert some semblance of power and control in shaping both their own individuality and the course of treatment they received. For most girls the exam process began in the courtroom and continued at the Juvenile Psychopathic Institute, or after 1917, the Institute for Juvenile Research (IJR). Another round of examinations began when the inmate arrived at Geneva. In most cases, experts repeated the examination process several times during the period of incarceration.

Experiences similar to that of Helen were not uncommon. Born in October 1921, Helen experienced her first examination at the IJR in November 1930, when she was nine years old. Psychologists assigned her an IQ of 89, or a "low average intelligence." At the time of her first exam, Helen was living with a cousin in Chicago. She was part of what caseworkers described as a "broken family." Her father was gone, and her mother had refused to take Helen with her to Indiana when she moved there with a new man.

In February 1931, the Cook County Juvenile Court sent Helen to the Illinois Children's Home and Aid Society (ICHAS), who ultimately placed her in the state foster care system. Helen's cousin had refused to care for Helen any longer, because of the girl's "misbehavior" and "nervousness." Helen remained in the foster care system until November 1937. During that time, she passed through several homes and institutions. She did not adjust well in her first home and was sent to the IJR in July 1934 for a second round of examinations. The psychologist obtained similar results with the IQ tests, but now the psychiatrist determined that Helen was "beginning a psychosis or soon would become psychopathic." The ICHAS placed their charge in a new home, where she remained for the next six months, during which time she went to the IJR twice a month for treatment to prevent a "manic depressive psychosis."

Helen entered her first institution, the Mary Judy Boarding School, in January 1935, where she once again had a difficult time. In November 1936, she was moved to the Evanston Receiving Home. A month later, the staff at the IJR examined her yet again. This time they declared that Helen was not psychotic and that she possessed an average intelligence. The IJR recommended that Helen be sent to yet another foster home, where she remained until November 1937. In October 1937, Helen's birthmother had returned to Illinois in search of her daughter, and after a brief investigation, the ICHAS allowed Helen to live with her. This, however, did not mark the end of Helen's experience with examinations or the state.

In July 1938, Helen returned to the IJR, apparently determined to use the only means she knew to escape the custody of her mother. During the subsequent examinations, Helen, whom experts had classified as "average intelligence" on three previous occasions, performed poorly on intelligence tests, resulting in a rating of "dull and backward." Helen was also initially "stolid and resistive" to the psychiatric interview, and when she finally began to cooperate, she was "sullen and resentful." Later she became "more friendly but very emotional." The examiner found that, "In spite of her tears she maintained a very suspicious paranoid attitude." Helen apparently felt that everybody hated her and nobody trusted her. She accused her probation officer and various workers from different social agencies of lying about her and of "wanting to get rid of her." She admitted to hallucinations, "particularly of God's voice which tells her that she is a very bad girl." According to the psychiatrist, Helen had "very definite ideas of influence"; she felt that people could read her mind and that certain "people" whom she refused to name were responsible for her misbehavior. The "impression" of the experts at the IJR was that Helen was a "case" of schizophrenia or dementia praecox and that she was in need of custodial care. Although the IJR wanted to send Helen to a state hospital for the psychopathic or insane, she refused to be sent anywhere but the state training school in Geneva, where she said she could be safe from the "evil influences" in her life. Helen got her way; she was sent to Geneva.

Helen entered Geneva at the end of July and one month later became the subject of yet another examination. This time the whole experience was different. According to the Geneva staff, Helen was a "very friendly girl who made herself at home as soon as she got in the examining room." The psychologist noted that the "situation and circumstances were familiar to [Helen] since she has been examined so often before." When the experts asked Helen why she was at Geneva, she replied, "Because I can't get along anyplace but in an institution." Helen felt so "at home" in the examination room that she "talked constantly for 2 1/2 hours and it was only when she was told that she had to eat that she was willing to leave." Her examiners noted that during the interview, Helen "made an attempt to diagnose her own difficulties and seemed to have some degree of insight." She even used some of the clinical language that she had heard the adults use when they were discussing her experience. Following the examination at Geneva, experts determined that Helen was not psychopathic or insane, but that she could benefit from talking to a psychologist "occasionally about her problems." The staff was not able to give Helen a Stanford-Binet intelligence test, because "she had had the examination three times before and knew all the questions." She was also familiar with most of the other written examinations. Helen remained at Geneva, and away from her mother, until she was twenty-one years old.[27]

As Helen's case shows, the ritual of the examination was fluid and dynamic, and though mental health experts, the state, and other adults held a considerable amount of power over their young subjects, that power was not absolute. Even within the severely constraining environment of foster homes, state institutions, and the Institute for Juvenile Research, Helen maintained some measure of influence over her own fate and the creation of her own identity. She did not passively receive her individuality from her examiners; she was not simply a "case" to be filed away with other similar "cases." She was, however, caught within a system, a modality of power and knowledge in which experts tried consistently to define her as unintelligent, as psychopathic, as deviant; as someone in need of custodial care; as all of those classifications that figured so prominently in the lives of most female delinquents and their families and had their roots in dominant understandings of "normal" intelligence and behavior. Helen, like so many of the young women labeled "feebleminded" or "mentally defective," did not accept the identity imposed upon her by experts uncritically, nor did she passively submit to incarceration. Although they rarely escaped the controlling, normalizing gaze of experts, judges, institution administrators, and parents completely, the girls incarcerated at Geneva possessed a measure of agency; some of them, in fact, were quite savvy.

Inmates at the state training school at Geneva were well aware of the importance of the examination and the power of examiners. They dubbed resident experts "brain touchers" and continually published articles in their school newspaper advising their fellow inmates on how to maintain their composure during the very tense testing process.[28] Despite distinct social and cultural disadvantages, as well as an acute sense of fear and anxiety brought on by the exam process, inmates rarely showed signs of being passive or powerless during their evaluations. Many of them, like Helen, were talkative during their exams. Inmates made excuses for themselves, they shared their experiences, and they sought their own explanations and interpretations of their incarceration and of the testing process and the results it supposedly revealed. In many cases, inmates who feared they might be classified as "mentally defective" attempted, in their own subtle ways, to undermine experts' authority and persuade mental testers that they were indeed "normal."

By taking an active interest in the exam process, by appropriating the language of their examiners, and by continually voicing their own concerns and insights, inmates shaped the evaluative process in very subtle but also very meaningful and powerful ways. An inmate's verbal banter, their posture, and their attitude during an exam sent clear messages to mental testers that inmates were not going to be pinned down in their own "particularity" and become part of an "observing hierarchy" without some level of contestation. Inmates' actions, moreover, make salient the looseness of mental classifications that most Americans saw as at once "natural" and "scientific." By going into the exam room with inmates like Helen and the female experts who examined them, we can begin to reveal the historical contingency of impairment itself.

"I ain't been reading while on parole"

There is little doubt that incarceration and the ritual of the exam proved stressful for inmates. Experts at Geneva administered a litany of physical and psychological examinations within the first two weeks of incarceration. In most cases, the staff performed all of the examinations within the first few days of admission, while the girls were still attempting to adjust to their new surroundings and cope with the stress of being incarcerated. Although inmates were given group tests, most exams were performed individually and in private—not en masse, as they were during World War I—which added stress to the exam process. Sixteen-year-old Evelyn, who was tested just three days after entering Geneva and who was found to possess a "dull borderline intelligence," was "extremely nervous when she came into the testing room." Psychologists noted that Evelyn's body "quivered as if an electric current were passing through it." She "began to cry before a word was said to her." Mental testers found that Daisy exhibited "poor attention" during her exam, in part because she was "still emotionally upset over being in the institution." Experts classified Daisy as a "borderline mental defective" and assigned her an IQ of 73.

Despite the stress of the ritual of the examination, many inmates assumed a confident, cooperative, and sometimes superior posture in the exam room. Elzina, whom experts described as "very talkative at the time of the examination," made many promises regarding her future behavior, but ultimately tried to convince her inquisitors that occasional delinquencies were unavoidable. Elzina ended her exam by stating, "but you know how it is, a girl will get into a little trouble now and then." Yvonne was also very talkative during her exam. Among other things, Yvonne attempted to convince experts at Geneva that although the doctors at the Institute for Juvenile Research "thought she was 'nuts,'" she really only had a 'psychopathic heart.'" Experts argued that Dora possessed "no insight into her limitations." Yet she remained very much at ease with her examiners. The staff at Geneva commented that Dora even assumed a "rather superior attitude" during her exam, and that she watched the scoring "very closely." When Daisy Mae did not perform well on her examination, she informed the psychologists that she was worried about her mother and unable to concentrate. She made it clear that she needed to be certain that her mother was "getting well." The Geneva staff recorded that yet another inmate, named Lillian, "smiled complacently" throughout her exam, as if "nothing which was being done could affect her." Mental testers noted, however, that Lillian frequently queried examiners regarding the quality of her answers and that toward the end of her exam, Lillian "grew solicitous for the welfare of the examiner." According to experts, Lillian wondered aloud if it was not tiring for the psychologists to "talk so much."[29]

Not all of Geneva's inmates coped in the same manner with the anxiety and stress involved with taking the exams. Although some inmates attempted to remain confident and cooperative, other young women such as Louise possessed a "quarrelsome nature," or like Eleanor, remained "stolid and defiant" throughout the testing process. Some inmates simply refused to talk about certain subjects. Experts at the IJR described seventeen-year-old Thelma, one of the few African American girls whom they encountered in their work, as a girl who presented "a very dull, inadequate appearance" and someone who was "dull and backward in intelligence." She had gonorrhea at the time of her examination and admitted to having had an abortion at the Cook County Hospital, but examiners noted that she refused "to discuss the reason for the abortion and also refuse[d] to name anyone as being responsible for her pregnancy." According to the experts,

Thelma stated "very frankly that she did not consider it necessary to discuss that particular phase of her troubles. She was very vague as to her sex activities and obviously did not wish to tell the truth." Thelma remained guarded during her interview, a survival technique she no doubt learned growing up in Chicago's black belt. Other girls, like Josephine, became "rather aggressive" or "moderately resentful" during the examination. Experts noted that Josephine also "blamed all of her delinquencies and her commitment on Dorothy Hughes, another Geneva ward." Blaming other girls for their apparent delinquencies was common among the young women at the IJR and Geneva. The psychologist at Geneva noted that Annabelle "blamed Helen Starck (committed to Geneva with her) for all of her difficulties and claims she 'never would done nothin' if Helen hadn't appeared."[30] Inmates knew they were at a disadvantage in the exam room. Yet this did not stop them from asserting themselves in their own distinct ways.

Some inmates, like Doris, exhibited signs that they simply did not value the exam process and were unconcerned about performing well on tests. Experts described Doris as "a small, white girl" who appeared "alert and much brighter than" test results indicated. Psychologists stated that Doris followed directions well, but that she was unable to concentrate. She grew restless during her exam and became tired; and when questions became "too difficult she became very bored and made no attempt to solve [them]." The Geneva staff also found that Doris "gave very poor attention" when taking a group intelligence test. She guessed at all of her answers and tried to copy from a neighbor. Experts concluded that Doris read well, but that she did not understand what she read. Doris's apparent unwillingness to participate in the ritual of the exam led experts to classify her as a "borderline defective."[31]

Other inmates knew that their lack of formal schooling would be detrimental to their performance on exams, and they frequently vocalized their concern to mental testers. Although young women such as Della and Evelyn were "very cooperative," they were also anxious to do their best on tests. Part of inmates' anxiety stemmed from the fact that they were very much, in the words of their examiners, "aware of their limitations." They frequently made comments such as, "I ain't been reading while on parole"; "I can't do much today"; "I ain't had much schooling"; or "Something is wrong with my brain." Psychologists noted that Evelyn was "anxious to be successful," and that she "covered her errors by statements concerning her 'dumbness' in comparison with her brother's brilliance." Experts also found that Evelyn "frequently" used her own nervousness to explain her failure on the exam. Fifteen-year-old Naomi, who had completed only the third grade, told her examiners that she did not like going to school because her teachers made fun of her. When Annabelle's testing began, she immediately explained to the psychologists that she was "not very smart at school." Although she tried every item on the exam, Annabelle frequently guessed at the answers. Another inmate, named Shirley, whom psychologists described as a "thin, pale white girl," was so "nervous" and "unsure of herself" that she grinned and giggled when she was unable to answer a question. She needed constant encouragement, and she added, "I think that is right," or "something like that" to the end of each answer. Geneva's inmates understood the importance that staff members placed on test results, and they recognized that they were not prepared to take the exams. Rather than accept their "failure" uncritically, they used every means at their disposal to challenge the outcome of the ritual of the examination.

Sixteen-year-old Sybil's experience is emblematic of the contestation that occurred in the exam room. Sybil had quit school after the sixth grade, but was "anxious" to complete the eighth grade when she entered Geneva. She articulated her desire to continue her schooling to her examiners, but because tests showed that she supposedly possessed a "mental age" of eleven and an IQ of 74, psychologists were hesitant to allow her to continue her education. They noted that Sybil was "quite ambitious for a girl of her mental ability and in this respect show[ed] no insight into her limitations." They concluded that she would "profit little from further academic work." What psychologists considered a lack of "insight into her limitations" was most likely a manifestation of Sybil's efforts to define her own identity, despite experts' diagnosis.

Sybil appears to have had some measure of success in her battle with the "brain touchers." Despite test results, Geneva staff placed her in the seventh-grade class, where she excelled. The following year the Geneva psychologists, who were determined not to abandon their original mental classification, recorded that "Sybil's academic progress has been very good in consideration of her mental ability." Eager to reassert their power over Sybil, the experts concluded once again that she had "reached her academic limit." They classified her as "a borderline defective, very close to dull." Although they grudgingly admitted that Sybil might show some future progress, experts maintained their conclusion that she did not possess the ability to complete the eighth grade. Sybil, who was determined to complete the eighth grade because she "found this very necessary in looking for a job," remained anxious to continue her education. Unfortunately, it is unclear from Sybil's records if she ever completed her schooling, but her experience remains revealing of the struggles between inmates and experts.[32]

Throughout the first half of the twentieth century, Geneva's inmates remained steadfast in their conviction to chart their own path through Illinois' juvenile justice and mental health systems. Some, like Sybil, sought to continue their education despite experts' official pronouncements concerning their "mental ability." Inmates did not always get their way and they did not always succeed in their endeavors; but their challenges to the authority of experts and staff at Geneva and the IJR cannot be denied.

The Ritual of the Examination and the Creation of Mental Deviance

Unfortunately for many inmates, experts often read the contestation that occurred in the exam room as further evidence of "mental defect." In virtually every instance, examiners based their assessment of an incarcerated individual's competence not only on test scores, which were problematic in themselves, but also on a subjective interpretation of inmates' actions during the examination, as well as on their own personal history.[33]

The most important marker of mental deviance, especially for female test subjects, was any evidence of experience in "sex matters." Goddard and Helen Hill cited, along with a litany of other characteristics, the fact that a sixteen-year-old woman whom they studied got "very much excited by the company of men," and "attracted the attention of workmen across the street" when the probation officer brought her in to be examined, as evidence of mental "defect." In the same study, Goddard and Hill stated that another "feebleminded" girl's employer found her to be "boy crazy."[34] The experts at the IJR noted that a Geneva inmate named Josephine "told of repeated sex relations" during her examination. In another exam, the IJR staff found Emily to be a "borderline defective" and "dull," in part because she exhibited "every indication" that she had "learned to turn to sexual delinquency for satisfactions which she has not been able to obtain at school or in the home." Emily's "dullness" combined with her "definite physical maturity" and her "crying need for affection and attention" led to her incarceration in Geneva.[35] She was, in the words of eugenicists, a "feebleminded menace." Well into the twentieth century, experts asserted that the apparent correlation between "feeblemindedness" and sexual "immorality" was evidence that "feeblemindedness" could be both the cause and the result of "immoral" activity.[36]

Young women who came into the exam room pregnant were especially likely to be labeled "mentally defective." Experts at the IJR noted that during her examination, Elizabeth, who was five or six months pregnant, appeared "attentive" and "cooperative," and indeed may have scored "slightly higher" if she were not pregnant. Yet they made no attempt to retest her after she delivered her baby. When Elizabeth arrived at Geneva, the psychologists there concluded that, "All examinations agree in classifying this girl as a borderline defective, close to the feeble-minded group." They described Elizabeth as someone who "appeared to be a shallow, superficial girl, completely lacking in insight or understanding"; all characteristics that no doubt influenced their classification, as well as their decision not to retest her. The Geneva staff concluded that "Elizabeth's adjustment will probably be typical of her classification." Although Elizabeth expressed a desire to continue her education in high school, the psychologists determined that she was "not capable of further academic work." They recommended institutionalization and "training in a more simple field."[37]

In many cases, Geneva staff also classified victims of sexual abuse as "mentally defective." Ruth is an example of an inmate whose evaluation was directly affected by the hardship brought on by rape. Psychologists recorded that Ruth appeared very anxious and expressed interest in wanting to talk to someone when they called her in for the examination. Yet they proceeded with the intelligence tests. Examiners later commented that Ruth gave them the "impression of being unstable, and possibly easily disturbed emotionally" during the tests. She also showed signs of "indecision" and "uncertainty." Ruth "blushed a good deal" and seemed disturbed and ashamed. It appeared to her examiners that Ruth wanted to tell them about the experience of being raped by her father, but that she "seemed quite disturbed over the situation and could not speak freely about it." Ruth eventually told her examiners about her rape, but it apparently did little to influence their diagnosis of her "mental ability." No further information concerning the rape was included in Ruth's case file. The file did, however, include the results of the intelligence tests. Psychologists found Ruth to be "dull to low average," and concluded that she had reached her academic limit, which was the eighth grade. They recommended high school vocational work in, of all things, domestic science.[38]

Ruth's experience was not uncommon. Other girls classified as "mentally defective" conveyed equally chilling stories of molestation and rape. Yvonne told her IJR interviewer that "a young man who represented himself as a police officer approached her, and under threat of arrest took her to a house . . . where he forced her to submit to sex relations." She claimed to have "screamed and hollered," but was unable to obtain any help. Yvonne stated that, "He finally let her go threatening he would shoot her if she told anyone." She admitted to being so upset by this attack that she "went to the home of a girl friend," and "did not return home until several days later." Thirteen-year-old Josephine told experts at the IJR of "repeated sex relations with a James Cole," who took her near Brookfield Zoo and forced her to have sex. Although twelve-year-old Elzina was suffering from syphilis at the time of her exam, she denied any "sex activities." She claimed that her only sexual experience "was when an elderly man handled her genitalia but did not attempt sexual relations."[39] In many cases, experts interpreted stories of sexual abuse as either a direct sign of an inmate's inherent inability to control both herself and the men she encountered, as the product of the overactive imagination of their young test subject, or as signs of the girl's willingness to deceive, all of which they classified as evidence of mental "defect."

Another important sign of mental "defect" was a girl's extreme "suggestibility." Della, who was in and out of Geneva between the ages of fifteen and nineteen, was another inmate who gave examiners the "impression of being brighter" than test results indicated. Yet when the psychologists examined Della, they found her to be a "high grade mental defective." Experts described Della as someone who was "talkative"; who was "quite alert to her surroundings"; and who showed "some degree of common sense." These factors, combined with Della's "earnest and sincere manner in speaking," gave them the "impression" that she was a "girl of a higher I.Q." According to the Geneva staff, Della's greatest fault was her "extreme suggestibility." They found that she was "willing to accept any response suggested to her and would change a correct response to an incorrect one if she thought she detected a sign of disapproval from the examiner."[40] Experiences similar to Della's were common among inmates at Geneva and the IJR. Experts cited "suggestibility" in nearly every case in which an inmate was found to be mentally "defective." Rather than acknowledge the asymmetrical power relations inherent in the testing process itself and alter either their methods or their findings, the experts at Geneva instead chose to highlight their subjects' "extreme suggestibility" as an obvious sign of mental "defect."

Although experts considered the majority of the girls at Geneva as white, native-born Americans, many of them lived in households where parents spoke little English. Inmates' general lack of formal schooling, combined with obvious language difficulties, contributed to their being labeled "mentally defective." One girl's experience is illustrative of the significance of language in the evaluative process. When psychologists examined fifteen-year-old Virginia, which was only two days after she entered Geneva, they found that she was "very quiet, very unemotional." Examiners recorded that there was "an immobility about [Virginia] which made testing very difficult." They explained that "Not by any sign would she show whether or not she grasped the directions." When the psychologists asked Virginia if she understood the directions, she invariably said "yes." The staff noted, however, that Virginia also frequently stated that she did not know the answers to their questions, and that she displayed "no embarrassment" when she could not answer their questions. Experts noted that outwardly, Virginia appeared cooperative and attentive. Yet they concluded that she seemed to "create a barrier between herself and the examination, which made it difficult to judge the extent of her real participation." Virginia explained that Dutch was spoken in her home, and "English hardly at all." Despite Virginia's plea, mental testers made no attempt to compensate in any way for their test subject's obvious language difficulties. In fact, they concluded that Virginia was a "high grade mental defective," and held that intelligence tests clearly showed that she had been "pushed in school beyond her capabilities." Virginia had been in the eighth grade before her incarceration at Geneva and expressed interest in completing her schooling. The Geneva staff concluded, however, that further academic training did not "appear to be indicated either by her attainment or by her intelligence level."[41] In Virginia's case, as well as other cases, cultural and linguistic differences between examiners and their subjects complicated the testing process and significantly affected both diagnosis and treatment.

The experts at Geneva and the IJR showed signs that they were aware of the complicated situations from which their test subjects emerged. Yet they were unwilling to abandon either the testing process or the information it supposedly revealed. Superintendent Amigh, who was one of the most outspoken proponents of eugenic commitment, observed that "Very few of the girls have had any training in the choice and use of good books, before entering."[42] The teachers at Geneva also acknowledged that many of their pupils never attended school, and knew "absolutely nothing in the line of a practical education."[43] Geneva's principal, Charlotte Dye, who was at Geneva the same time as Amigh, asserted that the majority of the girls who could not read or write were "not deficient but neglected."[44] Comments such as, "Her home environment was very unsatisfactory and she had very irregular attendance in school" appear in nearly all of the examination records of girls whom experts classified as "mentally defective." Equally prevalent, however, are comments such as ". . . will never be able to do high school work"; ". . . has reached her academic limit"; ". . . will profit little from further academic work"; and ". . . does not have the ability to complete the grades."[45] Mental testers at Geneva and the IJR recognized that their subjects came from abusive, neglectful homes and had little or no formal schooling. This alone, however, rarely affected either their diagnosis or their prescribed course of treatment for the young women they examined.

The ritual of the exam provided mental health experts with the means to minimize possible social and economic explanations of inmates' deviance, and in turn attribute it to some inherent mental "defect." If a subject's performance on an examination did not meet the expectations of the examiner, or if a subject exhibited behavior that was not defined by the examiner as "normal," then the subject was labeled "feebleminded" or "mentally defective." For example, in his examination of Dora, an inmate at the Lincoln State School and Colony, Dr. Edmund Huey found that she was a "good dancer" and a "satisfactory pupil" who could multiply, divide, and read a newspaper with "moderate fluency." Huey also found that Dora was "dull," "unstable," and possessed a "feeble mental span," in part because she could not define the terms "charity," "goodness," and "justice" in a manner that satisfied him. When Huey asked Dora to define "charity," she replied, "Aren't they the people that come here [to Lincoln] to look after things?" When Huey asked Dora to define "goodness," she replied, "Someone is kind to you." According to Huey, Dora was unable to define "justice." Although the Binet test only required that the subject define two terms "satisfactorily," Huey concluded that abstractions were "quite beyond" Dora.[46] New scientific evaluations created by emerging professionals enabled them to cast a group of young, working-class, native born, white women who engaged in sexually dubious behavior as inherently "deviant." In most cases, any nonnormative behavior or utterance during the ritual of the exam served as a powerful marker of some flaw embedded deep within the test subject.[47]

Outcomes

Experts' unwavering faith in science and in their own ability to discover "defect" often had dire consequences for young women who found themselves caught within the ritual of the examination, the worst of which was indefinite incarceration in a state institution. Geneva psychologists committed Shirley to the state institution at Dixon indefinitely, in part because she "classified as a high-grade mental defective according to two examinations, a group test and an individual test." Shirley, the experts concluded, was "completely lacking in insight and judgment." She was "not capable of taking care of herself" and would "always require strict supervision and care." In view of her previous history and her "present attitude combined with her low mentality," it appeared to her examiners that Shirley would "easily return to her previous delinquent habits." Commitment to an institution for the feebleminded would offer Shirley and the community "the necessary protection." Mental testers classified yet another Geneva inmate, Annabelle, as a "high grade defective" and assigned her an IQ of 61. They described her as "both intellectually and emotionally shallow" and as someone who had "little understanding of her delinquencies." Psychologists concluded that Annabelle would "require close supervision both outside of the institution and within it." They recommended that she also be committed indefinitely to an institution for the "feebleminded."[48] The materialization of a perceived "defect" through the ritual of the examination proved critical in the recommendation of indefinite commitment for both Shirley and Annabelle.

Though they possessed considerable power, mental health experts did not always have the last word in the diagnosis or treatment of their charges. Inmates who fought to have their voices heard during their examinations and struggled to succeed in Geneva's classrooms challenged the notion that they were "unfit" and ultimately played a role in transforming the diagnosis and treatment of adolescent "sex delinquents." Though subtle, the cumulative effect of young women's challenges contributed to the decline in the diagnosis of impairment at

Geneva and eventually to an abandonment of eugenic commitment in Illinois by the early 1950s. Other social and scientific factors played an important role in bringing about these changes, but the previously unacknowledged role of the young women themselves no doubt also had an effect.

Despite significant disadvantages, including being labeled "feebleminded" or "mentally defective," many Geneva inmates showed marked improvement in their schoolwork. From its inception, the staff at Geneva perceived their institution as an educational facility. That perception did not change with the advent of intelligence testing and the apparent realization that the majority of their inmates exhibited some degree of "mental defect." Upon the completion of a series of physical, mental, and psychological tests, administrators placed their charges in an appropriate grade level. The teaching staff then began to work with students in acquiring basic skills and knowledge, sometimes with positive results. "It has been the purpose of this school," Superintendent Amigh noted, "to give every girl, as far as she is capable of acquiring it, a good English education, and while the [progress] of many is slow, very satisfactory results have been obtained." Amigh explained that the staff at Geneva instilled a desire to learn in many of the girls through "story telling and by reading aloud to them" and by allowing them access to the books in the school's small library.[49] One of the teachers at Geneva explained that of the inmates with little schooling, which tended to be the majority, "many would ordinarily be considered incapable of learning, but by patience, infinite patience, sympathy and tactful management they acquire power to read and write, also to memorize choice selections." Some of her students, the teacher declared, advanced even further, and expressed interest in continuing their studies in high school.[50] Principal Dye declared in 1910 that the girls' progress in school had been "gratifying to both themselves and their teachers."[51]

Although the testimony of institution administrators and staff eager for state funds should be viewed with some skepticism, other evidence suggests that Geneva's inmates were indeed capable of functioning "normally" in the school setting. The State Training School for Girls held its first ever eighth grade commencement on July 31, 1912.[52] The staff at Geneva created a first-year high school class consisting of English literature, ancient history and English history, and higher algebra, in 1916. They added courses in stenography, typewriting, bookkeeping, business English, business spelling, and penmanship in 1917. The teaching staff, which consisted of one instructor in 1898, grew to thirteen by 1914.[53] Although the eighth grade class and the high school class remained small—the majority of the inmates were in the fourth, sixth, and seventh grade classes—their existence showed that at least some of the girls at Geneva were capable of advancing beyond their perceived academic limits. Geneva also created a permanent vocational curriculum for those young women who showed "great aptitude" for "mechanical work or fancy sewing."[54] By the mid-1930s, Geneva had all eight grades and three years of high school, as well as the vocational program. No one was incarcerated at Geneva who could not read or write.[55] Although the majority of the inmates who were in high school were in the ninth grade and many girls were in the vocational classes, it was clear that they were capable of learning despite their apparently degraded mental and physical state.

Conclusion

The mental testers at Geneva and the IJR, as well as their young subjects, played a vital role in the important, complex evaluative process that formed the core of the eugenic commitment debate and the social construction of mental "deviance." Experts used the results of intelligence tests and other *psy* examinations that they administered to sexually delinquent adolescent girls to argue that their subjects were "feebleminded" or "mentally defective" and incapable of living a "normal" life in the outside world. For some inmates, this meant a long process of training and reeducation that involved a combination of incarceration and parole, or probation that in many cases did not end until the inmate turned twenty-one years old. For other inmates, it meant indefinite incarceration in a state institution for the "feebleminded."

Eugenic commitment remained a very real option for experts and staff at Geneva because of the power and prestige afforded them by the ritual of the examination. Emboldened by the emergence of dozens of new mental and psychological examinations that ostensibly enhanced the precision of the testing process and numerous public school tracking systems during the 1920s, psychologists felt increasingly confident in their ability to diagnose and treat "mentally defective" delinquents after the First World War. Between 1915—the year Illinois passed its eugenic commitment law—and 1950, Geneva staff committed approximately 5–10 percent, or twenty-five to fifty inmates each year, to one of two state institutions for the "feebleminded." At the center of this process was the ritual of the examination; that critical moment, or series of moments, when all of the social, cultural, and scientific forces that defined the eugenic commitment debate collided in the form of the expert and their subject; the moment when theory met practice and practice informed theory, when cultural values became transparent and fears and desires became known; the moment in which identities were formed, negotiated, and redefined.

Experts held distinct advantages in the struggle to define their subjects, but their power was not absolute. The young women who found themselves entangled in the web of the expanding juvenile justice and mental health systems were not the passive recipients of their own individuality; they were not just a "case." The ritual of the examination opened a means through which female "sex delinquents" could make their voices heard; a place where they could express their demands, desires, concerns, and troubles. Though they often found it difficult to obtain the results they sought, inmates kept trying; and through their efforts to shape their own individuality and their own destiny, they ultimately helped to transform the ways in which experts and reformers viewed the causes of delinquency and the treatment of delinquents. Inmates were able to use the examination, no matter how constraining it may have been, to shape their own identity and in the process influence the definition of impairment itself.

5

"How a Girl of the Road Wins Rides and Influences Motorists"

> "The majority [of Geneva's inmates] chafe under enforced confinement, and in open defiance declare that they will never reform, and will do worse when they get out."
> —Dr. Esther H. Stone, 1918

> "It's too bad a kid can't go out once in a while and have a good time without having to pay for it."
> —Sixteen-year-old "sex delinquent," 1930s

Birdie was an inmate at Geneva during the 1930s, who according to Managing Officer Florence Monahan "could not resist the lure of the open road." The staff at Geneva diagnosed Birdie as a "chronic runaway" because of her incessant, unflagging desire to leave the institution. Monahan declared that it "finally got to the point where one matron would ask the other in making the evening checkup, 'Is this Birdie's night out?'" Birdie had become so proficient at "tramping" that in a confidential talk after one of her cross-country tours, she gave Monahan a lesson in the secrets of a successful hitchhiker: of "how a girl of the road wins rides and influences motorists." According to Monahan, Birdie explained that, "Cartoons to the contrary, experienced ladies of the highway," such as herself, did not "thumb rides." Instead, they sat "decorously" upon their upended suitcase by the side of the road and worked crossword puzzles until a motorist came along. That way, if a car pulled up and she did not like the looks of its occupants, she could simply continue doing her puzzle. Birdie explained that she preferred to ride with a couple and that her first choice was an elderly or middle-aged woman and man. She said that she never got in a car or truck with just one man and that she preferred not to hitchhike at night. Despite her candidness and her propensity to leave Geneva whenever she so desired, and despite the fact that she returned from one of her trips pregnant, Monahan did not consider Birdie a "bad" girl.

Instead, she recognized that Birdie's mother deserted her when she was a young girl, and that "tramping" had become a way of life for Birdie.[1] Unfortunately for Birdie and for many other girls who, for various reasons, did not conform to Geneva's elaborate disciplinary regime, not all of the staff at Geneva proved to be as understanding as Monahan.

This chapter focuses in more detail on the ritual of the examination as it occurred outside the exam room. It uses case files from the State Training School at Geneva and the Lincoln State School and Colony to analyze the ways in which the actions and utterances of young women and their families that occurred outside the exam room influenced the definition of impairment. Experts relied on much more than test scores and the psychiatric or psychological interview when diagnosing their patients. The ritual of the examination included every aspect of an inmate's life and their conduct both within and outside the institution. Very rarely did inmates and their families escape the penetrating gaze of experts and administrators, who seemed to process, analyze, and categorize every action and every utterance that came within their purview. All observable characteristics, including physical appearance, emotional condition, and behavior fell within the rubric of their evaluations. Once they had accumulated their data, experts would then use it to bolster their assertion that inmates who did not act "normally" were "feebleminded" or "mentally defective" and, in some cases, required indefinite institutionalization.

Geneva's Disciplinary Regime

All of those inmates defined by the Geneva staff as "feebleminded" or "mentally defective" were unable to meet the demands of Geneva's elaborate reform system. Although some administrators, such as Monahan, rooted young girls' "deviant" acts in a degraded environment and childhood neglect, most mental health experts saw them as yet another sign of embodied deviance.

From the beginning, Geneva administrators sought to model their institution after what historian Eric Schneider has referred to as "public family-style" institutions, which, among other things, were meant to evoke idealistic notions of the Victorian family. Public family-style institutions were constructed far away from cities, in bucolic settings. They consisted of a number of small cottages that—in the case of women's institutions—were governed by matrons who looked after their girls as if they were their own children. Inmates and staff alike frequently referred to members of the cottages as "family." The firm, but ostensibly loving, hand of the institution matriarch governed both inmates and matrons. Administrators and staff at family-style institutions sought to use strict discipline and a liberal education to instill dominant middle-class values in their charges and provide them with an alternative to the harsh custodial atmosphere of the state penitentiary.[2]

Illinois opened its first public family-style institution for young women in December 1893. It was located in Chicago and called the State Home for Juvenile Female Offenders. It received its first inmate on January 5, 1894. In her first annual report, Superintendent Margaret Ray Wickins declared that the purpose of the new institution was "to save the delinquent young girls of the State from the contaminating influences of a prison life and to surround them with influences which shall enable them to blot out of their lives the mistakes of the past, and to build characters for the future."[3] To carry out the founding principles of the institution, the state legislature moved it from its temporary location in Chicago to a new site approximately forty-five miles west of the city, in Geneva, near the picturesque banks of the Fox River. The new State Home for Juvenile Female Offenders, which initially consisted of a single building, opened in 1895. By 1902, it had a new school building, two new cottages, and a new engine house. It also had a new name, the State Training School for Girls, and a new superintendent, Ophelia L. Amigh.[4]

Amigh had come to Geneva in 1895 determined to carry out the institution's original mission. She hoped that, through strict discipline and constant encouragement, her charges would become "good, self-supporting women."[5] For nearly two decades, Amigh, along with her staff, which grew to include cottage matrons, teachers, physicians, and psychologists, kept a close eye on their girls, who had come to them in "a bad condition mentally, morally, and physically," with the intent that they would one day return their charges to "respectable citizenship."[6] Although it expanded significantly, the basic system put in place by Amigh remained intact for decades. Following a litany of physical, mental, and psychological examinations, and necessary medical treatment, the girls at Geneva began the long and, for some, arduous process of reform, which included domestic, moral, physical, industrial, and commercial education. Inmates attended their academic classes in the morning or the afternoon, depending upon their grade level. When they were not in class, inmates attended religious services and engaged in civic work. They organized their own units of the Junior Red Cross and the Girl Scouts.[7] Basic calisthenics were also part of their regimen. By the 1930s, they were playing croquet, baseball, and basketball, participating in track meets, and roller-skating around the institution's half mile of sidewalks.[8] They composed their own poems and stories, which they published in the school newspaper. Inmates produced special holiday performances; and when they found the time, they attended guest lectures.[9] Residents learned how to sew, knit, cook, and perform housework. Those inmates who did well in industrial and commercial classes also got to assist the staff with general office work. Keeping their girls occupied and maintaining a strict sense of discipline and order remained paramount among the Geneva staff. It was not until the 1930s, when Monahan became the managing officer at Geneva, that the disciplinary regime put in place by Amigh was relaxed somewhat, and even then the ultimate goal of training female juvenile delinquents to be "respectable" citizens did not change.[10]

But what exactly did that mean? What did it mean for young women living during the early twentieth century to become "respectable" citizens? This was something that proved difficult for Amigh and her successors to define. Throughout its history, Geneva's inmates received mixed, seemingly contradictory, messages concerning their role in society, which in some ways made it more difficult for them to meet the expectations of staff and administrators. As other scholars have shown, maternalists at Geneva and other similar institutions were deeply concerned with young women's domesticity and with controlling their sexuality.[11] They sought to mold those individuals whom they deemed capable of reform to fit within dominant, middle-class notions of a moral, virtuous wife and mother.[12] Yet the maternalists at Geneva also encouraged their charges to be financially and emotionally independent. They created business classes that taught basic clerical skills, as well as other courses that taught inmates how to wait on tables and assist in the management of tearooms. By the 1930s, Geneva also offered classes in "beauty-culture" for those young women who wanted to become part of the burgeoning beauty care industry.[13] Principal Ella Erlewine and the rest of the Geneva staff included business and commercial courses in the curriculum because they expected their girls to be "self-governing" by the time they left the school. At the graduation ceremony for the class of 1916, Erlewine declared that the aim of the staff had been to train the inmates "well in forming habits of self-reliance and self-control," so that they might become "useful, self-respecting citizens." She went on to state that the "educated girl properly trained in habits of self-control can take care of herself. She is worth much to the state."[14] Though maintaining women's "traditional" roles in society proved extremely important to the maternalists at Geneva, they envisaged more for their charges than a future filled only with domestic service, marriage, and motherhood.

The dualism with which the Geneva staff defined inmates' "proper" role in life was reflected in the school's student-run newspaper, the *Training School Chat*. Alongside articles with titles like, "Always Be Polite" and "Keep Sweet" were articles such as, "The Emancipation of Woman," which spoke candidly and favorably about the importance of women's suffrage. In one lengthy piece, inmates were allowed to debate whether "a woman really has more sense than a man." In addition to feature-length articles, the newspaper included a column entitled "Femininity" that provided readers with a series of factual tidbits that highlighted women's achievements in politics, business, law, and other public arenas, and pointed out societal shortcomings concerning gender equity.[15] In her address to the graduating class of 1916, which students reprinted in the *Chat,* Mrs. Frederick A. Dow, president of the Federation Committee on the Visitation of State Institutions, offered the following insight and encouragement to inmates: "There are so many definitions for the word, 'Illinois' but there is one I believe to be the real one. It was given by the old Indian Chiefs and means 'Manly Men.' To the girl graduate it may mean 'Manly Women' for the State of Illinois cannot need manly men any more than it needs manly women."[16]

Although much of inmates' education, training, and work experience remained focused on "traditional" women's roles, the maternalists at Geneva also expected them to be "manly" when it came to issues concerning self-control and self-reliance. For many Geneva inmates, especially those whom experts classified as "feebleminded" or mentally "defective," acting like a proper, middle-class lady and being "manly" all at the same time proved difficult.

Young women reacted differently to incarceration and their actions usually had serious consequences, not the least of which was being labeled "feebleminded" or mentally "defective" and facing indefinite commitment in a state institution. Fifteen-year-old Mary Elizabeth entered Geneva in June 1937. In September 1938 she was committed to Lincoln indefinitely. Geneva's psychologists found Mary to be a "high grade defective" and "committable as far as her intelligence [was] concerned"; but that is not the only reason why Mary was sent to Lincoln. Mary was sent to Lincoln because she "was unable to adjust well with the other girls," and "was considered by them as someone to 'pick on.'" Mary was "inclined to be nervous." She "told many untruths"; and "at times she would burst out crying at some imagined grief and with the same spontaneity laugh joyously." Mary "copied the work of other girls when she could manage to do it so that she would have a good grade." She "claimed lost handkerchiefs because she liked to own more things." She "wrote notes"; "carved initials on her body"; and in September 1937, she had to be sent to the "punishment cottage" for three weeks.[17] In documenting Mary's case, Geneva's psychologists, teachers, and administrators chose not to focus exclusively on her intelligence test scores or her demeanor during the examination, but on her actions outside the exam room, which for them carried equal weight in classifying an inmate's "mental ability" and determining a course of treatment.

Experts conveyed just how important an inmate's actions outside the exam room could be in their assessment of Althea. They described Althea as "a well-developed, white girl who was very polite" during her examination. Although she was "hesitant and unsure of herself," she "appeared easy going and passive," and "answered all questions freely." Experts concluded that, "In general conversation Althea appear[ed] to be much brighter than test results indicate[d]." Yet they classified her "as a high grade mental defective on three examinations and as a borderline defective on one examination." Althea's exam scores were not the only things that concerned the Geneva staff, however. Equally important was her behavior outside the exam room. During her stay at Geneva, Althea had displayed signs that her "attention was inclined to wander"; that her comprehension was "poor"; that she "gave up easily"; and that "all" her judgments were "poor." Based on exam scores and on their assessment of Althea's behavior outside the exam room, experts concluded that she would "continue to have difficulty adjusting in a normal environment, and this factor should be considered in making plans for her future." Psychologists noted that, "If Althea's behavior and adjustment here [at Geneva] are poor she can be considered as eligible for commitment to an institution for the feeble-minded."[18]

Culture, Conflict, and the Normalizing Gaze

The struggle for power between subjects and experts that figured so prominently in the ritual of the examination extended to every facet of institutional life, especially for those girls whom experts singled out as potential "problem cases." The youth-oriented peer culture that had come to dominate modern American life by the 1920s frequently found its way into the institution, often with dire results for inmates.[19]

Inmates who devised clever ways to resist incarceration rooted their nonconformity in an institutional peer culture that resembled a larger adolescent, urban, working-class culture that middle-class reformers and working-class parents already viewed with a considerable amount of suspicion. The commodification of leisure in American cities that began in the late nineteenth century shaped popular culture in ways that made it distinct from the gendered, separate spheres of earlier American life. Though gender and generational differences and power relations remained an important part of modern American life, they were muted by social interactions and peer relations that occurred outside the dominant gaze of parents, teachers, clergy, and watchful neighbors, who had monitored and regulated the actions of youth in earlier eras. Mass entertainment, increased encounters with, and dependence upon, one's peers, and heterosocial activity came to dominate the early twentieth-century urban social scene. Ritualized displays of one's self and peer relations took on new meanings as adolescents forged identities away from hearth and home.[20] Inside the institution, inmates formed friendships and engaged in sexual experimentation; they maintained their own dress codes; and they told stories and spoke candidly with one another, just as they would have outside the institution, in spite of the demands of Geneva's staff that they modify their behavior.

From the perspective of a staff attempting to mold responsible, self-governing adults, the adolescent subculture at Geneva appeared rebellious and deviant. Dr. Esther H. Stone characterized the girls in her study as "unreliable" and "noisy" and claimed that they were "never evenly balanced." She found that inmates were either "exuberantly happy, furiously angry, or mildly sad," and were "easily moved to tears or joy." A number of the young women were also "spiteful, cunning and untrustworthy." Stone argued that Geneva's inmates loved "display and trinkets" and that they were "lavish in outer adornment." According to Stone, inmates would not "hesitate to appropriate the belongings of others" in order to achieve the look they desired. Despite the staff's efforts to discourage their actions, many of Geneva's residents also teased and annoyed their companions, and were "highly pleased" if they succeeded in angering them.[21] Although psychologists found Yvonne to "be obedient and respectful to those in authority, willing and cooperative," she was also "inclined to be mischievous and like[d] to play pranks." Josephine was "loud, boisterous, a bully and defiant" toward her fellow inmates. Dora Mae was a "willing worker" but she was also "inclined to be quarrelsome" and did not get along well with the other girls. Hazel found it "a little difficult ... to mind her own business" and liked "tattling on people." Neva was "very silly when amused" but could also be "very sullen and ugly when depressed." Dorothy's fellow inmates accused her "of fighting, of leading the others into difficulties and of having difficulty adjusting with other girls." When the inmates were taking a group intelligence test, sixteen-year-old Evelyn "showed a tendency toward exhibitionism," which psychologists argued stemmed from her "aim ... to make herself outstanding, in some way, in a group situation." Experts and teachers found that although Mildred "had a refinement that suggested that she had had some good home training," she was "a bit neurotic, oversexed, impudent and indifferent to academic work with few inhibitions." Mildred was also "very flippant, with a flare for making herself conspicuous."[22] Experts classified all of these young women as "feebleminded" or mentally "defective."

One of the most troubling forms of behavior displayed by delinquent girls was to remain stolid and uncooperative in spite of staff attempts to reform them. In her study of Geneva, Stone complained that the inmates would not learn, and that they were not "amenable to law and order." She claimed that they lacked perseverance and quickly abandoned a task for something new or more alluring. According to Stone, Geneva girls could not be depended upon to complete anything, and they began their assigned tasks "only under pressure." Stone argued that the inmates she studied constantly sought diversion, "no matter at whose expense." She concluded that their attention was "very poor" and that they were "flighty and restless." "When instructed to do something," Stone complained, "they will return, stating that they forgot the order, and it must be repeated."

Stone found that Geneva's inmates "despised" much of their work—both in school and in other parts of the institution—and they feigned illness to avoid working. The practice of feigning illness to avoid work was so common that it came to be known throughout the institution as "laundry sickness."[23]

When they were not tormenting their peers, engaging in emotional outbursts, or being generally uncooperative, Geneva inmates reveled in telling elaborate tales and lying to staff. As Stone discovered, the craving for attention for the majority of the girls was so insatiable that they told incriminating tales about themselves, often simply to arouse investigation and inquiry. Stone attributed the incessant storytelling at Geneva to the fact that the inmates were "over excited" and "over stimulated" and that their concentration was "nil." According to Stone, the girls were highly imaginative. She claimed that they related the "most bizarre occurrences," in which they always played the most prominent role. Many of the inmates were so bold that when staff confronted them with what they considered the "true state of fact," the girls did not display any signs of embarrassment or remorse. Stone found that when caught in a lie, many inmates would "merely say, 'I did not want _____ to tell a better one than I did.'" Other inmates would not even admit to the lie, but adhere to their original story.[24] Storytelling became an effective means of shoring up one's identity vis-à-vis the thriving youth culture that existed both inside and outside the institution. Deceiving staff and fellow inmates became a way of bolstering one's position within the peer group. To the staff, storytelling was yet another indication that Geneva's charges did not possess the mental or emotional faculties to behave "normally."

In most cases, inmates' stories centered on the latest campus gossip or their own—usually somewhat embellished—life histories. Stone declared that "when unobserved," Geneva's inmates would tell each other of "their achievements in crime and immorality." She found that they reveled in "smutty talk," delighted in reading "obscene literature," and enlarged, "in most salacious style, upon their conquests of the unwary male, their sex attraction and physical make-up."[25] Not all of the inmates' stories centered on their sexual exploits, however. In some cases, girls contrived elaborate stories to conceal their plans to escape or engage in some other "illicit" activity. Stone complained that a "great source of annoyance" to the Geneva staff were inmates' "deceptions." She argued that inmates frequently made promises to "be good and do better" and that, in most cases, though they appeared determined to carry out their promises, they were actually laying plans to "escape or join a friend in some wrongful act." Stone referred to inmates who deceived the staff as "goody-goody girls." Storytelling, bragging, and deception were all tactics that the young women at Geneva developed to survive, and in some cases thrive, in the outside world. Inmates were simply continuing the behavior that led to their arrest and incarceration in the first place, which was yet another indication to Stone and her colleagues that many of them were incapable of reform.

Especially disconcerting for the Geneva staff were the "goody-goody girls" who managed to get released from the institution and promptly resumed their former lives. Frequently, psychologists and other institution staff expressed their disappointment with incarcerated women who had been released from Geneva and had not only returned to their "former haunts," but also intensified their "wrongdoing." Stone cited the case of seventeen-year-old N.B., who after a short stay at Geneva was paroled to "her people," as one example of an inmate's ability to deceive experts and staff. N.B. immediately left home, returned to her old associates, and, according to Stone, "indulged in immorality to a much greater extent than before." Shortly after M.F. was paroled, she robbed her employer and disappeared. Another "goody-goody," C.B., was paroled after a year at Geneva and "returned immediately to her former haunts and associates, was a permanent inmate of a very low dive, and from her earnings there, and the proceeds of thefts from her patrons, supported a paramour."[26] During her interview with psychologists, Doris stated that she liked it at Geneva and would "probably make a good adjustment." Doris was paroled at least three times, and each time she was returned to Geneva. Experts ultimately made the rather obvious conclusion that although Doris may have appeared to make "a good adjustment" while in the institution, she did not "appear to be sincerely interested in doing well on parole."[25]

Inmates, who were well aware of the benefits of being a "goody-goody," had become so prolific in their deceptions that the staff eventually grew skeptical of the girls' confessions and their promises. Psychologists' notes frequently included comments such as, "If her stories are true ..." or "... made a very poor impression as to telling the truth."[28] Evidence from Geneva suggests that experts' suspicions were not entirely misplaced. Many inmates, like Doris, made a conscious effort to be on their best behavior in order to be released from the institution.[29] As one inmate put it, "We have heard people say that it didn't pay to be good in this place, but we know better."[30] Other inmates made heartfelt promises to improve. Psychologists found that Mildred "tried very hard to make a good impression" during her interview. She spoke of "'turning over a new leaf,' 'making something of herself,' 'becoming a new person,' etc." Mildred said that she "had originally resented her commitment," but after spending some time in the institution she stated that she "like[d] the school very much" and believed that it would "do her good." The experts were not entirely convinced by Mildred's admissions. They concluded that she may have been "sincere in her intentions," but it would "remain to be seen what her behavior [would be]." Mildred's case file contained numerous reports of misbehavior, but she denied any misconduct; and although she appeared repentant, the psychologists noted that she had also appeared repentant at the IJR, "with poor behavior reported since that time."[31]

Many of the incarcerated women whom psychologists labeled as "feebleminded" or "defective" did not internalize middle-class reform rhetoric and resumed former social and work relations when they left Geneva. Although some parolees were the victims of abusive, malicious criminals and had little choice in the course their life took outside the institution, other girls actively sought out their "former haunts." Parolees who found their life choices severely constrained by crushing poverty, precarious employment, little formal schooling, and a chaotic, abusive, neglectful home life usually went back to the people and the places they knew best—as a means of survival, if nothing else. The Geneva staff, regardless of circumstance, frequently portrayed girls who returned to their "former haunts" as inherently deviant and rebellious. In her study of Geneva, Stone rather vaguely attributed young women's "wrong doing" while on parole to "long confinement and resultant violent reaction," which implied that its source came not from any external forces but from deep within inmates' bodies and minds. It is clear from case records that Stone and other members of the Geneva staff placed the onus for inmates' actions largely upon the girls themselves.

Frequently, inmates' penchant for storytelling and deception, as well as their desire for attention, manifested itself in the formation of sexual relationships with their peers. As Stone argued, the "loves and jealousies" of Geneva's inmates, though "trifling" to most of the staff, went beyond that stage at times. Many inmates formed attachments with one another and sent each other love notes, messages, and trinkets. They indulged in hugs and caresses, and tried to get into bed with each other. Stone found that "Nauseating love scenes, amounting to actual perversions [were] common" at Geneva. According to Stone, Geneva's inmates went through "vulgar pantomime and suggestive acts, even in broad daylight" that included, among other things, surreptitiously exposing one's self under the desks while at school.

Although they were troubling to the staff, same-sex relationships were not necessarily the primary concern at Geneva. The staff considered any sexual relations between inmates to be deviant and punished those individuals whom they discovered having affairs with their peers.[32] In most cases, however, the staff did not classify young women who experimented sexually with their fellow inmates as "inverted" or "lesbian."[33] As Charlotte Ruth Klein, a researcher from the University of Chicago, explained in 1935, the roots of the relationships formed at Geneva were not to be found in "any basic homosexuality but in the nature of institutional life."[34] Young women confined in a total institution invariably formed relationships that occasionally crossed the boundaries of "acceptable" or "normal" behavior.

Especially marked for Geneva staff were attachments made between white and "colored" girls. Black delinquents, who comprised about 10 percent of Geneva's inmate population and who boarded in racially segregated cottages, rarely attracted the attention of resident experts, who seemed preoccupied with the etiology of white girls' delinquencies, except when black and white girls became involved with one another. Klein and her colleagues found the formation of interracial relationships far more disconcerting than any sexual transgressions between white inmates. As historian Anne Meis Knupfer argues, the staff considered white girls' racial indiscretions to be "beyond redemption or repair."[35]

Much of the conflict within Geneva centered upon interracial relationships formed among inmates. In one incident, a white matron who discovered that her charges were "fraternizing" with a group of African Americans called them "white trash" and "nigger lovers." In an effort to spite the offending matron, the white girls decided to move into the black girls' cottage, causing a "minor scandal."[36] On a separate occasion, the power struggle between inmates and staff that was usually limited to small, isolated incidents erupted at a school dance. Apparently, the "mixing of the two races" in the days and months leading up to the dance had become such a serious problem in the minds of the Geneva staff that they forbade white and black girls from socializing together and made it clear to their wards that they disapproved of their actions. Despite stern warnings issued by the staff, the white girls insisted on dancing with the African American girls, resulting in even more severe restrictions. It was later discovered that both the black and white inmates had agreed in advance that they would be "partners" for the entire evening.[37] Both white and black girls did not hesitate to bend and stretch the parameters of "acceptable" female sexual behavior when it meant that they could usurp the authority of institution administrators and staff.

Even inmates, however, rarely expressed their relationships in anything other than heterosexual terms. In her study of Geneva, Klein found that relationships formed in the institution almost always took on a "hetero-sexual character," and that in an attachment formed between a "colored" girl and a white girl, the former "invariably" assumed the "masculine role."[38] In a separate study, Stone argued that the "usually more aggressive" African American inmates appealed to the "weaker white" inmates in a "masculine sense."[39] In some cases, residents at Geneva formed their own "self-styled," "make-believe families," in which African American girls filled the male roles and white girls filled the female roles.[40] Both black and white inmates rarely transgressed their own understanding of the boundaries of acceptable sexual expression and in the end had little reason to question their own sexuality. As one white sixteen-year-old inmate stated, if she were to take another white girl and give her a kiss, or put her arm around her, or pinch her, she would not be "counted decent," so she did not do such things.[41] There were white inmates at Geneva who formed "honey girl" relationships with one another, and in some cases white girls assumed the "masculine" aggressive role in an interracial relationship.[42] Yet all of the inmates at Geneva consistently defined their relationships in heterosexual terms. Even those young women who were involved with a "honey girl" expressed their desire to resume heterosexual relationships when they left the institution.[43]

Most often, inmates justified their temporary racial and sexual transgressions by couching them in a keen sense of desperation brought on by incarceration. The same sixteen-year-old girl who expressed concern that she would not be "counted decent" if she made sexual advances toward her white peers also stated that if she could not kiss or make love, she did not want to live. She then openly bemoaned the fact that all she could do while at Geneva was "take some Negro behind the screen at the Chapel or somewhere else. Kiss them for all we are worth."[44] This white inmate spoke of "taking" an African American inmate in a sexual manner that was usually reserved for men. Yet she did not consider her confession to be a violation of her decency or her heterosexual identity, partly because of her own sense of despair brought on by her confinement at Geneva. The sexual objectification of black bodies that had been a dominant part of colonial and American culture for hundreds of years also undoubtedly contributed to this young woman's sense of sexual privilege.[45] By describing their racial and sexual transgressions as a temporary means of expending heterosexual energy, inmates were able to gain the attention and power they craved without seriously jeopardizing their status within the peer group or their potential to become part of the larger society upon their release from the institution. To experts and staff measuring the minds of Geneva's inmates, their actions served as yet another marker of embodied deviance.

Equally alarming to psychologists, teachers, and administrators were those girls who acted out melodramatic scenes in which they suffered from imaginary maladies that "affected" their minds and bodies. Psychologists found that Hazel, whom they classified as a "borderline defective," had what they referred to as an "'ailment' complex." At one time or another, every one of Hazel's internal organs had "claimed its share of attention." Yet medical reports always confirmed the impression held generally that Hazel "was in excellent health." When the staff informed Hazel that there was nothing wrong with her, "tears were often in evidence," which suggested to psychologists that Hazel's "complex" was "a weapon she had always used to win her point and get her own way."[46] In an effort to frustrate B.F., whom they had learned was planning to escape, the staff at Geneva told her that she had a high fever and that she needed to go to bed at once. Upon learning of her fictitious fever, B.F. began to act in a delirious manner. She "failed to recognize her companions, and seemed [stupefied]; yet her temperature was perfectly normal." According to staff reports, B.F. "continued thus for about two days, and finally announced she was better." In another case, V.W. went into a trance and failed to recognize any of her associates until she was finally "humored out of her condition." V.W. also claimed that her bowels and bladder would not function properly for months at a time, during which time she would somehow manipulate the thermometer so that her temperature would reach the entire length of the instrument. Experts ultimately admitted that,

"Though closely watched, it was never determined how [V.W.] accomplished this feat."[47] In her study of Geneva, Dr. Anne Burnet found that many inmates exhibited signs of being "strongly hysterical" and some suffered from what she classified as "attacks of hysterical blindness." One girl had "spells" resembling "major hysteria," and another had "spells" that suggested "auto-hypnotism." One of Geneva's more creative inmates claimed she was clairvoyant and, according to Burnet, it became necessary to separate her from the other residents. Shortly after being separated from the other inmates, her health improved and her "spells" became less frequent.[48]

Though not all cases of "hysteria" can be attributed solely to a craving for attention and power, evidence suggests that some inmates staged their hysterical episodes in an effort to achieve a specific end.[49] In one study, Illinois' state criminologist, Dr. Herman Adler, recorded the cases of several Geneva inmates who were sent to one of the state mental hospitals because they exhibited signs of insanity. Once at the hospital, they "became suddenly very docile and friendly" and were quickly paroled. This suggested to Adler that the young women in his study were not suffering from any serious mental or emotional condition, but instead used mental "illness" as a means of leaving Geneva. According to Adler, there were "only a few cases" of young women at Geneva who were "actually insane," and the "mental disorders" in those cases were "of a very minor degree."[50] Young women, like those in Adler's study, possessed a working knowledge of Illinois' elaborate reform system and exploited it to their own ends.

Other inmates displayed aggressive and destructive behavior that was neither deliberate nor contrived, but was the outward manifestation of years of pent-up frustration, anger, and guilt brought on by an abusive and neglectful childhood. Violent fits of rage and self-mutilation were fairly common occurrences at Geneva. Burnet noted that in addition to having what she classified as "especially bad sex habits," many inmates displayed signs of self-mutilation. She found that inmates frequently came to her with "deep scratches" that they had inflicted upon their own bodies.[51] Stone also found evidence of self-mutilation in her study of Geneva. Psychologists noted that Hazel "cut initials on her flesh." Mary Elizabeth also "carved initials on her body."[52] C.K. "would deliberately stick fence wire into her arm and beg most piteously that her arm be saved from blood poison." She would also "stain her lips with iodine and claim that she swallowed a large quantity." Once, according to Stone, C.K. "actually frightened a small community by her cries for help, saying that she was poisoned." Another inmate, A.H., would carve the initials of her "sweethearts" into her flesh and "pretend to suffer intensely when her wounds were dressed."[53]

Stone attributed her subjects' self mutilation to their desire for attention, and argued that it was not uncommon for inmates to "act in inconceivable ways" to gain the attention they craved. According to Stone, girls who cut themselves did so to gain sympathy from fellow inmates and staff.[54] Although the desire to gain the attention of inmates and staff may have played a role in young women's self-destructive behavior, it was most likely what modern psychologists refer to as a "secondary gain," an unconscious desire to experience the feelings of power and importance brought on by their actions.[55] The primary motivation for girls to cut their flesh lay much deeper, most likely in their troubled childhood. Though the topic remains open for debate, scant case studies and statistical surveys conducted in the late twentieth century indicate that girls cut themselves and engage in other self-destructive behavior in an effort to block out or relieve physical, emotional, and psychological trauma experienced during childhood.[56] Although Stone and the rest of her colleagues at Geneva acknowledged their subjects' troubled pasts, they rarely considered them in any meaningful way when classifying the "mental ability" of the young women they studied.[57] Instead, they described inmates' actions as an "inconceivable" means of gaining attention and a sure sign of mental "defect."

Classifying prolonged fits of rage and self-mutilation as conscious acts of resistance or simply as a means of gaining attention, which both early twentieth-century experts and current historians have done, is not only a misrepresentation, but it also minimizes the severity of the trauma many girls endured, and the importance of the acts themselves, as perceived markers of embodied deviance.[58] Young women who cut themselves or engaged in other self destructive behavior most likely were not completely aware of the reaction that they would elicit from institution staff, experts, and court officials. In this sense, their actions were not conscious displays of resistance, but rather their own way of working through severe emotional and psychological pain. This, however, is not how most early twentieth-century experts and current historians have viewed these acts. Instead, they have classified them as a conscious effort to gain attention or defy authority, as blatantly defiant or "deviant" acts that posed serious challenges to administrators and staff intent on controlling delinquent women, which was at best a secondary effect of these desperate cries for help.

Perhaps the most potent display of nonconformity among inmates at Geneva was escape. Hundreds of girls attempted to escape from both private and state institutions each year. Many more inmates escaped while on parole.[59] Girls who escaped from state institutions did so because it was an effective means of asserting power in a situation over which they had very little control. As Monahan and other experts argued, some inmates escaped in protest of a particular situation, or to gain the attention of staff and administrators. Jane's experience was typical of many of the escapes from Geneva. Monahan later recalled that on one hot summer afternoon, Jane simply walked off the institution grounds. According to

Monahan, Jane was "trudging down the shoulder of a busy high-way a few miles from school when a parole officer, easily recognizing [her], stopped and picked her up." Adding her own bit of dramatic flair, Monahan later wrote that, "Jane smiled out through layers of dust," and sighed. "My," Jane said, "it took you an awfully long time. I'm getting tired." When the staff at Geneva asked Jane why she ran away, she apparently replied: "Oh, I just got disgusted." In her record of the escape, Monahan seemed empathetic to Jane's plight. She stated that simply walking away from one's problems was "not at all strange," and admitted to going out and buying a hat when things got "too bad" in her own life.[60]

Some inmates who felt that they had been incarcerated wrongfully, or that they were not being treated fairly in the institution, escaped in order to resume their lives outside the institution. Many of Geneva's inmates harbored feelings similar to those expressed by one sixteen-year-old sex delinquent, who stated that it was "too bad a kid can't go out once in a while and have a good time without having to pay for it." Judge Bartelme of the Juvenile Court complained that "many girls" came before her with an "insolent and defiant air," which she argued was usually the result of their "wrong idea" that the only purpose of the law and the court was to punish them.[61] Mrs. Lucy Ball, who served as the managing officer at Geneva in the 1920s, noticed a similar attitude in many of her charges. According to Ball, it was "very difficult for girls entering [Geneva] to think of it other than a place of punishment." Ball went on to explain that many of the girls could not "understand why they were so discriminated against. To them the court, the judge, the probation officer, and the state's attorney [were] their enemies."[62] One Geneva inmate stated that she knew many girls who "went out with young boys, go with everyone that comes along." She called it "puppy love" and said that it was "right." She went on to state that she felt bitter and resentful because she felt like she did not receive a "square deal." During her interview with psychologists, Katherine "spoke quite freely about her delinquencies and regarded them as the accepted type of behavior."[63] Another inmate explained that many of Geneva's residents ran away because they got "man hungry," as if it were a perfectly acceptable reason for leaving the institution.[64] Mary, who escaped while on parole from Geneva, was determined to carry on her life despite being incarcerated. According to Monahan, Mary met a sailor, got married, broke it off with the sailor, who was a widower with two small children, hitchhiked and prostituted her way to California with a friend, got in a fight with the friend, stayed with an aunt for a short time, and then returned to Chicago, where she was picked up and returned to Geneva—all in three weeks![65]

Not all of the inmates who attempted to escape from Geneva did so because they were disgusted with life in the institution. There were a number of inmates who characterized escape as an adventure and left the institution because they found it exciting to do so. In December 1912, A. L. Bowen, the executive secretary of the State Charities Commission, published a report of an investigation that he made into the attempted escape of Zoe, Lulu, and Vida. On the evening of September 6, as the other girls and the housekeeper and matron made their way to the second floor of Fabyan cottage, Zoe, Lulu, and Vida remained downstairs to do some work. As soon as they thought no one was looking, they jumped out the window in the day room. They ran as fast as they could toward the Fox River and darted into the underbrush just as the alarm was beginning to sound. Zoe, Lulu, and Vida wandered along the river and through the woods for some time, until they finally came upon the Aurora, Elgin, and Chicago Electric rail line and decided to follow it to the nearest town.

The girls' escape took a tragic turn when Zoe suggested that they walk hand in hand on the rails. As Vida later recalled, they had never heard of the "death rail." As soon as one of them stepped on the deadly third rail, they were all shocked and thrown to the ground. Lulu and Vida survived the incident. Zoe was not so fortunate. Her lifeless body lay stretched across the tracks. Lulu and Vida tried to rouse their friend, but when they reached for her, sparks and blue flame shot from her body, burning their hands and clothes and throwing them to the ground. Not knowing what to do, Lulu and Vida set out in search of help. They eventually came across a farmer, who let them stay at his house while he went to investigate the scene of the accident.

A short while later, police officers returned Lulu and Vida to Geneva, gathered the remains of Zoe's body, which had been run over by a train, and sent them to the undertaker, where they were prepared to make the long journey home to Zoe's mother and grandmother. According to Bowen, Zoe, Lulu, and Vida "had no grievance against any person." In an interview after the accident, Lulu and Vida claimed that they had been treated well at Fabyan cottage, which was Geneva's "honor cottage," and that they really had no explanation for their escape—other than their desire to accompany Zoe. As Bowen explained, the three girls attempted to escape from Geneva simply because they wanted to "see the world."[66] Unlike Mary and Birdie, who flaunted their blatant disregard for authority, and Jane, who became disgusted and escaped to vent her frustration, Zoe, Lulu, and Vida held no apparent grievances and were not angry or upset at the time of their escape. Their actions, however, were no less disconcerting to experts who studied female sex delinquents, because they reaffirmed the prevailing assumption that individuals who escaped or acted out in other ways were inherently "deviant," and that they did not need a reason to resist incarceration, because it was in their "nature" to do so.

Social Deviance Becomes Mental Deviance

Actions that current scholars and mental health experts would most likely characterize as teenage rebelliousness, desperate pleas for help, or even "normal" adolescent behavior were classified by early twentieth-century researchers as definitive signs of feeblemindedness and mental defect. There is no doubt that the majority of mental testers in Illinois agreed with Dr. Adler's assertion that the number of "feeble-minded" inmates at Geneva far exceeded that of any other institution, except, of course, Lincoln, where supposedly all of the inmates were "feebleminded." Experts also agreed with Adler's contention that the majority of Geneva inmates were there because of their "unruly, boisterous, and destructive behavior." Finally, most experts agreed with Adler's argument that "feeblemindedness" or "mental defect" was at least "one of the accessory factors," if not the main cause of delinquency.[67] All of these assumptions found some measure of legitimacy in the popular notion that "deviant" minds and "deviant" actions were intimately and inextricably linked, and that they shared a reciprocal relationship. Dominant scientific theories concerning the relationship between "feeblemindedness" and delinquency enabled maternalists at Geneva to cast a very wide net when searching for embodied deviance, which in turn reinforced their own power and authority as experts.

The staff at Geneva categorized any actions that deviated from their own understanding of "normal" behavior as signs of some sort of mental "defect." Mental testers at Geneva diagnosed Elizabeth as a "borderline mental defective" partly because she "demanded more attention than was due her," and because she "liked to gossip and repeated it with the inaccuracy typical of this level of intelligence." Experts categorized Elizabeth's sister Louise, who was also at Geneva, as a "high grade mental defective," in part because she possessed a "quarrelsome nature." The Geneva staff concluded that Louise could not be expected ever to assume any responsibilities or to adjust in a community "without the most careful supervision," and that she required a "simple routine environment." Maternalists at Geneva described Lorene, whom they also classified as a "borderline mental defective," as a "perfect pest" who "liked to gossip and tell her life history." According to the Geneva staff, Lorene "tried to be obedient and to work hard but she accomplished very little." The experts at Geneva based their diagnosis of Elsie, whom they classified as "dull normal," partly on the following evaluation: "Elsie had to be prodded constantly as she was very lazy. When in the library she didn't miss a thing that was going on but the lesson she was supposed to be studying. . . . She accepted correction poorly and she had to be corrected frequently for 'blurting' out. . . . At times she did very excellent work and at times very poor work. . . . Elsie is so very, very polite and plausible at times that I doubt her sincerity. She is not frank and honest. I wouldn't trust her much." Many of the behaviors exhibited by Geneva inmates frequently made their way into the official case records compiled by resident experts who, in most cases, interpreted them not as the manifestations of a group of abused and neglected adolescents but as the markers of some unalterable innate flaw imbedded deep within each inmate.[68]

No case better elucidates the power of a test subject's actions outside the exam room in influencing experts' diagnosis and their prescribed treatment than that of Della. Della gave mental testers "the impression of being brighter than test results indicate[d]." Yet they classified her as a "high grade mental defective." Experts at Geneva concluded that the results of three separate examinations undoubtedly supported their diagnosis. The tests, however, told only part of the story. An equally important part of the diagnostic process consisted of the staff's observations of Della outside the exam room. According to Della's school report, she was "too garrulous outside of school hours about school affairs." She gossiped "a great deal" and relayed stories, which were "not reliable from school to campus and vice versa." The Geneva staff determined that Della was the "verbalistic type feebleminded who will always do this sort of thing." They worried that people coming into contact with her might forget that she was "feebleminded" and "attach some credence to what she [said.]" The staff ultimately concluded that unless Della's gossiping was "checked," she could cause a "great deal of dissension." One sure way to check her gossiping and reduce the possibility of dissent among Geneva's inmates would be to transfer Della to the Lincoln State School and Colony for the Feebleminded, where under the new commitment law she could remain indefinitely. The staff at Geneva used Della's actions outside the exam room to justify their classification of her mental ability and her removal from Geneva, while also bolstering their own power and authority over the inmates under their care.

The maintenance of order and control remained an important part of the reform efforts at Geneva, but it was not the only concern of administrators and staff. Della's case clearly illustrates that the maternalists at Geneva were also very much interested in protecting a group of girls who seemingly could not care for themselves. Although she appeared "normal," experts at Geneva concluded that their tests and observations revealed that Della was incapable of "normal" reasoning and conduct. The staff found that Della was "easily flattered by the apparent interest of other people," and that she had "neither the academic background nor the natural ability to judge such things correctly." "This characteristic," psychologists argued, was "liable to make trouble for her because of relating other things." The staff did not specify what "relating other things" would give Della trouble. They did state, however, that she was "extremely suggestible," and given the high percentage of moral offenders at Geneva, it was very likely that Della was a "sex delinquent," or had at least some experience in "sex matters." It is also possible that Della came from an abusive or neglectful home. The maternalists at Geneva used their diagnosis to commit Della to Lincoln in part to protect her and keep her out of trouble, despite a marked improvement in her schoolwork—including an "A" in deportment![69]

As Della's case suggests, experts did not deny the existence of environmental causes of social deviance, but that did not stop them from using science to classify delinquent women who did not behave "normally" as impaired. As Drs. Louise Morrow and Olga Bridgman stated in their study of Geneva, they were well aware of "a popular idea that the cause of delinquency in girls is largely environmental." After a short stay at the institution, however, they were convinced that "environment alone" could not explain the young women's "transgressions of the laws of society."[70] In a separate study of the tragic escape attempt of Zoe, Lulu, and Vida, the experts at the *Institution Quarterly* argued that "Heredity was a force; environment augmented it, stimulated it, gave it impetus." Although the experts who investigated the escape acknowledged that Zoe, Lulu, and Vida had all come from degraded homes characterized by "broken" families, poverty, and neglect, the underlying cause of their rebelliousness lay much deeper than their environment. Experts concluded that Zoe was "possessed of a wanderlust; she could no more resist its prompting than the meteor can retrace its course in the skies." As for Lulu and Vida, the experts concluded that they followed Zoe "as under hypnotic influence," and that they "could never say 'No.'"[71] Even Monahan, who was much more tolerant of inmates' "deviant" behavior than many of her colleagues, emphasized the importance of acknowledging pathological causes of antisocial behavior.

Although Monahan later admitted that the "irritating behavior problems" that she encountered at Geneva were almost always "solved without trouble," she recalled that there were also many "really bad girls" at Geneva. Monahan defined the "really bad girls" as the inmates with "definite mental problems and psychopathic personalities."[72] Monahan admitted that she and the rest of her staff were "baffled" by "feebleminded" and "psychopathic" inmates, and argued that the "really bad girls" made life at Geneva more complicated and difficult. She asserted that they "took much of the valuable time and attention of the staff, and this time and energy, so completely wasted on them, could have been used constructively if given to the normal ones in the group."[73] Her conclusion, at least in part, was to segregate the "feebleminded" and "psychopathic" inmates from the rest of the inmate population, a "sorting process" that she argued should have been done well before any of the girls were sent to Geneva. The "feebleminded," Monahan declared, should have been committed to institutions established especially for their care, and the "psychopathic" should have been sent to hospitals equipped to treat them.[74]

Monahan, like the rest of the administrators, staff, and experts at Geneva during the 1920s, 1930s, and 1940s, did not explicitly address the eugenic elements inherent in her involuntary "sorting process," but that did not make it any less eugenic than earlier attempts to segregate "feebleminded" and mentally "defective" delinquents. Although most experts who associated themselves with the diagnosis and treatment of female juvenile delinquents stopped using the word "eugenics" during the mid-1920s, they did not completely abandon fundamental eugenic principles, nor did they stop using Illinois' involuntary commitment law to segregate young women whom they classified as "deviant."

Inmates, Families, and the Creation of Mental Deviance

By acting out or escaping, or simply doing nothing at all, delinquent girls incarcerated at Geneva attempted to maintain their identity, beliefs, and values, as well as their sense of connectedness to the communities from which they came. Inmates' families also resisted the incarceration of their loved ones by actively seeking their release from the institution. Though many relatives sought out the courts' and institution administrators' assistance in controlling their delinquent daughters, an equal if not greater number of relatives struggled to have girls released from institutions.[75] Inmates' relatives stood at a distinct disadvantage vis-à-vis the courts and institution administrators, but they were not powerless; many families fought successfully to have their relatives released from institutions. Unfortunately for inmates and their families, any type of resistance often exacted a heavy toll. By actively challenging the authority of the courts and institution administrators, inmates and their families opened themselves to experts eager to diagnose their "mental ability" and the quality of their "home life," which in most cases did not bode well for the young women incarcerated at Geneva and Lincoln.

While my focus here is on families' challenges to incarceration and the ways in which experts and administrators interpreted those challenges, there were many families who expressed a deep appreciation for the work being done by the state. Hundreds of letters sent to parole officers and institution administrators at Geneva suggest that many inmates and their families eagerly cooperated with the staff at that institution and viewed time spent both in the institution and out on parole as extremely beneficial. The letters were published in Geneva's school newspaper and its official reports, and were obviously selected for their glowing content, but they nevertheless provide valuable insight into the experiences and attitudes of individuals who, for various reasons, viewed time spent at Geneva and out on parole in a favorable light. Many girls who spent time at Geneva stated that they learned, as E.P. phrased it, "the great difference in leading a good life from a bad one," and expressed a great deal of thankfulness in their letters.[76] An uncle of one of Geneva's inmates wrote a very long letter to the staff, in which he offered the following praise:

> Fortunate, indeed, are the citizens of Illinois that the great establishment erected and dedicated by them for the care of their unfortunate daughters is ruled by the

wise hand of motherly love and righteousness. The velvet lawns, the great shade trees, the flowers, all the beauties of nature, the well kept buildings, the splendid discipline, are all reflected in the contented smiling faces of the groups of happy, healthy girls one meets at the Training School at Geneva; and far beyond the confines of this noble institution, the hearts of hundreds of paroled girls are truly grateful for all that has been done for them and for all there is being done for them through your excellent parole system, giving them that start in life that could never otherwise have been theirs.[77]

Although the motives of individuals who portrayed time spent at Geneva favorably are difficult to discern, it is apparent that a significant number of inmates and their families responded positively to incarceration and parole. There were, however, individuals who did not react positively to the notion of reform evinced by the Geneva staff or the administrators at Lincoln, and it was those individuals who most concerned mental testers. In most cases, experts used their evaluations of families who challenged their authority to keep relatives in the institution as a means of bolstering their initial classification of inmates and their assertion that certain inmates required indefinite commitment.

When family members decided to try to have their relatives released from institutions, it was usually for economic or emotional reasons. Working-class parents struggling to maintain their families, who depended upon their daughters' wages and their reproductive labor within the household, faced additional economic strain when one or more of their daughters were incarcerated.[78] Some parents missed their incarcerated children. Other parents were under the impression that their child would be "improved or restored to a normal condition" when they entered an institution, and when this did not occur they became discouraged.[79] If the emotional or economic need to regain custody of their relatives became too great to bear, parents or other close family members went to institution administrators and the courts and demanded the release of their loved ones.

Two cases taken from the Lincoln State School and Colony highlight what for relatives and institution administrators became an all-too-common exchange. The first case involved a "feebleminded" girl named Pearl and her mother. After being apart for some time, Pearl's mother went to Lincoln and demanded her daughter's release from the institution. Administrators who wanted to maintain custody of Pearl resorted to "[e]arnest pleading regarding the inadvisability of such a move," but much to the dismay of Lincoln's superintendent, Dr. Harry Hardt, administrators' "entreaty fell upon deaf ears." Hardt later explained that staff pleaded with Pearl's mother to keep Pearl in the institution because of her "past history." According to Hardt, Pearl was a "high grade moron of the moral degeneracy type" whom state officials had just recently "rescued from the clutches of crime and infamy." Hardt explained that Pearl had been institutionalized because she did not "recognize social responsibility." Despite the incessant pleading of Lincoln's staff to keep Pearl in the institution, her mother remained steadfast in her attempt to regain custody of her daughter, to which she said she had a perfect right. In demanding the release of her daughter, Pearl's mother "urged that a mother's love was stronger than all else."

Faced with Pearl's mother's determination to have her daughter released from Lincoln, Hardt and his associates resorted to less-direct tactics to maintain custody of their ward. They insisted that Pearl's mother secure written consent for Pearl's release from the county judge and from Pearl's father. Several months passed before Pearl's mother finally returned to Lincoln. When she arrived at the institution, she explained to the staff that she had in fact failed to obtain written consent for Pearl's release, because her husband had divorced her and the judge had granted custody of Pearl to him. Hardt later concluded that his encounter with Pearl's mother "clearly demonstrated" to him that her "judgment, prudence and reasoning were below par," and that the court was wise not to release Pearl into the custody of a woman of such "questionable character." Hardt and his colleagues managed to keep Pearl at Lincoln indefinitely, in large part because the court found her mother "unfit" for custody.[80] By attempting to have Pearl released from Lincoln, her mother had unwittingly become involved in the debate over eugenic commitment, both as an advocate for the release of an inmate and as an object of evaluation and examination.

The experience of another Lincoln inmate named Elsie further illustrates the extent to which family members inserted themselves into the eugenic commitment debate. The staff at Lincoln classified Elsie as a "fairly bright" fourteen-year-old girl who was "well placed" in the institution. Elsie's mother, who was thirty-five years old and unmarried, worked as a charwoman at a local bar. According to Hardt, a little more than a year after Elsie had been committed to Lincoln, she had made "such excellent progress in mental effort and physical appearance" that her mother and aunt came to take her from the institution, which the staff did not permit. Although they left that day without her, Elsie's mother and her aunt were determined to regain custody of Elsie. According to Hardt, they soon returned to Lincoln "armed with letters and affidavits certifying to their ability, honesty and integrity, and custody was granted, under protest." One year after her release, county authorities picked Elsie up again in the "slums" and sent her back to Lincoln after she had received medical treatment. The location of Elsie's mother and her aunt were unknown.[81] In fighting to have Elsie released from Lincoln, her mother and her aunt—like Pearl's mother—became pivotal players in the drama surrounding eugenic commitment. They had shown that they were able to have Elsie released from Lincoln in spite of protests from institution administrators. Yet they had also shown—by allowing Elsie to be returned to Lincoln—that they were incapable of preventing Elsie's delinquencies. To experts evaluating the mental status of female juvenile delinquents, relatives' pleas to regain custody of inmates appeared irresponsible, haphazard, desperate, and fraught with inconsistencies, which experts ultimately argued were all signs of some hereditary defect.

The cases of Pearl and Elsie illustrate the extraordinary measures that family members took to have their relatives released from a state institution. They also provide valuable insight into one of the main arguments that eugenicists used to justify involuntary commitment: namely, that without the legal means to maintain custody of "feebleminded" inmates indefinitely, institution administrators and the courts were forced to allow relatives, many of whom were of "questionable character," to return "feebleminded" girls to neighborhoods and situations that would invariably lead to future problems. Throughout the early twentieth century, reformers and administrators expressed their concern with "feebleminded" girls who were being released from Geneva and Lincoln simply because their relatives requested that they be released.[82] In its study of "mentally defective" children living in Chicago, the Juvenile Protective Association voiced its concern for a young woman who was released from Lincoln and was "brought back into a life full of danger, simply because her mother was 'lonesome' for her."[83] Experts at Lincoln and elsewhere argued that Illinois needed to remain vigilant in its implementation of a system of involuntary commitment because without such a system, the state would be powerless to stop eugenically "unfit" relatives from taking "feebleminded" inmates back into "degraded" homes and neighborhoods, where they were certain to encounter insurmountable obstacles.

The enactment of the involuntary commitment law in July 1915 was, of course, initially intended to provide institution administrators and other experts with the power they desired. Yet, as noted in chapter one, the committee that drafted the bill was so concerned with protecting the rights of allegedly "feebleminded" individuals that the law was difficult to enforce. The law enabled institution administrators and the courts to detain indefinitely any individual found to be "feebleminded" by a court-appointed expert. It also, however, provided parents, guardians, and other relatives of incarcerated individuals with the legal means to petition the court and institution administrators for the release of an inmate, which is exactly what George Bott did. Bott successfully sued the State Training School for Girls and its managing officer, Florence Monahan, in an effort to regain custody of his adopted daughter Marie, who had been sent to Geneva on charges that she was incorrigible, immoral, and growing up in idleness. After several months of litigation, the court found that Marie was being illegally detained at Geneva and released her to the custody of her parents.[84] Despite the passage of the involuntary commitment law, reformers, administrators, and judges found it difficult to maintain custody of incarcerated women, because relatives of inmates continually agitated for their release.

As these cases have shown, families of incarcerated women played a critical role in shaping eugenic commitment in Illinois. On one hand there were experts and administrators who, in an effort to retain their charges, argued that working-class individuals who sought the release of family members from institutions were too "unfit" to care for them. Although they remained committed to maintaining social justice and due process, experts and administrators invariably interpreted family members' challenges, as well as many aspects of their complicated lives, as signs of a heritable defect that warranted an inmate's prolonged stay in the institution. For their part, relatives who sought the release of Illinois' "feebleminded" charges for their own personal and economic reasons never wholeheartedly accepted the argument made by experts and administrators that involuntary commitment was an efficacious and beneficent reform measure. The lack of support displayed by relatives of the subjects of eugenic segregation undoubtedly contributed to the gradual abandonment of involuntary commitment in Illinois. Some experts and administrators reluctantly chose to forego a system of state-sponsored segregation when it became apparent that relatives of Illinois' "feebleminded" inmates would not tolerate such a program.

Conclusion

Although an analysis of young women's resistance to incarceration and the consequences they faced can be helpful in explaining the creation of deviant bodies, one must take care not to adopt a concept of resistance that is overly capacious and romanticized.[85] Using resistance as an analytical tool is only meaningful when it is defined in relation to its historical context and the social location of those individuals whom it encompasses. Young women at Lincoln and Geneva carried with them physical, emotional, and psychological scars caused by years of abuse and neglect that in some cases erupted into violent, self-destructive behavior.[86] The responses to institutionalization displayed by inmates and their families took different forms and had different outcomes. A number of relatives fought successfully for the release of an individual from an institution, others did not. Some inmates chose to remain stolid and defiant while others chose to act out. Inmates forged relationships in defiance of staff and administrators. They also told elaborate stories and contrived intricate schemes to hide their true motives and desires. Inmates became hysterical. They feigned blindness, illness, and even insanity, all as a means of exerting power and control in a situation in which they had very little of either. Other inmates took a more direct approach and escaped. Some inmates were so emotionally and psychologically upset that they abused their own bodies in an effort to ease their pain, and in the process gained the attention of their fellow inmates and the staff.[87] The immediate consequences inmates faced were as varied as the acts that provoked them and ranged from a stern chiding or restricted liberties to indefinite confinement in a state institution, and even death.

As one might suspect, the implementation of a state-sponsored system of eugenic commitment in Illinois was complicated and difficult, and involved much more than merely enacting House Bill No.655. In addition to overcrowding and a severe lack of funding, reformers in Illinois faced resistance from inmates and their families who, for their own reasons, were unwilling to accept life within an institution. Experts also encountered experiences in which inmates, who may not have had a conscious desire to resist incarceration, nevertheless presented them with serious challenges. Inmates and their families' interpretation of institutionalization differed significantly from that of middle-class reformers. They had different, often competing, goals and desires with respect to the purpose and function of the institution, as well as the involuntary commitment law, which in most cases complicated both the implementation of the law and the work of the institution as an effective means of social reform. Although they were not made privy to all of the scientific nuances of the debate, those working-class women and their families who challenged incarceration for their own personal and economic reasons contributed directly to the gradual abandonment of a state-sponsored system of eugenic commitment in Illinois.

By challenging institutionalization, inmates and their families also, however, unwittingly provided a multifarious group of experts with yet another point of entry into their lives. They opened themselves to investigation by researchers who, in most cases, used their actions to cast them as inherently "deviant." Despite earnest pronouncements of scientific objectivity and rigor, mental health experts and other researchers allowed their own understanding of "normal" behavior, which was obviously influenced by their class position, racial status, and gender, to influence their diagnosis of individuals who resisted their efforts to reform adolescent sex delinquents. The result, at least in part, was that experts, perhaps unfairly, emphasized "feeblemindedness" or "mental defect" as the cause of their subjects' actions, and not other environmental and emotional factors. Experts, in turn, relied upon their "discovery" of an exceedingly large number of "deviant bodies" among female sex delinquents and their families to use Illinois' involuntary commitment law to detain young women such as Della indefinitely.

6

"Little Savages" and "Psychopathic Deviates"

> "What each of these youngsters [born in 1954] will become is in no way determined at his birth. No child comes with built-in attitudes towards persons or property. . . . All these things he must in some way learn and acquire as he grows up, having made measured steps toward a life of delinquency and crime."
>
> —Richard C. Clendenen, staff director,
> Subcommittee to Investigate Juvenile Delinquency,
> Committee on the Judiciary, United States Senate, 1954

Geraldine was a sixteen-year-old white Catholic girl incarcerated at Geneva in 1955. The five-foot three-inch, ninety-five-pound teenager was sent to Geneva from the Cook County Family Court as a "sex delinquent." Geraldine first came to the attention of the police when nineteen-year-old Arnold, who was being treated for syphilis, reported her to the Chicago Board of Health. Upon investigation, authorities learned that Geraldine ran away for three weeks in December 1954. While she was on the road, she met a truck driver, with whom she had "sexual relations" on "several occasions" as they traveled throughout Colorado and Utah. When she returned home to Chicago, Geraldine renewed her relationship with Arnold. The police informed Geraldine's parents of the situation, who brought the matter to the attention of the court.

This was not the first time state officials had encountered Geraldine. She and her siblings had first come to the attention of caseworkers during the early 1940s, when their mother was admitted to the University of Chicago Lying In Clinic after an attempted abortion. Upon an investigation of their home, clinic staff concluded that Geraldine and her siblings were "neglected" and "undernourished," and that Geraldine's mother was "considerably disturbed, but unable to respond to treatment." Following the death of her first husband in early 1942, Geraldine's mother sent her four children to the Catholic Home Bureau, where they remained until

June of that year. In September 1942, four-year-old Geraldine was committed to the Catherine Casper Industrial School for Girls and remained there until she was released on probation in February 1945. Three months later, Geraldine was returned to the industrial school on a probation violation and was not released again until 1949. Geraldine's mother eventually remarried and regained custody of her three daughters; her son had died in 1948. The family moved to a small town outside Chicago, where they lived in a home with no running water or indoor toilet. Geraldine attended several grade schools, as well as Lyons Township High School. Although her grades were good, she was frequently absent from school. She left high school in February 1954. In December of the same year, Geraldine began receiving treatments for "secondary syphilis." Shortly thereafter, she ran away from home and when she returned, state officials wasted little time in sending the sixteen-year-old to the state training school in Geneva.

During her psychological evaluation and intelligence examination, Geraldine exhibited behavior that historically was common among Geneva inmates. She "appeared nervous, tense and tried desperately to make a good impression. She answered all questions in the light of what she thought would make a good impression in the interview. She expressed a desire to go home and live with her mother, later get married, have a family and be happy." In most respects, Geraldine could be considered a typical Geneva inmate. There was one critical exception, however. Although the psychologist found Geraldine to be "rather retarded academically," she determined that her young test subject was "functioning at the present time in the average range of intelligence." Historically, mental testers had conflated girls' delinquencies with their home life, their academic achievement, and their behavior during the ritual of the examination when assigning them an intelligence rating, often resulting in a diagnosis of "feeblemindedness" or mental "defect," a classification that proved both influential and damaging in the lives of young women. By the early 1950s, this was occurring with much less frequency.

As Geraldine's experience shows, mental health experts increasingly parceled out potential markers of "defect," which led to a redefinition of the impairment that underlay female juvenile delinquency. The transition can best be described as a shift away from a biological theory of delinquency to a psychoanalytic or personality theory of delinquency.[1]

In this chapter, I examine changing social attitudes and scientific theories that led to a rearticulation of the perceived causes and possible treatments of female juvenile delinquency by the early 1950s. Throughout the 1940s and 1950s, girls remained more likely to be arrested and incarcerated than their male counterparts, and their delinquent acts were more likely to be pathologized; but experts and reformers no longer promoted strictly hereditarian, biological, eugenic explanations of the causes of delinquency. The result was that only one inmate from a random sample of Geneva inmates was considered for commitment to one of Illinois' mental health institutions after 1950, and no evidence of eugenic thinking exists in that case. Though the circumstances under which young women were committed to Geneva had not changed much in the sixty-odd years of the institution's existence, the ways in which experts thought about the impairment that supposedly caused female juvenile delinquency and the possible consequences of female juvenile delinquency had changed considerably, so that explicitly negative eugenic measures no longer dominated discussions of possible treatment and prevention programs by the early 1950s.

The Community and the Delinquent

The scientific, social, and cultural forces that formed the movement away from eugenics, which began as early as 1915 in some of the more progressive parts of the country, were complicated, but the immediate catalysts were the two world wars. Both wars enabled scientists to assume a more formidable role nationally; the wars also created a heightened sense of urgency that revolved around increased national efforts to combat a perceived rise in youthful crime. Changes in the perceived prevalence of delinquency, as well as the social profile of the typical delinquent, which began during World War I and continued through the interwar period, accelerated and expanded during World War II, ultimately rendering feeblemindedness theory and eugenic segregation obsolete by 1950.[2]

All relevant data seemed to indicate to experts, lawmakers, and the reading public that delinquency had indeed increased during both world wars. Although complete national data on juvenile delinquency during World War I were difficult to obtain, evidence from cities around the country showed that the number of juvenile court cases increased during the war. Statistics gathered by the Federal Bureau of Investigation (FBI), the nation's courts, and other government agencies showed similar increases in delinquency during and after World War II. Delinquency cases continued to rise throughout the 1950s. Between 1956 and 1960, juvenile court cases increased four times faster than the growth rate of the American population between the ages of ten and seventeen.[3] Hindsight and decades of scholarly research leave little doubt that the domestic social upheaval caused by both wars, the nascent civil rights and feminist movements, and a burgeoning youth culture, as well as better record keeping and an ever-expanding juvenile justice and child guidance system, contributed to the rising numbers of so-called juvenile delinquents, but the popular perception among most Americans living between 1917 and 1960 was one of a nation of young people run amok. Juvenile delinquency, which first became a national concern during World War I, seemed to reach epidemic proportions during and after World War II.

The apparent rise in lawlessness among the nation's youth led in part to the creation of complex national systems of observation, analysis, rehabilitation, and prevention. The so-called child guidance movement, which emerged in the wake of World War I and continued to grow during the Great Depression, expanded in both size and scope during and after World War II.[4] Agencies such as the Federal Bureau of Investigation, the Federal Children's Bureau, the Social Security Administration, the Bureau of the Census, and the U.S. Department of Justice made elaborate studies of delinquency.[5] The United States Senate Committee on the Judiciary created a Subcommittee to Investigate Juvenile Delinquency, which in 1954 reported that youngsters ages ten to seventeen were being picked up by police at a rate of 2,700 per day.[6] J. Edgar Hoover announced in 1954 that crime cost American taxpayers $20 billion per year. Judge Thomas Kluczynski of the Family Court of Cook County (Chicago) reported in the same year that he handled an ever-increasing number of juvenile cases and that U.S. Children's Bureau statistics showed that he was not alone. According to the Family Court judge, delinquency was definitely on the rise, and could be found in rural as well as urban areas. In 1953 alone, the nation's juvenile courts handled 435,000 cases—a new all-time high, exceeding the peak of 400,000 during World War II. If things did not change, Kluczynski warned that in 1960 more than 1.5 million juveniles would be apprehended by police and more than 750,000 children would appear before the juvenile courts.[7] For those individuals involved in the study, control, and prevention of juvenile delinquency, the perceived social unrest embodied in the nation's youth foreshadowed a much larger, more serious crisis that threatened to overwhelm police, courts, and society if action was not taken to eliminate or redirect unwanted or "inappropriate" behavior.

Even more alarming to experts and the American public were studies that showed that delinquency was not limited to a particular class, gender, region, or social setting. Although delinquency remained most prevalent among what could be classified as the "urban underclass," rural areas were experiencing a rise in delinquency, and so were middle- and upper-class neighborhoods.[8] A study published in 1952 showed that 91 percent of 340 college juniors and seniors surveyed between 1943 and 1948 had "knowingly committed offenses against the law, both misdemeanors and felonies." The data collected showed that women students were just as "glaringly delinquent" as male students.[9] An extension of the same study, which sampled groups of successful professional women and men, including doctors and lawyers, found that they too had run "the entire gamut of run-of-the-mill delinquencies, as well as more serious offenses."[10] In a separate study, a professor at the University of Texas found that all of the 437 college students he surveyed had committed one or more offenses; the number of offenses reported yielded an average in excess of eleven offenses per student![11] Although these middle-class women and men were almost never apprehended and they generally did not consider themselves "delinquent," they forced experts, legislators, law enforcement officials, and the American public to rethink their ideas about delinquency and its causes.[12]

In December 1950, President Truman hosted the fifth decennial White House Conference on Children and Youth to bring leading experts and interested citizens together to discuss the most effective means of raising responsible, respectable sons and daughters. The conference was immensely popular: five thousand delegates from all over the country traveled to Washington. In contrast, the first conference called by Theodore Roosevelt in 1909 assembled only two hundred people. President Hoover's 1930 conference attracted close to three thousand people, but the 1940 conference drew only seven hundred conferees.[13] Among the five thousand attendees of the midcentury conference were five hundred young people. For the first time in the forty-one year history of the conference, children and young adults attended the White House Conference on Children and Youth. Conference organizers hailed the 1950 gathering as "the largest movement on behalf of children in the history of this country."[14] They were not wrong.

Historically, the White House conferences had proven influential in legitimizing and institutionalizing social reform measures and scientific theories that, in most cases, had been gaining momentum for years. The 1950 conference would be no different. According to Frank Woods, chairman of the Illinois governor's committee on the midcentury conference, the first meeting in 1909, though small, "expounded one of our basic principles of child welfare; namely, that children ought not be separated from their parents for reason of poverty alone." Within two years of Roosevelt's conference, Illinois passed the first Mothers' Pension Law in the world. Woods declared that Hoover's 1930 conference, which was primarily a meeting of "experts," produced "the most comprehensive statement of child needs ever assembled." The thirty-two volumes of material produced by the 1930 conference were still considered by Woods and his committee to be "authoritative source material for educators, pediatricians, social workers, nurses—in fact for all professions touching upon child development." With the advent of the 1950 conference, childhood development and delinquency prevention had "officially" become community concerns. President Truman's call to the midcentury conference asked organizers such as Woods to consider how to develop in all the nation's children "the mental, emotional, and spiritual qualities essential to individual happiness and responsible citizenship." The conference, moreover, was designed from the earliest stages as a grass-roots project. The White House expected conference organizers to make an "honest effort" to "secure the widest possible participation of citizens from every walk of life."[15] The 1950 conference's popularity, as well as its theme, which conference organizers summarized as furthering healthy personality development, mirrored changes in the fields of juvenile delinquency and childhood development that had been taking place since the early 1920s, but only really began to emerge at the national level during the late 1930s and 1940s.

Across the country, especially in the nation's cities, delinquency prevention and "healthy" childhood development were already well on their way to becoming community concerns when the United States entered World War II. Americans' experience during the war and the 1950 White House conference legitimized the need for those grass-roots efforts, and perhaps more importantly, helped to direct much-needed state and federal dollars in their direction. In 1945, the New York state legislature moved to combat rising delinquency rates by creating the New York State Youth Commission and charging it with the responsibility of "giving guidance and state aid to localities to help them cope with their youth problems."[16] In 1947, the New York City Board of Estimate created the New York City Youth Board under the provisions of the State Youth Commission Act. In a report issued in the tenth year of its existence, the youth board observed that juvenile delinquency was neither a new problem, nor was it unique to New York City. Since the beginning of World War II, however, there had been an increasing "instability of life," a "challenge to accepted values," and a "weakening of family ties," all of which had "made for an intensification of this serious social malady." The Youth Board remained confident, however, that the community and its leaders were not only "acutely aware of the problem of juvenile delinquency, but also [were] willing to encourage and support a full preventive program."[17]

Illinois experienced similar changes after the war. In 1947, the state's Division for Delinquency Prevention changed its name to the Division for Youth and Community Service. Two years later, Illinois' annual Conference on the Prevention of Juvenile Delinquency, which had been meeting since 1931, changed its name to the annual Conference on Youth and Community Service.[18] During the nearly two decades of its existence the annual conference, in the words of one of its organizers, had "evolved from academic studies of criminology and case work theories" to what was in 1950 "a workshop type of meeting for lay persons actively interested in young people and in community organization." In 1950, the conference had the endorsement and sponsorship of seventy agencies and organizations, both public and private, interested in the problems of youth.[19] The conference had become so large by the late 1940s that it had to be moved from its traditional downstate locations to Chicago hotels. "Downstaters" who could not make the trip to Chicago could attend one of several smaller, informal, one-day meetings held each fall. As one discussant put it in 1950, Illinois' annual conference "had grown up with the years." It no longer concerned itself only with the field of juvenile delinquency, but with services to all youth. The "proper adjustment" of the nation's youth, especially its middle-class citizens, had become paramount. Conferees in 1950 were considering such modern, youth-oriented, "mid-century topics" as television and comic books, and were talking about programs of national youth organizations. Yet conference organizers and participants had never lost sight of their original objective, which was the study, control, and prevention of juvenile delinquency.[20]

Following the 1950 conference, Illinois' local neighborhood committees for youth formed the Illinois Federation of Community Committees.[21] One year after they formed their federation, committee members met at the twentieth annual Conference on Youth and Community Service, held at the Hotel Sherman in Chicago, to discuss their experiences and plan for the future. General Frank Singer, the president of the federation, described the panelists as, "Just plain Mary and John Citizen from Chicago and downstate." Topics ranged from neighborhood improvement to the rehabilitation of parolees and centered on "the theory that ordinary people [had] within themselves the ability to solve their own problems by working together."[22] The session's keynote was given by Dr. Clifford Shaw, a pioneer in the "community committee movement," who more than twenty years earlier had started the Chicago Area Project.[23] The creation of the Federation of Community Committees, and the idea that delinquency itself was indeed a community problem, remained an important part of the public discourse on delinquency in Illinois and elsewhere throughout the 1950s.

The new thinking on delinquency, its causes, and its prevention received further state support in 1953, when the Illinois legislature created the Illinois Youth Commission in part to separate "officially" and administratively its "delinquent" population from its "mentally defective" population. Since its creation in 1917, the Department of Public Welfare had handled both populations. Following a preliminary study undertaken by the Illinois Commission on Youth, headed by state senator Walter Butler, the General Assembly passed Senate Bill No. 276 unanimously in 1953, placing the state's delinquency prevention, correction, and rehabilitation services in a single administrative unit separate from the Department of Public Welfare. The three-man Youth Commission, appointed by the governor with the advice and consent of the Senate, would work with the Division of Community Service and the Division of Correctional Services to prevent delinquency and rehabilitate the youthful offender.[24]

Primitive Hunters or Good Little Buddhists

According to dominant scientific theories, delinquency could be prevented and youthful offenders like sixteen-year-old Geraldine could be rehabilitated because delinquents were made by the environment and not heredity. In a revealing address entitled "Coming of Age in 1952," delivered at the banquet session of the annual Conference on Youth and Community Service in Chicago, renowned anthropologist Margaret Mead articulated dominant understandings of child development. In an effort to explain what most Americans perceived as a growing generation gap, Mead urged her listeners to accept the notion that their children were indeed different. "In the United States," Mead declared, "adolescents are not only different from adults (that is so in every society in the world in some way or other); they're different from what the adults *were*, and they're different from what *their* children will be." America was a "changing society," Mead explained, and because children were a product of the culture within which they were reared, generational differences were unavoidable. Accepting the idea of America as a changing society with all of its implications would allow adults to "realize that all the young people that we have to try to work with, to teach and understand, are something new, something different, something other than our own flesh and blood."[25]

For Mead and many of her colleagues, hereditarianism was dead. In the same speech, Mead dismissed any hint of hereditarianism entirely: "Of course we have a sort of mystical feeling that flesh and blood must somehow matter, although we know that you can bring children from the heart of Africa or Asia to [the] United States and they'll all grow up speaking English, and playing baseball, and chewing gum, and that we could take another group of children to the heart of Asia and Africa or somewhere, and they could grow up as primitive hunters or good little Buddhists."[26] Richard C. Clendenen, staff director of the Senate Subcommittee to Investigate Juvenile Delinquency, agreed: "What each of these youngsters [born in 1954] will become," he declared, "is in no way determined at his birth. No child comes with built-in attitudes towards persons or property.... All these things he must in some way learn and acquire as he grows up, having made measured steps toward a life of delinquency and crime."[27] Juvenile delinquents were made, not born.

Not all experts who associated themselves with the study of juvenile delinquency were such strict environmentalists; heredity remained important during the postwar period, but "hereditarianism" as it had been defined since the time of Galton held little scientific, cultural, or political power after the war. In their influential text, *Delinquency: The Juvenile Offender in America Today* (1956), Herbert Bloch and Frank Flynn argued that in order to "understand the problem [of heredity] adequately," students of delinquency needed to be familiar with the difference between the "structural characteristics of the organism and its functional possibilities." "At birth," Bloch and Flynn explained, "each child has a definite physical structure, which, however, can lend itself to a wide variety of forms of behavior. Physical structure, in its strictest meaning, indicates an enormous range of behavior potentials for any individual." According to the hereditarians of the 1940s and 1950s, an individual's "physical structure" or heredity was the scaffolding upon which individual character, or to use a more modern term, personality, was built. Heredity influenced development; it did not dictate behavior. If any doubt about this point remained in the minds of their readers, Bloch and Flynn assured them that "the ethnographic studies made by anthropologists for the last forty years should put a complete end to it."[28] Decades of scientific research, not Nazism, led to the decline of eugenic commitment after the Second World War.

As the "fact-finding" report of the midcentury White House Conference on Children and Youth indicates, personality, not heredity, had become the central focus of experts, legislators, and reformers. Edited by Dr. Helen Witmer, director of the Division of Research at the Children's Bureau, and Ruth Kotinsky, the report, entitled *Personality in the Making* (1952), brought together the work of a host of experts, including E. Franklin Frazier, Alain Locke, Benjamin Spock, and Margaret Mead. In the report's preface, the editors hailed it as a "benchmark in the upward and forward movement of our useful knowledge about children and youth." They added that information revealed in the report was "regarded as basic and essentially valid by large numbers of people who work directly with children in a professional capacity or who engage in studies in relevant fields."[29]

Steeped in scientific discourse and supremely confident of their own ability to affect change, the White House "fact-finding" committee had boldly and "officially" welcomed a new era in the study of juvenile delinquency, mental health, and childhood development. They claimed that their report, like the 1930 report before it, had set a new scientific standard in the seemingly endless march toward "Progress."[30] *Personality in the Making* was not a collection of the most recent, most innovative studies and findings, but rather a compendium of well-established scientific "facts"; a collection of data that had been gathered and theories that had been formulated, in most cases, since the publication of the 1930 White House report. By the early 1950s, scientists had established "personality" as a scientific "truth."

In an apparent effort to satisfy the disparate body of professionals represented in the report, its editors chose to develop a rather capacious definition of their new concept. Witmer and Kotinsky started with what they called the "philosopher's" notion that "personality is an inward awareness of the self as permanent and unchanging." Next, they added the view of the physiologist and psychologist that "personality is the organism itself in its most complex functioning, a system of reactions, physical and emotional, that has continuity but is indefinitely variable." To this the editors added the sociologist's "dictum that personality is the individual's peculiar embodiment of the ideas and customs of the culture to which he belongs." The final aspect of personality came from the psychiatrist's finding that "through all the flux of behavior and feeling there is consistency and that there are depths to the personality of which the conscious mind is not aware." The editors summarized their definition of personality as the "thinking, feeling, acting human being, who, for the most part, conceives of himself as an individual separate from other individuals and objects." Human beings did not have personalities; they were personalities.[31]

Critical in the report's definition of personality was the understanding that although it remained constrained by biology and culture, it was largely situational and developed throughout an individual's life. The intellectually, emotionally, and socially functioning human being, or personality, varied her behavior from time to time and from situation to situation. Yet this same personality developed in accordance with a pattern that was "set biologically for the human species"; set "culturally for the group to which he belongs"; and set in agreement with an infinite number of particular circumstances. Physical and intellectual factors set limits to an individual's variation, and responses to new experiences were conditioned by past experiences. In the end, the individual came to behave in a way that was "peculiarly his own." Because, by their own definition, personality existed only abstractly, the editors of the fact-finding report concluded that a "healthy personality" could only be measured by an individual's actions and the "relative success" of their efforts to "play [their] part in relation to other human beings and to the institutions through which social life is carried on."[32] Successful adaptation to dominant standards of normative behavior became the mark of a "healthy" personality.

In order to formulate a working thesis of "healthy personality development," Witmer and Kotinsky turned to prominent psychologist Erik Erikson. Erikson, who was born in 1902 near Frankfurt, Germany, to Danish parents, moved to the United States in 1933 and became one of Boston's first child analysts. In 1950, Erikson delivered a paper entitled, "Growth and Crisis of the Healthy Personality" at the annual Conference on Problems of Infancy and Childhood, which the editors of the White House report used to formulate their own thesis. They described Erikson's analysis as deriving from psychological theory, as well as his own knowledge of and experience in the fields of child development and cultural anthropology. Erikson, they argued, rooted his study of personality in two basic assumptions: that "healthy personality" had to be considered within the context of the "personality deviations" that had been studied so extensively in previous decades, and that one should only focus on those aspects of "healthy personality" that appeared to be universal and not restricted to one nation, culture, or faith.[33]

Ever mindful of the mental health profession's tumultuous beginnings, when the study of "deviations" of all types seemed to dominate the discourse, the editors of the White House report sought to employ an ostensibly modern, normalizing, universalist ethos in their definition of "healthy" personality development in an effort to reflect more accurately their growing interest in the middle-class that began largely during the interwar period. By constructing a "universal," that is a nondisabled, white, middle-class definition of "healthy" personality development, midcentury mental health professionals could at once cast themselves in a more detached, objective, "scientific" light and attract an ever-expanding base of "normal," middle-class clientele.[34]

Using Erikson's work, Witmer and Kotinsky argued that children developed in a series of distinct but interrelated stages. At each stage in a child's life a problem arose that she had to solve in order to advance to the next stage of development. A developing child never solved the problem or conflict completely; each new experience or change in environment brought about new conflicts. Witmer and Kotinsky asserted, however, that "each type of conflict appears in its purest, most unequivocal form at a particular stage in a child's development"; and that, "if the problem is well solved at that time the basis for progress to the next stage is laid and a degree of 'sturdiness' in personality secured for the future." Each "normal" child was born with a biological blueprint for healthy personality development, but the "constant interplay between organism and environment" meant that growing children needed the love, encouragement, and guidance of parents, teachers, and other adults to mature "properly."[35] In the end, the editors of the White House "fact-finding" report concluded that healthy childhood development could be affected negatively by numerous things, including congenital birth "defects," physical limitations, conflicted parent-child relations, income level, prejudice, and discrimination, and that the community needed to work together to raise healthy, well-adjusted, responsible citizens. Personality theory and delinquency prevention had become intimately bound with one another by the early 1950s.

The notion that delinquency stemmed from something other than biology was not new in 1950, but the movement toward a specific "scientific" personality theory of delinquency was a relatively novel concept that gained widespread acceptance following the 1950 White House conference and the publication of the "fact-finding" report two years later. Ideas about "personality" or "individual character" had been part of American culture for years, but it was not until William Healy's declaration in 1915 that delinquency researchers were "primarily students of personality" that delinquency experts began to take an interest in it.[36] Following World War I, personality research, like intelligence testing, became a lucrative endeavor. Paper and pencil personality measurements proliferated at a rate rivaled only by intelligence tests, and personality researchers who increasingly concerned themselves with "normal" subjects, as well as "delinquent" or "abnormal" individuals, spent the next fifteen years working out scientifically acceptable definitions of the new concept.

Ultimately, data collection proved much easier than defining personality. One 1919 definition of the elusive idea described it as "the habitual mode of adjustment which the organism effects between its own egocentric drives and the exigencies of the environment." Critics claimed that this definition, as it was phrased, "would include practically all of human behavior," which of course was not acceptable. Other attempts at defining personality were equally as unsuccessful. According to one 1924 researcher, personality was "the sum total of all the biological innate dispositions, impulses, tendencies, appetites, and instincts of the individual, and the acquired dispositions and tendencies." Another expert defined personality in 1924 as "so many important dimensions in which people may be found to differ." Yet another 1928 definition of personality described it as "the portrait or landscape of the organism working together in all its phases."[37] Despite their lack of a parsimonious definition of personality, researchers remained secure in their belief that they were indeed making "progress." The author of a 1931 text on personality began his foray into the subject with the caveat that, ". . . although personality is being variously defined from the different angles of approach, there is evidence throughout that we are moving toward a surer grasp of certain important principles."[38]

By the mid-1930s, experts had devised an understanding of personality that was quite similar to the one employed by Witmer and Kotinsky in the 1952 White House report. The author of a popular psychology textbook described personality in 1935 as the "most inclusive term available to the psychologist for the designation of an individual. Personality means the sum total of what an individual human being is. It includes all that is native and all that has been acquired."[39] Although this explanation of personality was just as far reaching as earlier attempts, it seemed to satisfy delinquency researchers enough that they began in the late 1930s to devise increasingly elaborate systems of intervention that centered upon the measurement and evaluation of "delinquent" personalities. With the advent of a new "impairment," the "maladjusted" or "delinquent" or, later, "antisocial" personality, delinquency itself became a "disability" that could "handicap" an individual and prevent them from living "normally."

The central role of personality theory in the study, prevention, and control of juvenile delinquency can be seen throughout the literature from the early 1950s. In a paper entitled, "Interpersonal Relationships in Behavior Control," which he presented at Illinois' 1951 Conference on Youth and Community Service, Dr. Bruno Bettelheim informed conferees of a relatively new personality theory of delinquency prevention that promised to be more effective than both hereditarian/eugenic and sociological approaches. "For a long time, as you know," Bettelheim told his audience, "delinquency was viewed as being due to heredity, meaning personality alone and the personality was then looked upon as unchangeable";

but new research was showing that personality was indeed malleable, so much so that it offered an even more effective means of preventing delinquency than both the eugenicists and the sociologists had favored. Bettelheim went on to argue that experts had learned, to their "disappointment," that "taking the delinquent away from his old life and providing him with better living conditions was by no means an assurance that he would give up his delinquent behavior." "So lately," Bettelheim observed, "we seem to have become more interested in changing the delinquent's personality," as well as changing his environment. Considering that personality development was largely the product of the sum of a number of emotional and environmental forces, Bettelheim concluded that, "Changing the one without the other will not get us very far."[40]

Proponents of the new approach to solving the country's social problems declared that focusing on healthy personality development had the potential to bring together a diverse array of specialists, community members, and governmental agencies in unprecedented ways. By their own admission, delinquency researchers recognized that they lacked an "inclusive personality theory" that would allow them to "determine with any degree of completeness either the detailed or the over-all interpretations [they] require[d] for adequate analysis of the causation of delinquency," but they remained optimistic that an interdisciplinary approach to the study of delinquency would yield such a theory.[41] Illinois' 1952 Conference on Youth and Community Service featured a keynote address entitled, "Teamwork in Building Personalities," as well as a lengthy panel discussion and small seminars on "Cooperation of the Specialties in Building Personality" that included experts from law, psychiatry, social work, education, theology, and sociology.[42]

It is no surprise that in the midst of the postwar Red Scare, McCarthyism, and the cold war, the community of experts and the community of concerned citizens and governmental organizations were able to build a consensus around a theory of delinquency prevention that focused on developing healthy individual personalities. Students of delinquency relied upon romanticized notions of democratic, patriotic teamwork and a palpable pressure to conform to dominant notions of normality in their efforts to create an internalized set of standards of behavior that would enable a burgeoning baby boom population to "overcome" the desire to misbehave. Critical in the postwar pathologization of delinquency was a new form of impairment, the notion of the "maladjusted" personality, which proved especially important for female delinquents.

Little Savages and Psychopathic Deviates

From the perspective of the experts, personality theory as it was articulated during the early 1950s went a long way in explaining the causes of delinquency, but it was not complete. The problem of motivation remained a salient issue for everyone involved in the study, prevention, and control of juvenile delinquency.[43] What, precisely, caused a child to act? It was not heredity, as the eugenicists had claimed. It was not external factors, as the sociologists had argued. Despite the alarming increase in delinquency during and after World War II, the total number of adjudicated delinquents in 1952 still only amounted to 2 percent of the total population of children between the ages of ten and seventeen.[44] Many children living in blighted areas ripe with environmental hazards were "overcoming" the apparent external pressure to engage in antisocial behavior. Even the "broken home" theory, which historically had held a tremendous amount of import for experts and reformers, was being challenged. Personality theory, it seemed, was the most effective way of integrating the collective strands of research into a coherent analysis of causation, which once again rooted delinquency in the mind of the individual, but even it did not fully address the issue of motivation. Inroads into this elusive area were being made, however.

Although many personality theorists, especially those interested in developing a more complex understanding of the interaction between personality and environment, approached Freudian psychoanalysis with an understandable degree of skepticism, experts interested in motivation, including those at the Illinois Youth Commission and the State Training School for Girls at Geneva, turned to Freud to explain the causes of delinquency.[45] Freudians began with the assumption that it would be "closer to the truth" to say that every human being was born with a "readiness for aggressive criminal behavior," but that obviously not everyone acted on that potential.[46] As the English psychiatrist Kate Friedlander argued, theories that ascribed the origin of criminal behavior to a "tangible difference" between the criminal and the law-abiding citizen "were erroneous." "Familiarity with the behaviour of very small children," Friedlander explained, "tends to make us formulate the question in a different way. . . . It seems really much more astonishing that so many of these little savages develop into socially adapted human beings than that some of them do not reach that stage."[47] Similarly, Dr. E. A. Stephens, an American psychiatrist and author of *Lawless Youth* (1953), argued that, "The many laws that have accumulated through the ages are ample proof of mankind's native aggressiveness. With bad example[s] existing everywhere, it is not surprising that youths become antisocial. What is surprising, is that so many do not become criminals."[48] For Freudians, small children normally exhibited antisocial thoughts and behaviors until they learned to repress or redirect their desires through a process of "social adjustment" that occurred relatively early in life. A child's urges were "neither bad nor good," but merely the "normal manifestations" of their "instinctive life."[49]

Unlike Erikson, who developed eight psychosocial stages that humans experienced throughout their lives, Freudians argued that the fundamental basis of an individual's personality formed by age eight. Friedlander found it "astonishing that the taming of the antisocial impulses" so freely expressed by children took place "in a comparatively short time: we have seen that a child of 8, even if not always able to do the expected thing, is already more or less socially adapted." According to Friedlander's reading of Freud, humans developed from a state of "pre-consciousness" at birth to a mental state at age eight that consisted of those basic Freudian components, the id, the ego, and the superego.[50] Freudians argued that because an individual's personality formed so early in life, a child's parents, especially her mother, played a critical role in her development.

For many Freudians, the child's "environment" was her mother. In his discussion of ego development, Stephens argued that, "The first step in maturation occurs when the environment (the mother) insists upon detachment from herself."[51] Stephens went on to argue that the "curtain" on a child's "struggle for emotional maturity and stability" arose "at the moment of fecundation," and that the "equipment" that the child brought to that struggle was acquired "during his residence in the mother."[52] For Freudians like Stephens, every subsequent developmental process hinged upon the initial mother-child relationship. Not all students of personality and delinquency adopted such a strictly Freudian conceptualization of "environment." Yet mothers remained a critical component in nearly every assessment of the development of "maladjusted" youth.

Although they usually grudgingly co-opted the Freudian concepts of the id, ego, and superego, most personality theorists took a slightly more expansive and amorphous view of "environment" than did the Freudians. Researchers sometimes referred to as neo-Freudians cited everything, including "deviant" homes, cultural conflict (usually in the case of recent immigrants), deteriorated neighborhoods, peer-age groups and associates, school, recreation, motion pictures, television, radio, comic books, and substandard economic conditions within their rubric of the "environment." According to experts, all of these things ultimately affected the formation of personality "sets" or "states" that in turn provoked young people to engage in antisocial behavior.[53]

By the early 1950s, researchers had delineated four personality "states" that they considered the primary causes of delinquency: the anxiety pattern, unsocialized aggression, the "acting out" neurotic, and egocentric waywardness. Bloch and Flynn described the anxiety pattern as a "diffuse," "invariant," and "abiding sense of insecurity" developed in early childhood that became an integral part of the whole personality. Children who developed an anxiety pattern displayed hostility toward themselves and a "furious resentment of all adult authority," both of which were grounded in a "chronic distrust." Experts defined unsocialized aggression as being cruel, defiant, and prone to destroy property and engage in fighting with little sense or feeling of guilt or remorse. The neurotic delinquent, or "acting out" neurotic, displayed what during the 1950s were considered "genuine" neurotic symptoms, namely a high level of anxiety and tension, a distorted social perspective rooted in a rich fantasy life, and a desire to avoid social contact. Experts defined egocentric waywardness as the arrested emotional development of a child at an extremely low level of maturity. Children who developed egocentric waywardness displayed a "generic hostility" that was "liable to run in different directions," like that of a child who had been "thwarted in pursuit of his immediate gratifications." Though these four personality "sets" or "states" were not the sole markers of social deviance, most delinquency researchers agreed that one or more of them could be "found" in most youthful offenders.

There were some delinquents, however, who seemed to defy pathologization. In addition to the four delinquent personality "states," experts also recognized what they called the "socialized delinquent," who possessed no "genuine pathological tendencies" but was considered pathological because they identified with "the deviant standards of a subcultural group or class." Bloch and Flynn labeled these individuals "cultural deviants."[54] The consensus among delinquency researchers was that "cultural deviants" were not nearly as dangerous as their pathological counterparts. While the former seemed to "outgrow" their delinquent tendencies, the latter required elaborate systems of intervention to live "normally." As we will see, "cultural deviants" were almost always gendered male, while young women tended to have their antisocial acts pathologized. Experts' creation of the four pathological personality "states," as well as the "cultural deviant," enabled them to set up a dichotomy between unacceptable/pathological (mis)behavior and acceptable/cultural (mis)behavior, which ultimately became a powerful gendered means of identifying and sorting individuals who violated dominant notions of normative adolescent conduct.

Although they sought to broaden the scope of their research to include other social and cultural forces and move away from a specifically Freudian explanation of development, the neo-Freudians continued to root delinquency in a maladjusted personality acquired early in life. Most psychologists began with the premise that "normative psychological development" was "seriously impaired" in those family situations and social settings in which a child had been afforded little or no opportunity for "normal identification with either or both parents, particularly the mother."[55] Like the eugenicists before them, both Freudians and neo-Freudians made mothers responsible for juvenile delinquency, but now it was the mother-child relationship and not the mother's "germ plasm" that was at fault.

Psychologists went to great lengths to associate specific types of mothering with the development of the four basic delinquent pathologies. According to the experts, the development of an anxiety pattern or unsocialized aggression could be traced to a sense of rejection "most noticeably expressed by the mother." Psychologists described the attitude of the mother of a neurotic delinquent as "ambiguous," and explained that although "seemingly affectionate in many instances," the mother's affection actually concealed a "fundamental indifference and casualness toward the child." The neurotic child, in turn, developed a "highly contingent relationship to the mother," the emotional content of which was "widely variable." The experts concluded that the neurotic delinquent's antisocial behavior developed in part out of "the need to assure himself of emotional response from the mother, whom he strongly distrusts." According to psychologist August Aichhorn, egocentric waywardness developed in most cases because the mother was "not equal to the task of rearing the child." "Weighed down by cares" for her child, the mother "worrie[d] continually about his welfare and [could not] demand from him any postponement or renunciation of pleasure. She clear[ed] out of his way all disappointments and obstacles which the child [needed to] learn to face and overcome in later life and thus she rob[bed] the child of initiative."[56]

Studies of so-called normal children, as well as those whom experts considered "maladjusted," conducted in the United States and abroad seemed to confirm the widely held belief among mental health experts that a "healthy" mother-child relationship played a critical role in childhood development. Witmer and Kotinsky devoted an entire chapter to the importance of mothering in the 1952 White House report, in which they cited the World Health Organization (WHO) study, *Maternal Care and Mental Health* (1951). According to the WHO study, which the editors of the White House report described as a "voluminous review" of the maternal care studies, one of the "most significant" contributions of psychiatry and psychology in the preceding quarter century had been the proliferation of "evidence" that seemed to corroborate the assertion that the "quality of parental care which a child receives in his earliest years is of vital importance for his future mental health."[57] Though this statement may have seemed rather innocuous and self evident—a child needs its parents—the notion that the "quality" of parental care, which experts almost always defined as maternal care, could somehow be measured objectively proved critical in the pathologization of "deviance."

Experts' own class, gender, and racial biases ensured that "quality" maternal care would be defined by a romanticized, middle-class, notion of child rearing that had been an important part of American culture since the 1920s. The WHO report stated that children needed to experience a "warm, intimate, and continuous relationship with his mother (or permanent mother substitute) in which both find satisfaction and enjoyment." It was within this "complex, rich, and rewarding relationship with the mother in the early years" that the child developed her "character" and "mental health."[58] The WHO report explained that in order to create a "healthy" mother-child relationship, the child needed to feel he was "an object of pleasure and pride to his mother." For her part, the mother needed to feel "an expansion of her own personality in the personality of her child." Both mother and child needed to feel "closely identified with the other." "Such enjoyment and close identification of feeling," the WHO report stated, was possible for either party "only if the relationship is continuous." Mother and child needed to feel as if they "belong[ed]" to one another. "The provision of constant attention" necessary to raise a mentally "healthy" child was "possible only for a woman who derives profound satisfaction from seeing her child grow from babyhood, through the many phases of childhood, to become an independent man or woman, and knows that it is her care which has made this possible."[59]

Embroiled in a cold war that, among other things, pitted idealized Western notions of home, hearth, and the nuclear family against Communist Russia, experts declared that a mother's relationship with her child needed to be "warm," "intimate," and most important, "continuous." She could not work or pursue other interests that may have taken her outside the home.[60] A good mother found her "satisfaction" and "enjoyment" not in other "worldly" pursuits, but in the "rich" and "rewarding" relationship she established with her child. "Quality" maternal care occurred only when a mother lost her own identity, or personality, in that of her child.

Though they created a seemingly endless array of variations, both Freudians and neo-Freudians rooted their pathologization of juvenile delinquency in three basic types of mothering, which they defined as overprotection or possessiveness, overindulgence, and rejection. Mental health experts reasoned that because humans passed through a longer period of dependency than any other mammals, breaking the bonds between parent and child proved difficult. According to the experts, mothers who sought, either consciously or unconsciously, to maintain their child's dependence became overprotective, or they granted every wish of the child, all in an effort to "enslave" them. The child, usually the son, became unable to escape his domineering mother, and ultimately developed a "neurotic" or "maladjusted" personality.[61] Although maternal rejection could occur with a child of either sex, experts considered it especially detrimental to daughters. Experts argued that mothers who were unable to accept their own "feminine role" in life rejected their daughters because they were a "constant reminder of what she [the mother] did not want to be." Daughters would, in turn, learn to "dislike being girls," and thus each new generation would transmit "neurotic conflicts without end."[62] According to the experts, a "maladjusted" personality could become a type of heritable "defect," or impairment, especially in the case of girls and women.

That female delinquents were more likely than their male counterparts to have their antisocial acts pathologized speaks to the perceived heritability of their "causes." The "socialized delinquent" who showed no "genuine pathological tendencies" was almost always male, while delinquency in young women was almost always seen as the outward manifestation of some internal "maladjustment." As Friedlander argued:

> In recent years girls who enter on an "immoral life" at the age of 14 or even earlier have come to present a difficult problem for parents and authorities alike. Not that this type of girl was unknown before the war, but under the external circumstances of increased opportunity their number has increased to a disquieting degree, and it has been recognized that the available methods of treatment are inadequate. On superficial enquiry it may appear as if the problem were one of environmental factors only. But in every case of this kind which has come to my notice, signs of an antisocial character formation have been present before puberty, and there was not one without a disturbance in the early family setting.[63]

Bloch and Flynn seemed to confirm Friedlander's argument when they stated that "the majority of girls will not engage in delinquent activities unless emotionally disturbed to begin with, whereas boys will do so under pressure of culture and environment."[64] Yet, another delinquency researcher found that his data suggested that "delinquency in females is more often the expression of personal inadequacies rather than a manifestation of cultural imperatives."[65] According to the experts, delinquent girls were, in every sense of the word, disabled.

Midcentury experts, like their eugenic predecessors, argued that they had the quantifiable scientific data to support their assertions. Though the eugenicists relied primarily on family studies and intelligence tests, more modern researchers used an instrument known as the personality inventory. In her 1945 study, "Personality Patterns of Adolescent Girls: Delinquents and Nondelinquents," Dora Capwell, director of the Psychological Services of Pittsburgh, Pennsylvania, was one of the first experts to find that two tests, the Minnesota Multiphasic Personality Inventory (MMPI) and the Washburne Social Adjustment Inventory, suggested that specific "personality aberrations" frequently were associated with delinquency in girls. According to Capwell, the "most conspicuous differences" between delinquents and nondelinquents appeared in their respective scores on the scales of the "psychopathic deviate" and "paranoia."[66] The MMPI, which experts considered the most reliable means of analyzing and predicting juvenile delinquency, defined the "psychopathic deviate" as an individual who always impressed the clinician "with their failure to be controlled by the ordinary mores of society. They seem little affected by remorse and do not appear to be particularly modified by censure or punishment. They are likely to commit asocial acts, but these frequently lack obvious motive." The paranoid delinquent was someone who displayed "undue interpersonal sensitivity; at its extreme this may be a paranoid feeling about other people in which the subject feels mistreated or threatened."[67]

From Theory to Practice

The importance of personality theory, with all of its attendant technologies of power, becomes readily apparent when we take a closer look at the experience of Geraldine, the "sex delinquent" incarcerated at Geneva in 1955, as well as the experience of her peers. Unlike earlier experts, the psychologists, psychiatrists, and social workers who evaluated Geraldine relied on psychoanalysis and personality theory, not eugenics, to explain her perceived delinquencies. The experts claimed that Geraldine was "an insecure dependent girl who need[ed] the support of a home environment." The psychologist found that a "good deal of conflict" existed within Geraldine as to "whether or not she deserve[d] the support and acceptance she need[ed]."

Experts rooted Geraldine's inner conflict in her troubled relationship with her parents, especially her mother. Geraldine was deprived of a relationship with her natural father, who died when she was four years old, and the psychologist concluded that Geraldine tended "to be suspicious of the father figure and his relationship with her." More important, however, was Geraldine's relationship with her mother. The psychologist reported that Geraldine seemed "to have gained much more from the mother figure than from the father, although a good deal more conflict exist[ed] in her relationship with the mother." The psychologist noted a "strong attachment" to the mother, but she also found that "a large component of hostility is present since so much frustration has been experienced as the result of mother's handling." The psychologist concluded that Geraldine possessed some "suspiciousness of the environment," which was caused by her "inability to cope with it."

According to the experts, Geraldine suffered from "separation anxiety," and "diagnostically" she appeared to be experiencing an "immaturity syndrome." All hope was not lost, however. The psychologist concluded that Geraldine possessed "good" ego controls and a "strong superego" that caused her "a good deal of guilt" concerning her "delinquent difficulties." "Since a strong super-ego appears to be present," the psychologist added, "it would appear that [Geraldine's] problem is neurotic in nature," and therefore was treatable. The experts concluded that a "period of stabilization in the training school [was] needed," and recommended that Geraldine be transferred to Geneva, where she remained until May 1957.[68]

As Geraldine's case shows, the pathologization of adolescent female behavior, and of women generally, continued during the 1950s. However, experts no longer relied on eugenics, hereditarianism, or feeblemindedness theory to construct the minds of women who violated prescribed gender and generational norms as deviant. Instead, a new generation of scientists, reformers, legislators, legal authorities, and concerned citizens worked diligently to imbue Freudian psychoanalysis and the newly emerging personality theory of human development with considerable social and cultural authority in their ongoing efforts to render the seemingly invisible and immeasurable visible and quantifiable.

The gender dynamics prevalent in earlier attempts to define delinquency and root social problems in the minds of a deviant "other" remained salient in the 1950s, but the eugenic elements that dominated earlier discussions of the causes and consequences of female juvenile delinquency no longer held scientific, cultural, or social import. Girls still had their delinquency defined in terms of sexual transgressions, and girls were still more likely than boys to face incarceration, but their actions and their subsequent incarceration no longer held any eugenic implications. The absence of eugenics, however, ultimately did little to alter the lived experience of young women who continued to find themselves at the center of a seemingly endless array of professional, governmental, and community-based systems of intervention.

The circumstances under which girls like Geraldine were committed to Geneva had not changed much in the sixty-odd years of the institution's existence; neither had the general profile of its inmates. Approximately 65 percent of a random sample of young women at Geneva during the 1950s was white.[69] Over half the sample came from "broken homes"; 30 percent were "sex delinquents"; 34 percent had run away from home; 16 percent were "incorrigible"; 16 percent had been truant from school; 10 percent came to Geneva pregnant; approximately 5 percent had been caught shoplifting; and 4 percent were the victims of sexual assault. Geraldine's religion was the only thing that placed her in the minority of Geneva inmates; she was Catholic. Only 16 percent of inmates in the sample claimed to be Catholic, while nearly half of those girls who claimed to be religious stated that they were Protestant.[70]

National data show patterns of arrest and incarceration similar to those at Geneva. The average age of the female juvenile offender had remained unchanged, at 15.6 years. Boys were still about five times more likely than girls to appear in juvenile court, but girls were more likely to be incarcerated or placed in the care of one of the numerous child guidance agencies. Data collected by the United States Children's Bureau in 1945 showed that girls were arrested for "being ungovernable" (incorrigible), running away, sex offenses, truancy, and stealing, in that order. As one postwar study explained, national concern over the misbehavior of girls still revolved largely around the possibility of "sexual and other forms of molestation" and "incipient or actual forms of sexual laxity."[71] Delinquency remained gendered after the war.

The marked difference in the post–World War II period lay not in young women's offenses or their home life, but in the ways in which experts thought about the causes and possible consequences of female juvenile delinquency. Although researchers still found a significant percentage of female offenders possessed below-average intelligence, they no longer considered "feeblemindedness" or "mental defect" heritable in most cases, nor did they consider intelligence a primary cause of delinquency. As one of the most thorough and influential postwar surveys of delinquency research stated in 1956, Americans' perspectives had "changed radically" regarding the function of intelligence in contributing to delinquency. "Until 1930," the authors argued, "most of our studies appeared to confirm that delinquents were either defective in intelligence or borderline cases." The authors found that twenty years later, "a considerable number of research conclusions seem[ed] to indicate that delinquents, by and large, [did] not differ radically in intellectual capacity from non-delinquent children coming from the same social and economic environments." The authors found it interesting that "many of the delinquency analysts who previously maintained the earlier position [had] actually reversed themselves." They attributed the change in thinking about intelligence and delinquency to an increased awareness among experts and the reading public of the "inadequate methods of investigation" employed by earlier analysts, "particularly the misuse of statistical samples."[72] Although the forces that lay beneath the shift in thinking concerning intelligence and delinquency involved much more than merely the exposure of the "misuse of statistical samples," the point remains that by the mid-1940s experts no longer considered juvenile delinquents by definition "feebleminded" or mentally "defective."

Test results from Geneva confirm this shift in perspective. In the same random sample of cases taken from Geneva for the 1950s, only one inmate was recommended for commitment to one of Illinois' mental health institutions. Experts classified more than half of the girls in the sample as "average" intelligence; an additional 10 percent of inmates scored in the "above average" range on intelligence tests. Although psychologists determined that approximately 40 percent of the sample cases functioned in the "below average" range of intelligence, they argued that nearly half of the so-called subnormal group were actually "underachievers" who were performing poorly on tests and in school for reasons other than a lack of innate ability.

Unlike eugenicists and the late-twentieth-century authors of *The Bell Curve*, experts working with juvenile delinquents in the 1950s made no causal inferences based on the perceived intelligence of their subjects, nor did they define delinquency as an indisputable marker of mental deficiency.[73] The shift within the scientific discourse on delinquency to a semi-Freudian psychoanalytic model that relied on personality theory rather than older hereditarian explanations of mental and psychological "deviance" no longer afforded experts the room to incorporate "negative" eugenic measures, such as indefinite commitment, into the prevention and control of juvenile delinquency. This, however, did not stop them from rooting delinquent behavior within the individual offender, especially in the case of adolescent women, who proved much more likely than their male counterparts to have their delinquencies pathologized. The important distinction in post–World War II scientific and social reform discourse can be found not necessarily in the ends to which experts and other interested individuals aspired, which included the consolidation of gender and generational relations and familial and sexual norms through the social construction of impairment, but rather the means by which they hoped to reach those ends.

Conclusion

The eugenic institutionalization of adolescent female sex delinquents ended by 1950, but the pathologization of female minds and bodies endured. Experts who considered themselves too modern and scientific to use family studies, feeblemindedness theory, and intelligence tests to construct girls who violated gender and generational norms as inherently flawed created new tests and new theories to explain the causes of young women's aberrant behavior. By the end of the 1940s, new systems of intervention that centered upon the development of "healthy," "well-adjusted" personalities had come to dominate the social-scientific discourse on delinquency. The movement away from eugenic institutionalization as a treatment for female sex delinquency was a gradual process that began in the wake of World War I and gained momentum throughout the interwar period, World War II, and the immediate postwar period. It involved complex, interrelated, and subtle social, cultural, and scientific shifts. There was no great epiphany, no precise moment when the shift in thinking occurred, and there is no evidence that the rise of Nazism or the revelation of Nazi atrocities contributed to the demise of this particular strand of eugenic thinking.[74]

In an era dominated by white suburban flight, loyalty oaths, and Senator Joseph McCarthy's crusade to root out "internal subversives," a group of white, middle-class experts, reformers, legislators, legal authorities, and concerned citizens couched their reform discourse in scientific language that once again rooted "deviance" in the minds of individual female offenders. By the end of the 1940s, however, those individuals were almost always able to be "redeemed," "reeducated," and reintegrated into society with little or no long-term consequences, provided they did not stray too far from dominant understandings of morally acceptable behavior. Before the First World War, eugenic reformers, who, like other middle-class reformers took a more collectivist, "progressive" approach to solving social problems, constructed a group of white working-class youth as inherently defective and unalterable and sought to use science and the state to improve society and the race by segregating female juvenile "sex offenders" who found themselves entangled in the growing juvenile justice and mental health systems. During the interwar period, as mental health researchers and juvenile delinquency experts increasingly concerned themselves with the middle class, the biologically deterministic, collectivist bent that dominated earlier reform efforts gradually gave way to a more holistic approach to reforming individual offenders through supposedly less intrusive and coercive therapeutic measures, as well as specific state-sponsored programs designed to alter the offender's environment—the community, neighborhood, and family. During the 1920s and 1930s, experts utilized an emerging child guidance movement, as well as a rapidly expanding welfare state, to control and prevent delinquency.[75] The politically, culturally, and socially conservative cold war years following World War II witnessed a decline, especially ideologically, of any overt attempts at direct state intervention in the lives or the communities of individual offenders. Individual families, neighborhoods, communities, towns, and cities bore the burden of controlling and preventing juvenile delinquency. In a culture dominated by antifederalism and social conformity, the state became a "facilitator" and the so-called layperson assumed center stage in the battle against delinquency. Experts were continually close by, however, expanding and institutionalizing knowledge/power systems that began to emerge during the interwar period and centered upon the pathologization of female juvenile delinquency through a newly ascendant personality theory of human development and something that historians refer to as "mother blaming."[76]

Like all social-scientific endeavors, the transition from a biological theory of delinquency to a personality theory of delinquency was played out in different cultural locations, with multiple variations and distinct levels of exchange. Rather than privilege one part of the discourse over another, I have attempted to show how a continuously interactive process involving scientific and legal experts, institution administrators, legislators, reformers, concerned citizens, and perhaps, most importantly, delinquent girls and their families shaped the history of the cultural construction of mental "deviance" (impairment) and juvenile delinquency in the United States. Categories of mental deviance—much like current definitions of impairment—were not fixed scientifically or biologically; they were fluid and dynamic and deeply rooted in the social, political, and economic context within which they were developed.[77]

The notion that certain forms of behavior that fell outside socially acceptable parameters had to be identified, categorized, labeled, pathologized, or otherwise medicalized and ultimately "cured" or permanently modified speaks to the centrality of disability in the burgeoning modernist impulse to "rebuild" the nation first articulated by Dr. Evans in November 1915.

EPILOGUE

Defining Deviance in the Late Twentieth Century:
The New "New Girl Problem"?

As we have seen, early twentieth-century eugenic reformers were deeply concerned with what they referred to as the "new girl problem." In some ways, surprisingly little has changed. Girls in trouble with the law in the late twentieth century have many things in common with their early twentieth-century counterparts.[1] Delinquent girls are still largely urban. They still come from abusive and neglectful homes, and what one scholar calls "empty" homes, complicated by poverty, unemployment, frequent moves, unstable adult relationships, death, desertion, divorce, drug addiction, and adult incarceration. Many delinquent girls still endure incest, rape, molestation, sexual assault, and sexual harassment from family members, peers, and adult acquaintances. Many become involved in relationships with older men and many delinquent girls are themselves mothers. The majority of delinquent girls are no longer labeled "sex delinquents," though they still find themselves punished for what modern researchers now call "status offenses"—usually truancy, disorderly conduct, incorrigibility, and running away. In addition, the number of girls adjudicated for so-called violent crimes and crimes against property has been rising steadily since 1980.[2]

Despite the lamentations and dire warnings of modern media and some politicians, however, girls appear to be no more violent than their early twentieth-century counterparts. At first glance, the statistics appear alarming: total girls arrested 1980–2003, up 42.7 percent; violent offenses up 75.7 percent; simple assaults up a whopping 318.5 percent.[3] Statistics, however, can be misleading. First, the basics: 75 percent of *all* juvenile offenders commit nonviolent or status offenses; boys comprise 71 percent of *all* juvenile arrests, and states detain four times as many boys as girls. Violent crime referrals comprised less than 5 percent of total cases referred to the juvenile court in 2000, and 64 percent of those violent crimes were "aggravated assault." Statistics from 2000 show, moreover, that girls comprised less than one-fifth (19 percent) of violent crime referrals to the juvenile court.[4]

Although the causes of girls' delinquency remain as complex now as they were one hundred years ago, juvenile delinquency scholars are quick to point out that reports of "skyrocketing" rates of girls' violence are at least in part a reflection of neo-liberal policy changes that arose during the 1980s and 1990s and were part of a larger response to reforms enacted during the early 1970s.[5] In the early 1970s, Supreme Court decisions, state law reforms, and the passage of the federal Juvenile Justice and Delinquency Prevention Act (1974) enabled the decriminalization of status offenses and the deinstitutionalization of status offenders, both of which greatly affected girls. By 1988, the number of status offenders detained by the juvenile court declined 95 *percent* from pre-1974 numbers. With the advent of neo-liberal "get tough" policies and the "crackdown" on youth crime that began with the election of Ronald Reagan in 1980, juvenile courts adopted what one scholar has called "subversion strategies" to evade many of the reforms enacted during the early 1970s, which were designed to prevent incarceration.

In many states, courts began relabeling status offenses. Disorderly conduct and incorrigibility became "simple assault," for example. Experts call this "bootstrapping," because offenses are, in a sense, "pulled up" to a more serious charge, allowing the court to incarcerate the offender. Another strategy employed by judges relied upon imposing strict court orders for treatment and behavior, and charging youthful violators of those orders with contempt of court. Approximately one-third of delinquent girls were detained for these "technical violations." Courts also increasingly confined status offenders in both private and state-funded secure mental health and chemical dependency facilities.[6] Although these changes in policy and procedure cannot fully explain the incarceration of all delinquent girls, it is possible that they contributed to rising incarceration rates and to the sense among many Americans, including modern media, that girls were becoming more violent (simple assault up 318.5 percent) in the last quarter of the twentieth century.

Class and race continue to play an important, though undertheorized, role in girls' delinquency. The majority (67 percent in 2000) of delinquent girls are white, and most are working class. Yet black girls remain overrepresented in both the juvenile justice system and in modern media portrayals of "criminal youth." Black girls comprised 16 percent of the juvenile population in 2000, but they accounted for 29 percent of referrals to the juvenile court. The remaining 4 percent of delinquent girls came from other ethnic backgrounds. Race and class also seem to play an important role in the disposition of delinquent girls by the court. White girls with economic means, who comprise the majority (86 percent in 2000) of drug-related referrals to the juvenile court, tend to be medicalized and hospitalized more than racial/ethnic minorities, while girls of color tend more often (than whites) to experience incarceration through bootstrapping and technical violations.[7]

In some ways, at least according to those scholars who engage in a critical assessment of the United States' juvenile justice system, the role of the juvenile court has changed little in the last 110 years. Two current researchers note the historical continuity in the treatment of delinquent girls. "Many girls," they argue, "are still being arrested, detained, judged, and institutionalized for behavior that is overlooked when boys do it. Likewise, girls' genuine problems with families are being ignored because the judicial system that was established to 'protect' them has not really been interested in their physical or emotional safety. Instead, it has served to shore up the boundaries of a girlhood that shaped and forced young women into being future second-class citizens."[8] Sexism, racism, crushing poverty, patriarchy, the sexual double standard, and an often misplaced sense of paternalism continue to dominate the experience of delinquent girls; so too do medicalized and pathologized explanations of their behavior.

Delinquency Meets the DSM: Social Deviance Embodied?

It is undeniable that the adjudication, incarceration, parole, and probation of "bad" girls and women continue to rely, at least in part, on increasingly complex scientific and medical discourses of disablement, most of which have their roots in the *Diagnostic and Statistical Manual of Mental Disorders* (DSM). Yet disability activists and scholars are only beginning to explore the pathologization of social deviance.[9] In this last section, I will offer some preliminary thoughts on the connections between a growing list of mental disorders and girls' delinquency.

In the midst of a growing interest in the medical, biochemical, neurological, and genetic "causes" of a whole host of social phenomena, as well as a dominant neo-liberal political and economic order that relies upon slashing social services and bolstering problematic and culturally freighted notions of accountability, court and mental health officials and modern *psy* discourses increasingly place the responsibility for girls' delinquencies—especially when they result in "illegitimate" births—squarely in the bodies and brains of delinquent girls. Evolutionary psychologists, for example, remain especially fond of studying "early onset puberty" and age of menarche as correlates of delinquent behavior in girls. Without the slightest nod toward the sexual objectification, alienation, exploitation, molestation, harassment, and abuse that many girls and women endure almost daily, psychologists argue that "early pubertal maturation" in young girls results in "precocious body development" and the potential for increased conflict with parents, exposure to peer deviance, and involvement in "romantic" relationships, all of which correlate strongly with delinquent behavior and a greater risk of developing various conduct "disorders."[10]

Evolutionary psychologists are not alone in their claims. Researchers in a number of fields, as well as judges, prosecutors, politicians, and many parents, maintain the assertion that an overwhelmingly high percentage of delinquent girls manifest "signs" of a broad array of mental "disorders"; and many psychologists and criminologists continue to explore what they call the "IQ-delinquency link." *Psy* researchers and practitioners have also created a number of new disorders with which they label and through which they are able to medicate, incarcerate, and otherwise surveil delinquent girls.

The last quarter of the twentieth century brought with it a marked rise in the number of documented mental "disorders," a proliferation of diagnostic categories that has not gone unchallenged by those scholars who take a critical approach to the study of psychiatry and psychology. Allan Horwitz, for example, argues that a broad range of historical actors influenced by an increasingly dominant medical model of mental health, by burgeoning pharmaceutical companies, and by *psy* practitioners and researchers desire to expand their client base, engaged in a "categorical revolution" during the late twentieth century. Equally important in this categorical revolution were clients, patients, inmates, relatives, advocates, allies, and disability rights groups, who in seeking recognition, politicization, and empowerment became part of what Horwitz calls a "shared culture of medicalized mental disorders."[11] This confluence of social, political, economic, and medical forces contributed to an exponential increase in the number of diagnosable—and perhaps more important, medically "treatable"—"diseases," "disorders," and "conditions." During the 1980s, the number of "discrete diagnoses" in the DSM-III— the third edition of psychiatry's diagnostic and statistical manual—increased to 265 diagnoses, up from fourteen basic diagnoses two decades earlier. The number of categories expanded to 292 in the DSM-III-R and to nearly four hundred in the recently published DSM-IV. Though most researchers and practitioners see this as progress, the development of a more subtle, sophisticated, and ultimately more accurate means of diagnosing, critics—especially those who take a social constructivist approach—see the proliferation of mental disorders at the end of the twentieth century as highly problematic.

Though the majority of social constructivists do not seek to deny the existence of mental disorder or minimize the material realities that both give rise to and result from living with a *psy* label, they seek to lay bare the social and historical processes that give rise to various classificatory schemes, so that we might begin to think differently about previously taken-for-granted scientific "truths" and reassess the social consequences of being labeled with a particular disabling condition. The list of disorders involved in girls' delinquency is long, but it is well worth citing. It includes but is not limited to: "conduct disorder," "disruptive behavior disorder," "anti-social personality disorder," "anxiety disorder," "bipolar disorder," "depression," "attention deficit hyperactivity disorder," "substance abuse disorder," and "oppositional defiant disorder." One recent study found that 71.2 percent of delinquent girls met the "diagnostic criteria for a psychiatric disorder." A separate study found that 57 percent met the "criteria for at least two disorders."[12] This alarmingly high percentage of disordered delinquents must be taken up and analyzed by disability studies scholars and disability historians so that they might offer a counter-narrative (or counter-hegemony) that reveals both the strengths and the weakness of relying on a medicalized understanding of social deviance.

Rather than dismiss or deny the existence of impairment, disease, or disorder, disability scholars need to meet these accusations head on; we must document and trace the genealogy of modern definitions of mental deviance, all the while remaining sensitive to the specific social and historical contexts from which modern-day "defective delinquents" emerge. Disability historians must engage in a critical analysis of the formation of the diagnostic regimes so readily deployed by researchers, practitioners, pundits, politicians, and parents in their efforts to understand and explain the behaviors of our nation's teenagers.

Barry Feld, one of the America's leading scholars of juvenile justice, has, in many ways, already begun this dialogue. Feld has argued that both rising incarceration rates and the high percentage of "disordered" delinquent girls can be attributed at least partially to both "psychiatric hospitals quest for profits" and "malleable diagnostic categories [that] enabled entrepreneurs to 'medicalize' adolescent deviance and parents to incarcerate troublesome children without any meaningful judicial supervision."[13] Feld's claims are not the only points of intervention into this discussion, but they are points that must be addressed directly by disability historians.

Through a critical assessment of this understudied strand of disability history we can begin to rethink the social and cultural work of defining deviance and analyze the creation of scientific "truths" within a specific social and historical context. Such an argument would not deny delinquent girls' embodiment. Instead, it would begin with a critical analysis of the social, medical, scientific, and juridical discourse at the root of taken-for-granted *psy* classifications. Such an analysis would also place delinquent girls themselves, their homes, families, and friends at the center of this new discourse of disablement.

APPENDIX A

Illinois' Involuntary Commitment Law

FOR THE LEGAL COMMITMENT OF FEEBLE-MINDED

Section 1. Be it enacted by the people of the state of Illinois represented in the general assembly: The words "feeble-minded person" in this Act shall be construed to mean any person afflicted with mental defectiveness from birth or from an early age, so pronounced that he is incapable of managing himself and his affairs, or of being taught to do so, and requires supervision, control and care for his own welfare, or for the welfare others, or for the welfare of the community, who is not classifiable as an "insane person" within the meaning of "An Act to revise the law in relation to the commitment and detention of lunatics, and to provide for the appointment and removal of conservators, and to repeal certain Acts therein named," approved June 21, 1893, in force July 1, 1893.

2. From and after the taking effect of this Act, no feeble-minded person shall be sent to any public institution for the feeble-minded except as herein after provided.

3. When any person residing in this State shall be supposed to be feeble-minded, and by reason of such mental condition of feeble-mindedness, and of social conditions, such as want of proper supervision, control, care and support, or other causes, it is unsafe and dangerous to the welfare of the community for him to be at large without supervision, control and care, any relative, guardian or conservator or any reputable citizen of the county in which such supposed feeble-minded person resides or is found, may, by leave of court first had and obtained, file with the clerk of either the circuit court, or of the county court of the county in which such supposed feeble-minded person resides or is found, or with the clerk of a city court, including the municipal court of Chicago, when the supposed feeble-minded person resides or is found in the city, a petition in writing, setting forth that the person therein named is feeble-minded, the fact and circumstances of the social conditions, such as want of proper supervision, control, care and support, or other causes, making it unsafe or dangerous to the welfare of the community for such person to be at-large without supervision, control or care; also the name and residence, or that such name or residence is unknown to the petitioner, of some person, if any there

be, actually supervising, caring for or supporting such person, and of at least one person if any there be legally chargeable with such supervision, care or support, and also the names and residences or that same are unknown of the parents or guardians.

The petition shall also allege whether or not such person has been examined by qualified physician having personal knowledge of the condition of such alleged feeble-minded person. There shall be indorsed on such petition the names and residences of witnesses known to the petitioner by whom the truth of the allegations of the petition may be proved, as well as the name and residence of a qualified physician, if any is known to the petitioner, having personal knowledge of the case. All persons named in such petition shall be made defendants by name and shall be notified of such proceedings of summons, if residents of this State, in the same manner as is now or may hereafter be required by law in proceedings in chancery in this State, except only as herein otherwise provided. All persons whose names are stated in the petition to be unknown to the petitioner shall be deemed and taken as defendants by the name and designation of "all whom it may concern." The petition shall be verified by affidavit, which shall be sufficient if it states that it is based upon information and belief. Process shall be issued against all persons made parties by the designation of "all whom it may concern," by such description and notice given by publication as required in this Act, shall be sufficient to authorize the court to hear and determine the suit as though the parties had been sued by their proper names.

4. The summons shall require all defendants to personally appear at the time and place stated therein, and to bring into court the alleged feeble-minded person. No written answer shall be required to the petition, but the [ ] shall stand for trial upon the petition on the return day of the summons. The summons shall be made returnable at any time within twenty days after the date thereof, and may be served the same as summons in chancery is served by any officer authorized by law to serve processes of the court issuing such summons. No service of process shall be necessary upon any of the defendants named, if they appear or are brought before the court personally without service of summons.

Whenever it shall appear from the petition or from the affidavit filed in the [ ] that any named defendant, other than the alleged feeble-minded person, resides or hath gone out of the State, or on due inquiry cannot be found, or is concealed within this State, or that his place of residence is unknown, so that process cannot be served upon him, and whenever any person is made a defendant under the name and designation of "all whom it may concern," the clerk of the court shall cause publication to be made once in some newspaper of general circulation published in his county, and if there be none published in his county, then in a newspaper of general circulation published in the nearest place to his county in this State, which publication shall be substantially as follows:

(Give names of such defendants and) To all whom it may concern (if there be any defendant under such designation):

TAKE NOTICE— that on the _____ day of _____ A.D. _____ petition was filed by _____ in the _____ court of _____ to have a certain person named _____ declared feeble-minded and to have the court provide for the care and the detention of such person.

Now, unless you appear within twenty days after the date of this notice and resist the granting of the prayer of such petition, the petition will be taken for confessed and a decree entered.

Dated _____ Clerk _____

and the clerk shall also within ten days after the publication of such notice send a copy thereof by mail, addressed to such defendants whose place of residence is stated in the petition and who cannot be served with summons. Notice given by such publication shall be as effectual for every purpose as if such person or persons were duly served with summons personally. The certificate of the clerk that he has sent such notice pursuant to this section shall be conclusive evidence thereof. Every defendant who shall be duly summoned shall be held to appear and answer either in writing or orally in open court, on the return day of the summons, and if the summons be served less than one day prior to the return day thereof, then on the following day. Every defendant who shall be notified by publication, as herein provided, shall be held to appear and answer, either in writing or orally, within twenty days after the date of the publication notice. The answer shall have no greater weight as evidence than the petition.

In default of an answer at the time herein specified or at such further time as by order of the court may be granted to the defendant, the petition may be taken as confessed against all defendants, except the alleged feeble-minded persons.

5. Upon the filing of the petition, or upon motion at any time thereafter, it shall be made to appear to the court by evidence given under oath that it is for the best interests of the alleged feeble-minded person and the community that such person be at once taken into custody, or that the service of summons will be ineffectual to secure the presence of such person, a warrant may issue on the order of the court, directing that such person be taken into custody and brought before the court forthwith or at such time and place the judge may appoint, and pending the hearing of the petition, the court may make any order for the detention of such feeble-minded person, or the placing of such feeble-minded person under temporary guardianship of some suitable person, on such person entering into a recognizance for his appearance, as the court shall deem proper. But no such alleged feeble-minded person shall, during the pendency of the hearing of the petition, be detained in a place provided for the detention of persons charged with or convicted of any criminal or quasi-criminal offense.

6. At any time after the filing of the petition and pending the final disposition of the case, the court may continue the hearing from time to time, and may order such alleged feeble-minded person to submit to the examination of some qualified physician or psychologist, and the court may also require by rule or order that the petitioner answer under oath such interrogatories as may be propounded, in a form to be prescribed by the Board of Administration.

7. The hearing on petition shall be by the court and a commission to be appointed by the court, of two qualified physicians or one qualified physician and one qualified psychologist, residents of the county, to be selected by the judge on account of their known

competency and integrity, and evidence shall be heard and proceedings had as in any other civil proceedings.

Evidence shall also be heard and inquiry made into the social conditions, such as want of proper supervision, control, care or support, and other causes making it unsafe or dangerous to the welfare of the community for such person to be at large, without supervision, control and care. The commission shall also make a personal examination touching the mental condition of the alleged feeble-minded person. Upon the conclusion of the hearing, inquiry and examination, the commission shall file with the clerk of the court a report in writing, showing the result of their examination of the mental condition and social conditions aforesaid, setting forth their conclusions and recommendations, and shall also file with such report their sworn answers to such interrogatories as may be propounded in a form to be prescribed by the Board of Administration. Such answers may be based upon their best knowledge and belief.

8. The report shall have the same effect as reports of masters in chancery, and shall be subject to be set aside or overruled by the court the same as reports of masters in chancery: Provided, however, that there shall be no need of making objections and taking exceptions to the same, and the court shall have the power to dismiss the proceedings, order a new hearing by the same or a new commission, or make such findings of fact and lieu of the findings in such report as may be justified by the evidence heard, and on the review by the court of the findings and recommendations of the commission, the court may hear such further evidence as it thinks fit.

9. If the court shall find such alleged feeble-minded person not to be feeble-minded as defined in this Act, he shall order the petition dismissed and the person discharged. If the court shall find such alleged feeble-minded person to be feeble-minded, and subject to be dealt with under this Act, having due regard to all the circumstance appearing on the hearing, the guiding and controlling thought of the court throughout the proceedings to be the welfare of the feeble-minded person and the welfare of the community, it shall enter a decree, appointing a suitable person to be the guardian of such feeble-minded person, or directing that such feeble-minded person be sent to a private institution qualified and licensed under the laws of the State to receive such person whose managers are willing to receive him, or may direct that he be placed in a public institution for the feeble-minded and such decree so entered shall stand and continue binding upon all persons whom it may concern until rescinded or otherwise regularly superseded or set aside.

Provided, however, that any guardian appointed under this Act shall be subordinate to any guardian or conservator previously or subsequently appointed, pursuant to "An Act to revise the law in relation to idiots, lunatics, drunkards and spend thrifts," approved March 26, 1874, and in force July 1, 1874, or "An Act in regard to guardians and wards," approved April 10, 1872, in force July 1, 1872.

10. An order that the feeble-minded person be placed under guardianship shall confer on the person named in the order as guardian such powers, subject to the regulations of the Board of Administration, as would have been exercisable if he had been the father of the feeble-minded, and the feeble-minded person had been under the age of fourteen.

11. Where an order has been made that a feeble-minded person be placed under guard-

ianship, the guardian may be removed by the court that appointed him, on the application of the feeble-minded person, or of any relative or friend of the feeble-minded person, or of any reputable citizen or of the Board of Administration; and when the guardian dies, resigns or is removed, the court may, on a like application, appoint a suitable person to act in his stead. And on application of the guardian, or of the feeble-minded person, or of any relative or friend of the feeble-minded person, or of any reputable citizen, or of the Board of Administration, the court that appointed the guardian, on being satisfied that the case is, or has become one unsuitable for guardianship, may order that the feeble-minded person be discharged from guardianship and set free, or be sent to a private institution qualified, and licensed under the laws of the State to receive him, whose managers are willing to receive him, or be sent to a public institution for the feeble-minded, [ ] seems best to the court, having regard to all the circumstances appearing in the hearing. No order shall be made discharging or varying a prior order placing the feeble-minded person under guardianship without giving one or more of the relatives or friends of the feeble-minded person, his guardian and the Board of Administration notice and an opportunity to be heard.

12. Upon the entry of an order directing that a feeble-minded person be sent to an institution for feeble-minded persons, the clerk of the court shall send a copy of the order to the superintendent of the institution to which such feeble-minded person is ordered to be sent, and such superintendent shall receive such feeble-minded person as a charge in such institution: provided, that if on account of the crowded condition of a public institution it is impossible to accommodate such feeble-minded person, the superintendent shall inform the court with the promise that the court be notified at once when the next vacancy occurs, and that such feeble-minded person be then received as a charge in such public institution.

13. For the conveyance of any feeble-minded person to any public or private institution for the feeble-minded, admission thereto having been ordered by the court as herein provided, the clerk shall issue a warrant in duplicate directed to petitioner, or to some suitable reputable person, as the judge may select, commanding him to take such feeble-minded person and deliver him to the superintendent of the institution. When the judge thinks necessary, he may direct the clerk to authorize the employment of one or more assistants, but no feeble-minded female shall be taken to the institution by any male person not her husband, father, brother or son, without the attendance of some woman of good character and mature age chosen for the purpose by the judge. Upon receiving the feeble-minded person, the superintendent of the institution shall endorse upon the warrant his receipt, naming the person or persons from whom the feeble-minded person is received, and one copy of the warrant so endorsed shall be returned to the clerk of the court to be filed with the other papers in the case, and the other shall be left with the superintendent and the person delivering the feeble-minded person shall endorse thereon that he has so delivered him, and said duplicate warrant shall be prima facie evidence of the facts set forth therein and in said endorsement.

14. No feeble-minded person admitted to an institution for the feeble-minded pursuant to an order of the court as herein provided shall be discharged therefrom except as herein

provided, except that nothing herein contained shall abridge the right of petition for the writ of habeas corpus. At any time after the admission of the feeble-minded person to an institution for the feeble-minded, pursuant to an order of the court as herein provided, the feeble-minded person, or any of the relatives or friends of the feeble-minded person, or any reputable citizen, or the superintendent of the institution having the feeble-minded person in charge, or the Board of Administration, may petition the court that entered the order of admission, to discharge the feeble-minded person, or to vary the order of the court sending the feeble-minded person to an institution. If, on the hearing of the petition, the court is satisfied that the welfare of the feeble-minded person, or the welfare of others, or the welfare of the community requires his discharge, or a variation of the order, the court may enter such order of discharge or variation, as the court thinks proper. Discharges and variations of orders may be made for either of the following causes: Because the person adjudged to be feeble-minded is not feeble-minded; because he has so far improved as to be capable of caring for himself; because the relatives or friends of the feeble-minded person are able and willing to supervise, control, care for and support him and request his discharge, and in the judgment of the superintendent of the institution having the person in charge, no evil consequences are likely to follow such discharge; but the enumeration of grounds of discharge or variation herein shall not exclude other grounds of discharge or variation which the court, in its discretion, may deem adequate, having due regard for the welfare of the person concerned, or the welfare of others, or the welfare of the community. On any petition of discharge or variation, the court may discharge the feeble-minded person from all supervision, control and care, or may place him under guardianship, or may transfer him from a public institution to a private institution, or from a private institution to a public institution, as the court thinks fit under all the circumstances appearing on the hearing of the petition. The superintendent of the institution having the feeble-minded person in charge, must be notified of the time and place of hearing on any petition for discharge or variation, as the court shall direct, and no order of discharge or variation shall be entered without giving such superintendent a reasonable opportunity to be heard; and the court may notify such other persons, relatives and friends of the feeble-minded person as the court may think proper of the time and place of the hearing on any petition for discharge or variation of prior order. The denial of one petition for discharge or variation shall be no bar to another on the same or different grounds within a reasonable time thereafter, such reasonable time to be determined by the court in its discretion, discouraging frequent, repeated, frivolous, ill-founded petitions for discharge or variation of prior order. On reception of a feeble-minded person in an institution pursuant to an order of the court under this Act, the superintendent of the institution under regulations of the Board of Administration shall cause the feeble-minded person to be examined touching his mental condition, and if upon such examination is found the person is not feeble-minded, it shall be the duty of the superintendent to petition the court for a discharge or variation of the order sending him to the institution. Any person sent to an institution pursuant to order of the court under this Act shall have the right to at least one hearing on a petition for discharge or variation within one year after the date of the order sending him to an institution.

15. Every person admitted to any institution for the feeble-minded shall have all reasonable opportunity and facility for communication with his friends, and be permitted to write and send letters, providing they contain nothing of an immoral or personally offensive character and letters written by any charge to any member of the Board of Administration, or to any member of the State Charities Commission, or to any State or county official, shall be forwarded unopened. But no leave of absence shall be granted except for good cause to be determined and approved by the Board of Administration in each case who shall take appropriate measures to secure for the feeble-minded person proper supervision, control and care during such leave of absence, and no leave of absence shall be for a longer period than two weeks in one calendar year.

16. In the event of a sudden or mysterious death of a charge of any public or private institution for the feeble-minded, a coroner's inquest shall be held as provided by law in other cases. Notice of the death of such person, and the cause thereof, shall in all cases be sent to the judge of the court having jurisdiction, over such person, and the fact of the death, with the time, place and alleged cause shall be entered upon the docket.

17. Any person who shall knowingly contrive, or who shall conspire to have any person adjudged feeble-minded under this Act, unlawfully and improperly, or any person who shall violate any provision of this Act, shall be deemed guilty of a misdemeanor, and upon conviction thereof shall be fined not exceeding $1,000, or imprisoned not exceeding one year, or both, at the discretion of the court in which such conviction is had.

18. The costs of proceedings in feeble-mindedness shall be defrayed from the county treasury, unless otherwise ordered by the court as herein provided. But when on the hearing of the petition, the person alleged to be feeble-minded is found not to be feeble-minded, the court, in its discretion, may require that the costs shall be paid by the person who filed the petition, and may render judgment against him therefor, except that no judgment for costs shall be rendered against the petitioner who filed the petition pursuant to the direction of a court as provided in sections 20 and 21. The fees paid for attendance of witnesses and execution of legal process, shall be the same as are allowed by law for similar service in other cases. For service as commissioner, the sum of $5.00 per day and the actual and necessary traveling expenses shall be allowed, to each person so employed. But when the proceedings are instituted in a court of any county of which the alleged feeble-minded person is not a resident, in case a judgment for costs is not rendered against the petitioner as above provided, the judge of the county court of the county in which the said feeble-minded person resides shall be furnished with a transcript of the record and findings in the case, and thereupon the said county shall be liable for the costs of the proceedings.

19. Where an order that a feeble-minded person be placed under guardianship, or be sent to a private or public institution, is made under this Act, the court entering the order, or any court having jurisdiction under this Act, may at any time on the application of the petitioner, or of the guardian, or of the managers of the institution or of the Board of Administration, as the case may be, make an order requiring the feeble-minded person, or any person liable or undertaking to maintain him, to contribute such sums towards expenses of his guardianship, or of his maintenance in the institution, and any charges

incidental thereto, including the costs of the proceedings in feeble-mindedness, of his conveyance to the institution, and in the event of his death in the institution his funeral expenses, as seems reasonable, having regard to the ability of the feeble-minded person, or of the person liable or undertaking to maintain him. Any such order may be enforced against any property of the feeble-minded person, or of the person liable or undertaking to maintain him, in the same way as if it were a judgment or decree for temporary alimony in a divorce case. When a conservator of the estate of the feeble-minded person under guardianship, or in an institution under this Act, has been, or is appointed pursuant to, "An Act to revise the law in relation to idiots, lunatics, drunkards, and spendthrifts," approved March 26, 1874, in force July 1, 1874, any such order for contribution to maintenance may be made and enforced against such conservator only by the court that appointed such conservator and in the mode and manner prescribed by said last named act.

20. When a child is brought before a "juvenile" court as a dependent or delinquent child if it appears to the court, on the testimony of a physician or a psychologist or other evidence that such person or child is feeble-minded within the meaning of this Act, the court may adjourn the proceedings and direct some suitable officer of the court or other suitable reputable person to file a petition under this Act; and the court may order that pending the preparation, filing and hearing of such petitions, the person or child be detained in a place of safety, or placed under the guardianship of some suitable person on that person entering into recognizance for his appearance.

21. On the conviction by court of record of competent jurisdiction of any person of any crime, misdemeanor, or any violation of any ordinance which is in whole or in part a violation of any statute of this State; or on a child brought before a juvenile court for any delinquency, being found liable to be sent to a reformatory school, a training school or in industrial school, the court if satisfied on the testimony of a physician or a psychologist or other evidence that the person or child is feeble-minded within the meaning of this Act, may suspend sentence, or suspend entering an order sending the child to a reformatory, training or industrial school, and direct that a petition the filed under this Act. When a court directs a petition to be filed it may order that pending the preparation, filing and hearing of the petition, the person or child be detained in a place of safety, or be placed under the guardianship of any suitable person on that person entering into a recognizance for his appearance. If upon the hearing of said petition or upon any subsequent hearing under this Act the person is found not to be feeble-minded the court shall impose sentence.

22. When the mental condition of a person under guardianship or in an institution for feeble-minded persons, pursuant to an order of the court under this Act, becomes or is found to be such that he ought to be transferred to an institution for lunatics, the guardian or managers of the institution, or the Board of Administration, as the case may be, shall cause such steps to be taken as may be necessary for his removal to an institution for lunatics under, " An Act to revise the law in relation to the commitment and detention of lunatics and to provide for the appointment and removal of conservators, and to repeal certain Acts therein named," approved January 21, 1893, in force July 1, 1893. And when the mental condition of a person in an institution for lunatics under such lunacy act of 1893 becomes, or is found to be such that he ought to be transferred to an institution for

feeble-minded persons, or placed under guardianship under this Act, the managers of the institution for lunatics, or the Board of Administration may cause such steps to be taken as may be necessary for having an order that he be sent to an institution entered by the court of original jurisdiction for feeble-minded persons, or placed under guardianship under this Act.

23. No person shall be discharged from a public institution for the feeble-minded without suitable clothing and some of money not exceeding $20, sufficient to defray his expenses home, which shall be charged to the county in which the person resides, and collected as other debts due the institution are collected. But the court ordering the discharge may dispense with this requirement if the court, in its discretion, thinks it fit and proper under the circumstances.

24. If any feeble-minded person shall escape from an institution for the feeble-minded, it shall be the duty of the superintendent of the institution and his assistants, and of any sheriff or constable, or other officer of the peace in any county in which he may be found, to take and detain him without a warrant, and report the same at once to the county judge of said county, who shall return him to the institution at the expense of the county from which he was admitted.

25. Each court having jurisdiction under this Act shall keep a separate docket of proceedings in feeble-mindedness upon which shall be made such entries as will, together with the papers filed, preserve a complete and perfect record of each case, the original petitions, writs, and returns made thereto, and the reports of commissions shall be filed with the clerk of the court.

26. The Board of Administration shall keep a record of all persons adjudged to be feeble-minded, and of the orders respecting them by the courts throughout the State, copies of which orders shall be furnished by the clerk of the court without the board's application or upon the board's application.

27. The invalidity of any part of this Act shall not be construed to affect the validity of any other part capable of having practical operation and effect without the invalid part.

28. All Acts and parts of Acts inconsistent with this Act are hereby repealed.

APPENDIX B

Illinois' Model Sterilization Law

Draft of Sterilization Law for Illinois. —An Act to prevent the procreation of the feeble-minded, insane, epileptic, inebriate, criminalistic and other degenerate persons by authorizing and providing by due process of law for the sterilization of persons with inferior hereditary potentialities, maintained wholly or in part by public expense.

Section 1. Be it enacted by the People of the State of Illinois, represented in the General Assembly: There is hereby established for the State of Illinois a Eugenics Commission, whose duties are hereinafter defined, and which shall be composed of three persons possessing respectively expert knowledge in biology, pathology, and psychology.

Sec. 2. Immediately after the passage of this act the governor shall appoint the members of the Eugenics Commission, one of whom he shall designate as chairman. Any determination or order concurred in by two members of the commission shall be deemed an order of the commission. The members of the commission shall hold office at the pleasure of the governor, and vacancies in the commission shall be filled by him as they occur. Immediately after their appointment the commission shall assemble, shall organize their body and shall proceed to carry out the provisions of this act. The members of the Eugenics Commission shall be required to devote their entire time and attention to their duties as herein contemplated, and for their services shall be compensated from state funds not otherwise appropriated; and for the performance of their duties as herein contemplated, the aforesaid commission shall be directly responsible to the governor.

Sec. 3. It shall be the duty of the Eugenics Commission to examine into the innate traits, the mental and physical conditions, the personal records, and the family traits and histories of all prisoners, inmates, and patients of all the county and state institutions for the insane, feeble-minded, the epileptic, the inebriate, the criminalistic and pauper classes, and of all individuals of such classes in private institutions supported in whole or in part by state funds, excepting always permanent custodial cases, excepting also any persons in any county jail pending trial or serving a sentence of less than ninety-one days, with the view of determining whether in each particular case the individual is a person potential to producing offspring who, because of the inheritance of inferior or anti-social traits, would probably become a social menace, or a ward of the state. If after such investigation the commission is of the opinion that a given inmate is a person potential to producing such offspring, it shall be the duty of the commission to make its findings of such persons and record the same in a book to be kept by such commission together with a record of the nature of the extent of such examination and the recommendation by such commission; said commission shall also record its findings and recommendations, including a recommendation of an appropriate type of sterilizing operation to the county or circuit court of the county in which said person shall be located, at least thirty days before the day set for the release of such person from the custody of the state.

Sec. 4. The aforesaid court to which the aforesaid report shall be filed, shall thereupon set a date for hearing of the facts of the case, and shall immediately order that either the person nominated for the operation, his nearest kin, lawful guardian, or close friend, shall be notified forthwith in writing, the time, place and nature of the aforesaid hearing; provided that in cases wherein on account of the mental or physical conditions of the person so nominated, such notification would, in the opinion of the commission, be inadvisable, and wherein, in the same case, the whereabouts of neither of the aforesaid mentioned nearest of kin, lawful guardian, nor close friend within the state be known to the commission, it shall be sufficient for the said commission to indorse the notification statement with a statement of the reasons why such notification was not served.

Sec. 5. On the date previously set for the hearing as herein contemplated, the aforesaid court, shall, with all speed consistent with thoroughness, examine the findings and recommendations of the commission, and shall hear any objections that may be offered thereto. The commission shall be represented at the hearing by the state's attorney, and shall defend their recommendation, and in all subsequent litigation incident to the execution of their duties as herein contemplated, the commission shall have the services of the state's attorney. The court may at its discretion appoint council to represent the person nominated for sterilization, and shall fix the compensation for such services, which compensation shall be paid from the funds from which other similar court expenses are now paid. If after due consideration the court is satisfied that the individual prisoner, inmate, or patient nominated sterilization is a person as found by the commission, namely, one who is potential to reproducing offspring who would probably, because of the inheritance of inferior or anti-social traits, become a social menace, or a ward of the state, it shall be lawful and it shall be the duty of the aforesaid court to authorize and to order the Eugenics Commission to order the responsible head of the institution, in whose charge the particular person nominated for sterilization may be, to cause to be performed on such person, in a safe and humane manner, before his or her discharge or release from the custody of the state, an operation for the prevention of begetting or of conception, as the case may be; and the type of operation may be made a part of the order of the commission in each case; provided that said operation shall not be had within five days after the giving of the order therefor; and the aforementioned responsible head of the institution in whose custody the person subject to a particular order for sterilization may be, shall be directly responsible to the Eugenics Commission for the execution of the operation as ordered: provided that in such proceedings the report of the said Eugenics Commission shall be competent evidence in the proceedings before the said court.

Sec. 6. In case of a decision by the court contrary to the recommendations of the Eugenics Commission, said commission may at its discretion order an appeal to the Appellate Court, and the execution of any such original order for sterilization as herein provided for may be suspended by any judge of the Circuit Court in the county in which the particular prisoner, inmate or patient may be confined, until the hearing and determination of objections to the said order, which hearing shall be had not later than the next special term for motions of the court, and an appeal will lie from the determination of such objections by either party as from an order in a special proceeding. Pending the final determination of such suspended order or of an appeal, the subject of the particular order for sterilization shall remain in the custody of the state.

Sec. 7. After ordering the operation as hereinbefore provided for, any such operation may be performed by any skilled surgeon licensed in the state, who may be designated by the responsible custodian of the person ordered sterilized, and any expenses incurred by the operation shall be borne by the institution in whose custody the person sterilized may be. The aforesaid order shall constitute complete authority for the performance of said operation, and no skilled surgeon, duly licensed in the state, performing the same, shall be questioned in any place or held responsible for the performance of the same.

Sec. 8. It shall be the duty of the managing head of all the state and private institutions subject to the provisions of this act to co-operate with the Eugenics Commission in the execution of their duties as herein contemplated, and to secure appropriate data concerning innate traits, personal records, and family histories and traits of the prisoners, inmates or patients of their respective institutions subject to the provisions of this act, and to furnish said data to the Eugenics Commission at least 60 days before the date set for the release of each particular inmate.

Sec. 9. The Eugenics Commission shall have full authority to make further study of the personal and family histories of persons subject to the provisions of this law furnished as herein contemplated by the managing head of institutions; and in the prosecution of such investigations the commission shall have the right to summon persons and to administer oaths, and shall have free access to all court and institution records of this state likely to be of service to such investigations.

Sec. 10. It shall be the duty of the Eugenics Commission to keep a permanent record of all business transacted by them, including a record of all cases, histories examined into, and of all reports and recommendations made by them, and of all orders made and received by them, and annually to report a history of all such transactions to the governor.

Sec. 11. All records of investigations, examinations, reports, recommendations, orders, and personal and family histories made, entered, or secured by the commission are hereby declared to be the property of the state, and shall not be opened to public inspection except upon an order made by a judge of a court of record; provided, however, that all such records may be used for scientific study by the commission.

Sec. 12. Each commissioner and each person appointed to office by the commission shall, before entering upon the duty of his office, take and subscribe the constitutional oath of office. Before entering upon the duties of his office, each commissioner shall give bond, with security, to be approved by the governor, in the sum of twenty thousand dollars, conditioned for the faithful performance of his duty as such commissioner. Every person appointed or employed by the commission, may, in the discretion of the commission, before entering upon the duties of his office, be required to give bond for the faithful discharge of his duties in such sum as the commission may designate, which bond shall be approved by the commission.

Sec. 13. There shall be appointed by the commission a clerk, whose duty shall be to keep all records of the commission, and who shall at all times be and in charge of, and keep open the office of the commission between the hours of eight in the morning and five in the evening throughout the year. The office of the commission shall be in the State Capitol. The commission shall have power upon the consultation with, and the approval of the governor, to appoint and employ counsel and such additional officers and assistants as it may deem necessary to carry out the provisions of this act, and shall fix the salaries, together with the salary of the clerk, by and with the approval of the governor.

Sec. 14. The annual salary of each commissioner shall be ten thousand dollars, to be paid as heretofore provided, and the commission may also incur necessary expenses for office furniture, stationery, printing and other incidental expenses.

Approved_____, 191____

Notes

Introduction

Epigraph. Goldberg and Goldberg, *Girls on City Streets,* 198.

1. I examined an unprocessed collection of five hundred case files from Geneva for the period 1930–1960 and two hundred discharge cards for the period 1895–1930, as well as business office correspondence, internal letters, memos, and publications from 1895 through the 1950s. Most of the archival material for Geneva was being stored at the St. Charles male juvenile facility at the time of this study. Some material related to Geneva can also be found at the Illinois State Archives, the Chicago Historical Society, and the University of Illinois, Chicago Special Collections. All cases taken from the unprocessed collection of Geneva records located at St. Charles included "Permanent Final Grade School Record," "Educational Recommendations," psychological and psychiatric evaluations, case history, and social workers' notes, as well as other miscellaneous ephemera, such as letters. All IQ scores were based on the Stanford-Binet unless otherwise indicated.

2. Unprocessed Geneva Case Files.

3. Ibid.

4. E. C. Hayes, "Mental and Physical Efficiency as a Sociological Problem," *Institution Quarterly* 7 (June 1916): 182–83.

5. W. A. Evans, "How to Keep Well: Rebuilding a Nation," *Chicago Daily Tribune* (November 7, 1915): A4.

6. Two of the most well-known scholars in the history of "mental retardation" are Noll, *Feeble-Minded in Our Midst,* and Trent, *Inventing the Feeble Mind.*

7. Rose, "Power and Subjectivity: Critical History and Psychology," in Carl F. Graumann and Kenneth J. Gergen, eds., *Historical Dimensions of Psychological Discourse.* For Rose's discussion of "regimes of truth" see pp. 109–11; on discursive psychology see Rapley, *The Social Construction of Intellectual Disability.*

8. Many disability theorists and activists have viewed impairment as something separate from disability, as a prediscursive state of being, as politically neutral, given, natural, and timeless. The separation of impairment and disability is a result of the rise of the social model of disability, which put simply defines disability as "a form of [socially constructed] disadvantage which is imposed on top of one's impairment, that is, the disadvantage or restriction of activity caused by a contemporary social organization that takes little or no account of people with physical impairments." The Union for the Physically Impaired Against Segregation (UPIAS) quoted in Shelley Tremain, "On the Government of Disability: Foucault, Power, and the Subject of Impairment," in Lennard J. Davis, ed., *The Disability Studies Reader,* 187. Though the social model of disability has been vitally important in the disability rights movement and foundational in disability studies, it, as Tremain argues, leaves impairment untheorized.

9. Some of the more recent work on women reformers in Illinois includes: Clapp, *Mothers of All Children;* Costin, *Two Sisters for Social Justice;* Curry, *Modern Mothers in the Heartland;* Gittens, *Poor Relations;* Goodwin, *Gender and the Politics of Welfare Reform;* Knupfer, *Reform and Resistance.*

10. Gordon, *Woman's Body, Woman's Right,* 110, 114–32; Kline, *Building a Better Race;* Larson, *Sex, Race, and Science;* Larson, "'In the Finest, Most Womanly Way': Women in the Southern Eugenics Movement," *American Journal of Legal History* 39 (1995): 119–47; Rafter, *Creating Born Criminals;* Stepan, *The Hour of Eugenics,* 56, 103–11. See also Franks, *Margaret Sanger's Eugenic Legacy.*

11. Kline refers to these women as the "moron" girls and argues that a group of male eugenicists portrayed them as sexual predators and a threat to dominant notions of morality and the prevailing sex/gender system. Kline, *Building a Better Race,* chapter 2.

12. Evans, "Rebuilding a Nation," A4.

13. Schoen, *Choice & Coercion,* 15; Ladd-Taylor, "The 'Sociological Advantages' of Sterilization: Fiscal Policies and Feeble-Minded Women in Interwar Minnesota," in Noll and Trent Jr., eds. *Mental Retardation in America.*

14. Some of the more recent works on eugenics and the *psy* discourses include: Black, *War Against the Weak;* Deutsch, *Inventing America's "Worst" Family;* Dorr, *Segregation's Science;* Dowbiggin, *The Sterilization Movement and Global Fertility in the Twentieth Century;* Dowbiggin, *Keeping America Sane;* Franks, *Margaret Sanger's Eugenic Legacy;* Gallagher, *Breeding Better Vermonters;* Kevles, *In the Name of Eugenics;* Kline, *Building a Better Race;* Kluchin, *Fit to be Tied;* Largent, *Breeding Contempt;* Lunbeck, *The Psychiatric Persuasion;* Ordover, *American Eugenics;* Paul, *Controlling Human Heredity;* Rafter, *Creating Born Criminals;* Schoen, *Choice & Coercion;* Selden, *Inheriting Shame;* Selden, "Resistance in School and Society: Public and Pedagogical Debates About Eugenics, 1900–1947"; Selden, "Educational Policy and Biological Science: Genetics, Eugenics, and the College Textbook, c. 1908–1931"; Snyder and Mitchell, *Cultural Locations of Disability;* Stern, *Eugenic Nation;* Winfield, *Eugenics and Education in America.*

15. Rose, "Power and Subjectivity," 106.

16. Danziger, *Constructing the Subject;* Rapley, *The Social Construction of Intellectual Disability;* Rose, "Power and Subjectivity." On disability studies' "second wave" see Da-

vis, *Bending Over Backwards,* introduction, chapters 1 and 2; Davis, *Enforcing Normalcy.* For examples of the second wave of disability theory see: Brownworth and Raffo, eds., *Restricted Access;* Emens, "Shape Stops Story"; Ingstad and Whyte, eds., *Disability and Culture,* part I; McRuer, "We Were Never Identified"; Smith and Hutchison, eds., *Gendering Disability;* Tremain, ed., *Foucault and the Government of Disability.*

17. Rapley, *The Social Construction of Intellectual Disability,* 2.

18. Ibid., 139.

19. Numerous scholars, journalists, and activists, including those who incorporate gender and disability into their work, have written about sterilization and restriction—by which Laughlin meant immigration restriction. Similar accounts of segregation remain marginal in the literature on eugenics. Mark Haller argued more than four decades ago that eugenic institutionalization was one of the most popular eugenic measures. Haller, *Eugenics.* Yet most authors, with the exception of Noll and Trent, have given it only cursory treatment.

20. Snyder and Mitchell, *Cultural Locations of Disability.*

21. McGerr, *A Fierce Discontent.*

22. Recchiuti, *Civic Engagement,* 18.

23. Gillham, *A Life of Sir Francis Galton;* Kevles, *In the Name of Eugenics,* preface and chapter 1; Paul, *Controlling Human Heredity,* 3.

24. Snyder and Mitchell, *Cultural Locations of Disability.*

25. Danziger, *Constructing the Subject;* Davis, *Bending Over Backwards;* Davis, *Enforcing Normalcy;* Rapley, *The Social Construction of Intellectual Disability;* Rose, "Power and Subjectivity."

26. Davis, *Bending Over Backwards,* 38–39; Davis, *Enforcing Normalcy.*

27. See Davis, *Enforcing Normalcy;* Foucault, *The Birth of the Clinic;* Hughes, "What Can a Foucauldian Analysis Contribute to Disability Theory?"

28. Rapley, *The Social Construction of Intellectual Disability,* 15.

29. W. A. Evans, "How to Keep Well: Eugenics. The Baby Science," *Chicago Daily Tribune* (March 10, 1912): B2.

30. Ibid.

Chapter 1. "Segregation of Mental Defectives as a Preventive"

First Epigraph. Martin, *The Rapid Multiplication of the Unfit.*

Second Epigraph. "Report of Committee on Eugenics," *Institution Quarterly* 6 (March 1915): 228.

1. Edward H. Ochsner, "Some Observations of the Care of the Feebleminded," *Institution Quarterly* 6 (September 1915): 16.

2. "Illinois' Law for the Commitment of the Feeble-Minded," *Institution Quarterly* 6 (September 1915): 8.

3. "Segregation of the Feebleminded," *Institution Quarterly* 7 (June 1916): 33. Rafter asserts that the Progressive Era was "evidently the first time in U.S. history that the body itself was criminalized. Previously only prohibited acts could be punished; now the category of

punishable phenomena expanded to include a condition, the state of degeneracy." Rafter, *Creating Born Criminals*, 47.

4. E. C. Hayes, "Mental and Physical Efficiency as a Sociological Problem," *Institution Quarterly* 7 (June 1916): 180–83.

5. Clara Harrison Town quoted in "How Mental Abilities of Children Are Tested," *Institution Quarterly* 3 (December 1912): 135.

6. Letter from Dr. Edward H. Ochsner, President Illinois State Charities Commission, to Judge Harry Olson, Chief Justice Chicago Municipal Court (March 29, 1915), Chicago Municipal Court Collection, box 4, folder 27, Chicago Historical Society.

7. Clara Harrison Town, "Mental Types of Juvenile Delinquents, Considered in Relation to Treatment," *Journal Criminal Law and Criminology* 4 (May 1913): 83–89; Letter from Dr. Edward H. Ochsner, President Illinois State Charities Commission to Judge Harry Olson, Chief Justice Chicago Municipal Court (March 29, 1915), Chicago Municipal Court Collection, box 4, folder 27, Chicago Historical Society; "Legislative Department," *Illinois Federation of Women's Clubs Bulletin* 6 (May 1915): 28–30.

8. Although the history of turn-of-the-century women reformers has been well analyzed, there remains a tendency among some scholars to disassociate them from eugenics. Most scholars of eugenics, with the exception of Nicole Rafter and Edward Larson, argue that women's ability to shape eugenic policy was, at best, marginal and that women served as the audience for a eugenic discourse articulated by men. For gender and reform in Illinois, see Clapp, *Mothers of All Children*; Curry, *Modern Mothers in the Heartland*; Gittens, *Poor Relations*; Goodwin, *Gender and the Politics of Welfare Reform*. For women and eugenics, see Bix, "Experience and Voices of Eugenics Field-Workers;" Chase, *The Legacy of Malthus*, 111–175; Franks, *Margaret Sanger's Eugenic Legacy*; Hasian, *The Rhetoric of Eugenics in Anglo-American Thought*, (chapter 4); Kevles, *In the Name of Eugenics*, 64; Larson, *Sex, Race, and Science*, 71–79; Larson, "'In the Finest, Most Womanly Way': Women in the Southern Eugenics Movement"; Paul, *Controlling Human Heredity*, 54–57; Rafter, *Creating Born Criminals* (chapter 2); Stepan, *The Hour of Eugenics*, 56, 103–11.

9. Clapp, *Mothers of All Children*, 4.

10. On maternalist reformers, see Baker, "The Domestication of Politics: Women and American Political Society, 1780–1920"; Clapp, *Mothers of All Children*; Koven and Michel, eds., *Mothers of a New World*; Mink, *Wages of Motherhood*.

11. "Looking Backwards," *Illinois Federation of Women's Clubs Bulletin* 7 (February 1916): 29.

12. "Lines of Reform," *Illinois Federation of Women's Clubs Bulletin* 1 (January 1910): 4. On women reformers, see Blair, *The Clubwoman as Feminist*; Muncy, *Creating a Female Dominion in American Reform*; Scott, *Natural Allies*.

13. "Legislative Department," *Illinois Federation of Women's Clubs Bulletin* 6 (May 1915): 28–30.

14. "Legislature of Women Demand Eugenics Law," *Chicago Daily Tribune* (December 11, 1914): 3; "Flood of Bills Marks Close of Women's Congress," *Chicago Daily Tribune* (December 13, 1914): 1.

15. "Legislative Department," *Illinois Federation of Women's Clubs Bulletin* 7 (December 1915): 38–40.

16. In the 1870s alone, the percentage of women among students in colleges and universities grew from 21 percent to 35 percent; that proportion increased to 47 percent by 1920, a high point not reached again until the 1970s. There were thirty-two women lawyers in 1880 and 1,341 in 1910. The number of women physicians in the United States increased from two thousand in 1880 to ten thousand in 1910. The proportion of women professionals in the United States reached 41 percent by 1910 and increased to 45 percent by 1930. In 1900, the Bureau of the Census identified at least a small female presence in all but nine of 303 occupations. Evans, *Born for Liberty*; Filene, *Him/Her/Self*, 32, 238; More, *Restoring the Balance*, 148; Smith-Rosenberg, *Disorderly Conduct*, 245–96; Weiner, *From Working Girl to Working Mother*, 4, 27–28.

17. Moldow, *Women Doctors in Gilded-Age Washington*; More, *Restoring the Balance*, 54–69; Scarborough and Furumoto, *Untold Lives*.

18. Kunzel, *Fallen Women, Problem Girls*; Lunbeck, *The Psychiatric Persuasion*; More, *Restoring the Balance*; Moldow, *Women Doctors in Gilded-Age Washington*; Scarborough and Furumoto, *Untold Lives*. According to More, 2.5 percent of physicians were female in 1900. The percentage of female physicians reached a high point in 1920 at 5 percent, and then declined slightly. By 1940 4.6 percent of physicians were female. More, *Restoring the Balance*, 98. According to Scarborough and Furumoto, 62 percent of women who were members of the APA in 1928 reported that they worked in "applied" fields of psychology. Moreover, 40 percent of women in the APA reported that they did not engage in instruction, versus only 14 percent of men who made the same claim.

19. Clapp, *Mothers of All Children*; Curry, *Modern Mothers in the Heartland*; Gittens, *Poor Relations*; Goodwin, *Gender and the Politics of Welfare Reform*; Knupfer, *Reform and Resistance*.

20. See Clapp, *Mothers of All Children*, 4; Danziger, *Constructing the Subject*; Department of Public Welfare 19th Annual Report (1935/1936): 84; Dowbiggin, *Keeping America Sane*; Hale, *Freud and the Americans*; Kunzel, *Fallen Women, Problem Girls*; Lunbeck, *Psychiatric Persuasion*; Scarborough and Furumoto, *Untold Lives*; Sokal, ed., *Psychological Testing and American Society, 1890–1930*; Tice, *Tales of Wayward Girls and Immoral Women*.

21. Gordon, *Woman's Body, Woman's Right*, 110, 114–32; Stepan, *The Hour of Eugenics*, 56, 103–11.

22. As one popular graphic put it, eugenics was like a tree that drew its material from many sources and organized them into "an harmonious entity." Eugenics, the caption declared, was the "self direction of human evolution." "Eugenics Tree Logo," ERO, MSC77, Ser 10, box 1 (n.d.), American Philosophical Society Library, Philadelphia.

23. "Why Not Improve the Human Race?" *Chicago Daily Tribune* (January 26, 1908): E3.

24. Montague Crackenthorpe, "Parents May Improve the Race," *Chicago Daily Tribune* (July 5, 1908): G5.

25. "Would Eliminate Unfit Humanity," *Chicago Daily Tribune* (January 29, 1909): 2.

26. W. A. Evans, "How to Keep Well: Eugenics," *Chicago Daily Tribune* (December 8, 1912): H4.

27. "Predicts A 'Loveless' Age," *Chicago Daily Tribune* (December 19, 1913): 5.

28. Black, *War Against the Weak*, 75, 76; Dowbiggin, *Keeping America Sane*; Hasian, *The Rhetoric of Eugenics in Anglo-American Thought*; Kevles, *In the Name of Eugenics*; Lunbeck, *Psychiatric Persuasion*.

29. "Defies Eugenics By Common Law," *Chicago Daily Tribune* (January 8, 1914): 2.

30. "May Mate Best of Sexes," *Chicago Daily Tribune* (October 12, 1913): 2.

31. "Are You Fit to Be Parent? Query on New York Signs," *Chicago Daily Tribune* (October 23, 1915): 7.

32. "Super-Babies To Be Studied By Eugenists," *Chicago Daily Tribune* (March 19, 1916): 5.

33. W. A. Evans, "How to Keep Well: New Fashions in Babies," *Chicago Daily Tribune* (October 17, 1915): A4.

34. W. A. Evans, "How to Keep Well: Collecting Eugenic Data," *Chicago Daily Tribune* (July 5, 1914): A4.

35. W. A. Evans, "How to Keep Well: Growth of Eugenics," *Chicago Daily Tribune* (November 2, 1916): 6.

36. Rosen, *Preaching Eugenics*, 74, 75, and notes; Selden, *Inheriting Shame*; Selden, "Resistance in School and Society: Public and Pedagogical Debates About Eugenics, 1900–1947"; Selden, "Educational Policy and Biological Science: Genetics, Eugenics, and the College Textbook, c. 1908–1931."

37. W. A. Evans, "Among the New Books. Lectures on Heredity and Eugenics," *Chicago Daily Tribune* (September 12, 1912): 8.

38. "Says Eugenics Threatens Race," *Chicago Daily Tribune* (December 19, 1913): 1.

39. "Dr. Alice B. Stockham Dies," *Chicago Daily Tribune* (December 3, 1912): 2.

40. "Women See Eugenic Setback After War," *Chicago Daily Tribune* (December 20, 1914): F7; "News of the Women's Clubs," *Chicago Daily Tribune* (February 20, 1916): D3.

41. "News of the Women's Clubs," *Chicago Daily Tribune* (March 23, 1913): H9; "News of the Women's Clubs," *Chicago Daily Tribune* (November 26, 1916): D8; "News of the Women's Clubs," *Chicago Daily Tribune* (December 31, 1916): E3; "News of the Women's Clubs," *Chicago Daily Tribune* (March 11, 1917): F3; "News of the Women's Clubs," *Chicago Daily Tribune* (January 12, 1913): E5.

42. Between 1910 and 1924 the Eugenics Record Office (ERO) trained 258 students, 85 percent of them women, to be eugenic fieldworkers. The majority of the middle-class women whom the ERO trained as fieldworkers possessed an undergraduate education and many of them had obtained graduate degrees. While at the ERO, fieldworkers received an introduction to psychology and laboratory instruction in physical anthropology, as well as instruction in the administration of the Binet intelligence tests. Upon completion of their training, ERO fieldworkers traveled throughout the country, working with medical doctors, psychologists, and institution administrators to collect, sort, and analyze valuable mental

and psychological data. Bix, "Experience and Voices of Eugenics Field-Workers." In 1920, 44 percent of women who were members of the American Psychological Association (APA) reported that they worked in the applied fields of psychology, which meant that they worked in the field conducting examinations and administering services to various segments of the general population. Scarborough and Furumoto, *Untold Lives,* 160–61, 175–76.

43. Alexander, *The "Girl Problem"*; Gould, *Mismeasure of Man;* Hobson, *Uneasy Virtue;* Kunzel, *Fallen Women, Problem Girls;* Peiss, *Cheap Amusements.*

44. Dowbiggin, *Keeping America Sane;* Grob, *The Mad Among Us;* Grob, *From Asylum to Community;* Grob, *Mental Illness and American Society, 1875–1940;* Grob, *Mental Institutions in America;* Kunzel, *Fallen Women, Problem Girls;* Lunbeck, *Psychiatric Persuasion;* Trent, *Inventing the Feeble Mind.*

45. Gittens, *Poor Relations,* 185; Haller, *Eugenics;* Kevles, *In the Name of Eugenics,* 101; Larson, *Sex, Race, and Science;* Paul, *Controlling Human Heredity;* Pickens, *Eugenics and the Progressives.*

46. Breckinridge and Abbott, *The Delinquent Child and the Home,* 145.

47. Alexander, *The "Girl Problem"*; Kevles, *In the Name of Eugenics;* Kline, *Building a Better Race,* 19; Ladd-Taylor, *Mother-Work;* Larson, *Sex, Race, and Science;* Odem, *Delinquent Daughters,* 5, 99–100, 103, 105; Pernick, *The Black Stork* (chapter 2); Pickens, *Eugenics and the Progressives;* Sangster, "Incarcerating 'Bad Girls.' "

48. Wilson, "Chicago and Its Cess-Pools of Infamy and Chicago's Dark Places, Investigation by a Corps of Specially Appointed Commissioners."

49. "Eugenics Remedy for Race Suicide," *Chicago Daily Tribune* (November 16, 1913): 10.

50. Illinois State Training School for Girls, Biennial Report (June 30, 1910): 6.

51. On Amigh, see Gittens, *Poor Relations,* 119; Monahan, *Women in Crime,* chapters 7, 8.

52. "Y.M.C.A. Launches Lectures on Eugenics by Dr. Evans," *Chicago Daily Tribune* (November 14, 1912): 14; "Chicago Woman's Clubs for Good Cheer Spirit," *Chicago Daily Tribune* (November 28, 1912): 13.

53. "The Menace of the Feeble-Minded," Illinois State Charities Commission, Third Annual Report (1912): 4–5.

54. Key, "Better American Families, 1–3," *Journal of Heredity* 10 (January 1919): 13.

55. Jathro, "The Feeble Minded—An Ever Present Problem," *Training School Bulletin* 16 (May 1919): 38.

56. "A National Movement in Behalf of the Feeble-Minded," *Training School Bulletin* 12 (December 1915): 183.

57. "The Slum—Is it the Cause or the Result of Delinquency?" *Training School Bulletin* 10 (October 1913): 88–89.

58. Reeves, *Training Schools for Delinquent Girls,* 246; "The Menace of the Feeble-Minded," Illinois State Charities Commission, Third Annual Report (1912): 4–5.

59. "For Care of a Dangerous Class," *Chicago Daily Tribune* (May 12, 1915): 6.

60. Trent, *Inventing the Feeble Mind.*

61. "For Care of a Dangerous Class," *Chicago Daily Tribune* (May 12, 1915): 6.

62. "How Mental Abilities of Children Are Tested," *Institution Quarterly* 3 (December 1912): 134–35.

63. Ibid.

64. Kite, "Method and Aim of Field Work at the Vineland Training School," *The Training School Bulletin* 9 (October 1912): 82. Kite conducted most of the research for Goddard's famous Kallikak study. See Chase, *The Legacy of Malthus*, 144–75.

65. Quoted in "How Mental Abilities of Children Are Tested," 135.

66. Leonard, "The Feeble-Minded Problem as We See It at Lincoln," *Institution Quarterly* 7 (June 1916): 179–80.

67. Quoted in "How Mental Abilities of Children Are Tested," 135. See also Huey, Backward and Feeble-Minded Children; Johnstone, "What Shall We Try to Do?" *The Training School Bulletin* 13 (October 1916): 142.

68. Quoted in "How Mental Abilities of Children Are Tested," 134–35. See also C. B. Caldwell, "The Classification and Treatment of the Feebleminded," *Institution Quarterly* 3 (December 1912): 10–11.

69. Superintendent's Report, Illinois State Training School for Girls, Biennial Report (1902): 6.

70. Superintendent's Report, Illinois State Training School for Girls, Biennial Report (1904): 6. See Dr. Clara Harrison Town quoted in "How Mental Abilities of Children Are Tested," 135.

71. "The Story of Tin Town," *Institution Quarterly* 8 (March 1917): 24–25.

72. Ibid., 22, 34.

73. Ibid.

74. Ibid., 25–26.

75. "The Situation as to Feeble-Mindedness," *Institution Quarterly* 7 (December 1916): 19.

76. Town, "Mental Types of Juvenile Delinquents, Considered in Relation to Treatment," *Journal of Criminal Law and Criminology* 4 (May 1913): 87.

77. Illinois State Training School for Girls, Biennial Report (1910).

78. Hayes, "Segregation of Mental Defectives as a Preventive of Crime, Immorality and Inefficiency," *Institution Quarterly* 6 (June 1915): 98.

79. Hayes, "Segregation of Mental Defectives as a Preventive of Crime, Immorality and Inefficiency," 98.

80. "Report of Committee on Eugenics," *Institution Quarterly* 6 (March 1915): 228. Illinois State Charities Commission, Third Annual Report (1912): 4.

81. Hayes, "Segregation of Mental Defectives as a Preventive of Crime, Immorality and Inefficiency," 99.

82. "Declares Girls of Poor Stock Often Go Wrong," *Chicago Daily Tribune* (January 31, 1917): 17.

83. Ibid.

84. Hayes, "Segregation of Mental Defectives as a Preventive of Crime, Immorality and Inefficiency," 99.

85. Reeves, *Training Schools for Delinquent Girls*, 246.

86. "Illinois' Law for the Commitment of the Feeble-Minded," *Institution Quarterly* 6 (September 1915): 8.

87. "For Care of a Dangerous Class," *Chicago Daily Tribune* (May 12, 1915): 6.

88. "House and Senate Bills Ready for Gov. Dunne's Signature," *Chicago Daily Tribune* (June 19, 1915): 7.

89. "Feeble Minded Boys Committed Under New Law," *Chicago Daily Tribune* (November 19, 1915): 5. For more on the Haiselden case see Pernick, *The Black Stork*.

90. "Feeble Minded Boys Committed Under New Law," *Chicago Daily Tribune* (November 19, 1915): 5.

91. Caldwell, "Illinois' Commitment Law for the Feeble-Minded," *Institution Quarterly* 8 (March 1917): 69; Harley, "Observations on the Operation of the Illinois Commitment Law for the Feeble-Minded," *Institution Quarterly* 8 (December 1917): 96.

92. Harley, "Observations on the Operation of the Illinois Commitment Law for the Feeble-Minded," 95–102; "Segregation of the Feeble-Minded," *Institution Quarterly* 7 (June 1916): 32–33; "One Year of the Commitment Law: The Next Step," *Institution Quarterly* 7 (September 1916): 69–71; "State Faces Big Crisis in Care of Feebleminded," *Chicago Daily Tribune* (February 4, 1919): 10; "Thorne Gives Figures to Show Illinois Needs in Care of the Mentally Defective," *Chicago Daily Tribune* (February 5, 1919): 6.

93. "State Faces Big Crisis in Care of Feebleminded," *Chicago Daily Tribune* (February 4, 1919): 10; "Thorne Gives Figures to Show Illinois Needs in Care of the Mentally Defective," *Chicago Daily Tribune* (February 5, 1919): 6; see also: Clapp, *Mothers of All Children*; Gittens, *Poor Relations*; Knupfer, *Reform and Resistance*.

94. Superintendent's Report, Illinois State Training School for Girls, Biennial Report (1902): 6.

95. Harley, "Observations on the Operation of the Illinois Commitment Law for the Feeble-Minded."

96. "Illinois' Law for the Commitment of the Feeble-Minded," *Institution Quarterly* 6 (September 1915): 8. Letter from A. L. Bowen to Hon. Harry Olson (March 27, 1915), Chicago Municipal Court Collection, box 4, folder 27, Chicago Historical Society.

97. "Objections to the So-Called Schofield Bill," Chicago Municipal Court Collection, box 4, folder 29 (1915).

98. Maria Dean, "The State and the Child, With Special Reference to the Defective Child," *The Training School Bulletin* 13 (October 1915): 143.

99. Illinois State Charities Commission, Fourth Annual Report (1913): 8.

100. "Illinois' Law for the Commitment of the Feeble-Minded," *Institution Quarterly* 6 (September 1915): 8. Letter from A. L. Bowen to Hon. Harry Olson (March 27, 1915), Chicago Municipal Court Collection, box 4, folder 27, Chicago Historical Society.

101. Leonard, "The Feeble-Minded Problem as We See It at Lincoln," *Institution Quarterly* 7 (June 1916): 175–80.

102. Hayes, "Segregation of Mental Defectives as a Preventive of Crime, Immorality and Inefficiency," *Institution Quarterly* 6 (June 1915): 96–99; Hayes, "Mental and Physical Efficiency as a Sociological Problem," *Institution Quarterly* 7 (June 1915): 182–83.

Chapter 2. "Defective Children in the Juvenile Court"

First Epigraph. A. L. Bowen, "Legislative Provision for the Feeble-Minded: What Should it Be?" *Institution Quarterly* 7 (December, 1916): 68.

Second Epigraph. Superintendent's Report, Illinois State Training School for Girls, Biennial Report (1902): 6.

1. The Juvenile Psychopathic Institute was renamed the Institute for Juvenile Research and became part of the Department of Public Welfare in 1917.

2. Elsie Struble, Court Record, box 92-15, folder 4-75A "Social Work Delinquency," Judge Bartelme Papers, UIC Special Collections.

3. For more on female juvenile delinquency, see Alexander, *The "Girl Problem"*; Devlin, "Female Juvenile Delinquency and the Problem of Sexual Authority in America, 1945-1965," in Inness, ed., *Delinquents and Debutantes*; Odem, *Delinquent Daughters*.

4. For two historical critiques of eugenics, see Kline, *Building a Better Race;* Rafter, *Creating Born Criminals*.

5. Scholars have come a long way in documenting and analyzing America's growing obsession with the "feebleminded menace." Yet the identity of those individuals targeted for commitment remains elusive, they are a "feeble mind," to use Trent's words. In his excellent institutional history of "mental retardation" in America, Trent consistently refers to inmates in state institutions as "feeble minds." Trent, *Inventing the Feeble Mind*.

6. Meyerowitz, *Women Adrift*, 5.

7. Alexander, *The "Girl Problem"*; Peiss, *Cheap Amusements*.

8. Illinois was one of the first states to create juvenile and civil court systems. See also Knupfer, *Reform and Resistance;* Willrich, *City of Courts*.

9. Purcell-Guild was also a practicing attorney, a social investigator, and the "head worker" in a settlement. After the passage of a new set of child labor laws, children had to at least finish the fifth grade. Purcell-Guild, "Study of One Hundred and Thirty-One Delinquent Girls Held at the Juvenile Detention Home in Chicago, 1917," *Journal of Criminal Law and Criminology* 10 (November 1919): 441-76. See also Breckinridge and Abbott, *The Delinquent Child and the Home*.

10. In 1912, Dr. Anne Burnet published a study of delinquent girls at the Detention Home. She found that the average age of her 106 subjects was fifteen years, eight months, and that nearly all of her subjects were sex delinquents. Burnet, "Study of Delinquent Girls," *Institution Quarterly* (June 30, 1912), cited in Bronner, *A Comparative Study of the Intelligence of Delinquent Girls*, 72, 73.

11. Purcell-Guild, "Study of One Hundred and Thirty-One Delinquent Girls Held at the Juvenile Detention Home in Chicago, 1917."

12. "Convention Report," *Illinois Federation of Women's Clubs Bulletin* 1 (January 1910): 5.

13. Breckinridge and Abbott, *The Delinquent Child and the Home*, 76-78.

14. Breckinridge and Abbott, *The Delinquent Child and the Home*, 38, 39, 53, 54, 314-32; Juvenile Court of Cook County, Annual Report (1906-1919); Schlossman and Wallach. "The Crime of Precocious Sexuality."

15. Breckinridge and Abbott, *The Delinquent Child and the Home*, 36–37.
16. Ibid., 53–54.
17. Ibid., 96.
18. Burnet, "Study of Delinquent Girls," *Institution Quarterly* (June 30, 1912), cited in Bronner, *A Comparative Study of the Intelligence of Delinquent Girls*, 72, 73.
19. Purcell-Guild, "Study of One Hundred and Thirty-One Delinquent Girls Held at the Juvenile Detention Home in Chicago, 1917." See also Breckinridge and Abbott, *The Delinquent Child and the Home*.
20. UIC Special Collections, JPA-Supplement I, Case Studies (restricted), folders 7, 8, and 9. Although the cases documented by Hull House workers occurred within the space of two or three years, they are emblematic of the types of cases that state officials and reformers encountered throughout the period under investigation. See Breckinridge and Abbott, *The Delinquent Child and the Home*, 314–32; Juvenile Court Case Records; Annual Report of the Cook County Juvenile Court; Unprocessed Collection of Geneva Case Files.
21. UIC Special Collections, JPA-Supplement I, Case Studies (restricted), folders 7, 8, and 9.
22. In addition to Purcell-Guild, see Geneva Biennial and Annual Reports for the period 1893–1940. Approximately 93 percent of the young women admitted to Geneva between 1893 and 1916 were either American or from northwestern European countries or Canada. Approximately 80 percent were American. That 80 percent included African Americans, who comprised between 5 and 10 percent of the native-born inmate population in any given year. Geneva was incorporated into the Department of Public Welfare when the latter was created in 1917, and thereafter the annual report of the State Training School for Girls at Geneva appears as part of the annual report of the Department of Public Welfare. Demographic figures were not recorded in every annual report issued by the training school, as they were before 1917. The figures reported from Geneva, along with figures from Juvenile Court Records, indicate, however, that the nativity of young women admitted to Geneva remained relatively stable between 1917 and 1940. For example, of the 257 young women admitted to Geneva between July 1, 1928, and June 30, 1929, 250 were born in the United States; 138 fathers and 169 mothers of young women admitted to Geneva were also born in the United States.
23. Of the 2,588 parents who reported their nativity, 735, or 28 percent, claimed to be American, 1,145, or 44 percent, claimed to be from northwestern Europe (specifically English, French, German, Irish, Scandinavian). The remaining 708 parents, or 27 percent, claimed to be from eastern or southern Europe. Breckinridge and Abbott, *The Delinquent Child and the Home*, 57–63.
24. UIC Special Collections, JPA-Supplement I, Case Studies (restricted), folders 7, 8, and 9.
25. Mary W. Pickerill, "State Training School for Girls," in 23rd Annual Report of the Department of Public Welfare, Springfield: State of Illinois (June 30, 1940): 681–89; Elizabeth H. Lewis, "State Training School for Girls," in 24th Annual Report of the Department of Public Welfare, Springfield: State of Illinois (June 30, 1941): 34–41; Elizabeth H. Lewis,

"State Training School for Girls," in 25th Annual Report of the Department of Public Welfare, Springfield: State of Illinois (June 30, 1941): 38–49; Elizabeth H. Lewis, "State Training School for Girls," in 30th Annual Report of the Department of Public Welfare, Springfield: State of Illinois (June 30, 1947): 178–81. The report covers the years 1942/43 to 1946/47—annual reports were not published for 1943–1946 because of the war. Elizabeth H. Lewis, "State Training School for Girls," in 31st Annual Report of the Department of Public Welfare, Springfield: State of Illinois (June 30, 1948): 137–39; Elizabeth H. Lewis, "State Training School for Girls," in 32nd Annual Report of the Department of Public Welfare, Springfield: State of Illinois (June 30, 1949): 209–12.

26. See Knupfer, *Reform and Resistance,* 143. Illinois State Training School for Girls, Biennial Report (1898–1916); Department of Public Welfare, Annual Report (1917–1940).

27. Mary W. Pickerill, "State Training School for Girls," in 23rd Annual Report of the Department of Public Welfare, Springfield: State of Illinois (June 30, 1940): 681–89; Elizabeth H. Lewis, "State Training School for Girls," in 24th Annual Report of the Department of Public Welfare, Springfield: State of Illinois (June 30, 1941): 34–41; Elizabeth H. Lewis, "State Training School for Girls," in 25th Annual Report of the Department of Public Welfare, Springfield: State of Illinois (June 30, 1941): 38–49; Elizabeth H. Lewis, "State Training School for Girls," in 30th Annual Report of the Department of Public Welfare, Springfield: State of Illinois (June 30, 1947): 178–81. Elizabeth H. Lewis, "State Training School for Girls," in 31st Annual Report of the Department of Public Welfare, Springfield: State of Illinois (June 30, 1948): 137–39; Elizabeth H. Lewis, "State Training School for Girls," in 32nd Annual Report of the Department of Public Welfare, Springfield: State of Illinois (June 30, 1949): 209–12.

28. Letter from Margaret Cooper (c/o Mr. G. P. Christ) to Lucy Ball (Managing Officer, Geneva), November 9, 1930. The letter is part of an unprocessed collection of Geneva documents that at the time of this study were being stored in the old industrial arts building at the Illinois Youth Center at St. Charles, formerly the State Training School for Boys.

29. Letter from Lucy Ball (Managing Officer, Geneva) to Margaret Cooper (c/o Mr. G. P. Christ), November 15, 1930.

30. UIC Special Collections, JPA-Supplement I, Case Studies (restricted), folders 7, 8, and 9. See also: Breckinridge and Abbott, *The Delinquent Child and the Home,* 314–32; Juvenile Court Case Records, as well as the Annual Report of the Cook County Juvenile Court.

31. Schlossman and Wallach. "The Crime of Precocious Sexuality," 65–94.

32. Breckinridge and Abbott, *The Delinquent Child and the Home,* 35–41.

33. The disparity between the percentage of men who were incarcerated and the percentage of women who were incarcerated declined over the course of the first two decades of the twentieth century, so that by 1920, the Juvenile Court was committing 34 percent of women and 35 percent of men to institutions. Juvenile Court of Cook County, Annual Report (1920): 9–10.

34. Juvenile Court of Cook County, Annual Report (1909–1919).

35. Morrow and Bridgman, "Delinquent Girls Tested by the Binet Scale," *The Training School Bulletin* 9 (May 1912): 33.

36. Bronner, *A Comparative Study of the Intelligence of Delinquent Girls*, 1.

37. Trent, *Inventing the Feeble Mind*, 73–77; Rafter, *Creating Born Criminals*; Rafter, "The Criminalization of Mental Retardation," in Noll and Trent Jr., eds. *Mental Retardation in America*, 232–57.

38. See Superintendent's Report, Illinois State Training School for Girls, Biennial Report (1902): 6; Superintendent's Report, Illinois State Training School for Girls, Biennial Report (1906): 9; Superintendent's Report, Illinois State Training School for Girls, Biennial Report (1910): 5–9; "Discussion by Miss Amigh," *Institution Quarterly* 3 (March 1912): 185–86; See also Clara H. Town, "A General Survey of the Six State Schools," *Institution Quarterly* 4 (March 1913): 119.

39. "Discussion by Miss Amigh," *Institution Quarterly* 3 (March 1912): 185–86.

40. Morrow and Bridgman, "Delinquent Girls Tested by the Binet Scale," *The Training School Bulletin* 9 (May 1912): 33–36.

41. Walter Clarke, "Prostitution and Mental Deficiency," *Social Hygiene* 1 (June 1915): 373.

42. The Ordahl's study of "delinquent" and dependent girls at Geneva was conducted in July, August, and September 1915 and published in the *Journal of Delinquency* in March 1918. It was reprinted in *Institution Quarterly* in September 1918. The Ordahls examined 432 girls who were at Geneva during the period of the investigation. The Ordahls used the Faribault and Stanford revisions of the Binet-Simon scale to test the "general intelligence" of their subjects. They found that 22.9 percent of the girls examined were "definitely feebleminded"; 19.9 percent were "doubtfully feebleminded"; 24.7 were "borderline"; and 27.3 were "dull normal." Only 5 percent of the girls examined were classified as "average normal." None of the girls examined scored in the "superior normal" range. Louise E. Ordahl and George Ordahl, "A Study of Delinquent and Dependent Girls at Geneva," *Institution Quarterly* 9 (September 1918): 56–60.

43. Addams, George S., "Defectives in the Juvenile Court," *The Training School Bulletin* 11 (June 1914): 49.

44. Emile Renz, "A Study of the Intelligence of Delinquents and the Eugenic Significance of Mental Defect," *The Training School Bulletin* 11 (May 1914): 37–39. Renz's study indicates that the same cohort of young women was being incarcerated for the same types of offenses in Ohio as in Illinois. She states, "The Courts may sentence to the Girls' Industrial School girls from the ages nine to seventeen, the prevalent charges being incorrigibility, disorderly conduct, larceny, street walking, immorality." (p. 37).

45. Mrs. E. Garfield Gifford and Henry H. Goddard, "Defective Children in the Juvenile Court," *The Training School Bulletin* 8 (January 1912): 132–35.

46. Ordahl and Ordahl, "A Study of Delinquent and Dependent Girls at Geneva," 56–60.

47. Walter Clarke, "Prostitution and Mental Deficiency," *Social Hygiene* 1 (June 1915): 373.

48. "Study of Delinquent and Dependent Girls at Geneva," *Institution Quarterly* 9 (September 1918): 56–60.

49. I use McGerr's "associational thesis" when thinking about Progressive Era reformers and experts. McGerr, *A Fierce Discontent*.

50. William Healy, "Criminalism and Mental Defects," *Institution Quarterly* 6 (March 1915): 184–85.

51. Thomas H. Leonard, "The Feeble-Minded Problem as We See It at Lincoln," *Institution Quarterly* 7 (June 1916): 178, 179.

52. A. L. Bowen, "Legislative Provision for the Feeble-Minded: What Should it Be?" *Institution Quarterly* 7 (December 1916): 68.

53. Thomas H. Leonard, "The Feeble-Minded Problem as We See It at Lincoln," *Institution Quarterly* 7 (June 1916): 178, 179.

54. Amos W. Butler, "The Burden of Feeble-Mindedness," *The Training School Bulletin* 5 (May 1908): 4, 8–10. See also "In Memoriam," Department of Public Welfare, 21st Annual Report (1937/1938): 637–38.

55. Laura S. Abrams, "Guardians of Virtue: The Social Reformers and the 'Girl Problem,' 1890–1920," *Social Service Review* 74 (September 2000): 436–52; Odem, *Delinquent Daughters*.

56. Emphasis in original. Tremain, "On the Government of Disability," 188.

57. Clara Harrison Town, "Mental Types of Juvenile Delinquents, Considered in Relation to Treatment," *Journal Criminal Law and Criminology* 4 (May 1913): 88. Clara E. Hayes, "Segregation of Mental Defectives as a Preventive of Crime, Immorality and Inefficiency," *Institution Quarterly* 6 (June 1915): 98.

58. For more on female juvenile delinquency, see Alexander, *The "Girl Problem"*; Devlin, "Female Juvenile Delinquency and the Problem of Sexual Authority in America, 1945–1965"; and Odem, *Delinquent Daughters*. See also Kunzel, *Fallen Women, Problem Girls*.

59. Elizabeth G. Evans and Mary W. Dewson, "Feeble-Mindedness and Juvenile Delinquency: A Study from Experience," *Charities and the Commons* 20 (May 2, 1908): 183–91. Evans was a trustee of the Lyman and Industrial Schools in Boston. Dewson was the superintendent of the Parole Department for Girls, also in Boston.

60. Mrs. Lucy L. Flower and Mrs. Alzina P. Stevens formed the Juvenile Protective Association, which was originally known as the Juvenile Court Committee, at the first session of the newly established Cook County Juvenile Court in 1899. From its inception, the Juvenile Court Committee, and later the JPA, worked closely with the Juvenile Court to direct and pay probation officers and raise funds for new building projects. The JPA also conducted investigations of working conditions, public forms of entertainment, and city neighborhoods, in an effort to assess the causes of juvenile delinquency and recommend changes that would improve the lives of the children that came under its purview. By 1909, the JPA, an organization founded, staffed, and directed primarily by women, had become one of the most prominent children's reform associations in Illinois. Although the Juvenile Court Law outlined a system of probation, it failed to provide for the salaries of probation officers. At the first session of the court, Mrs. Flower offered to raise a fund to pay probation officers and Mrs. Stevens offered to serve as the first probation officer. See "History and Survey of Work," in Juvenile Protective Association, JPA (folder 125a). See also JPA letter "To the members of the board, Juvenile Protective Association Chicago, Illinois." (July 11, 1911) JPA (folder 15). For the underlying assumptions and conclusions of the JPA

studies, see "How to Prevent Delinquency," from the Proceedings of the Two Hundred and Twenty-second Regular Meeting of The Commercial Club of Chicago. (January 13, 1912). Hull House Association Papers, box 32 folder 299, UIC Special Collections.

61. In order to conduct their study, the JPA obtained, through the cooperation of a number of different state institutions, as well as the Juvenile Court and the "boy's branch" of the Municipal Court, the names of approximately four thousand children who had been pronounced "feeble-minded or subnormal by some competent authority." The JPA had three goals for their research: provide an accurate estimate of the number of "mentally defective" children living in Chicago; investigate what was being done for them; and make recommendations for future treatment. John Edward Ransom, "A Study of Mentally Defective Children in Chicago," *Institution Quarterly* 6 (June 1915): 47–50.

62. John Ransom, "A Study of Mentally Defective Children in Chicago: An Investigation Made by the Juvenile Protective Association," UIC JPA Papers, folder 127 (no date): 3.

63. John Edward Ransom, "A Study of Mentally Defective Children in Chicago," *Institution Quarterly* 6 (June 1915): 47–50. John Ransom, "A Study of Mentally Defective Children in Chicago: An Investigation Made by the Juvenile Protective Association," UIC JPA Papers, folder 127 (no date): 3.

64. John Ransom, "A Study of Mentally Defective Children in Chicago: An Investigation Made by the Juvenile Protective Association," UIC JPA Papers, folder 127 (no date): 8, 36, 46, 57.

65. Ibid., 48.

66. Ibid., 46, 49, 53.

67. "3,000 Mentally Defective Children in City, Says Report," *Chicago Daily Tribune* (December 20, 1914): A1.

68. "Amentia and Prostitution," *Institution Quarterly* 7 (June 1916): 74–75.

69. Bronner, *A Comparative Study of the Intelligence of Delinquent Girls*, 1, 86–87. See also Walter I. Trattner, ed., *Biographical Dictionary of Social Welfare in America* (New York: Greenwood Press, 1986), 138–40.

70. Augusta F. Bronner, "A Research on the Proportion of Mental Defectives Among Delinquents," *Journal Criminal Law and Criminology* 5 (November 1914): 561–68. Dr. Anne Burnet had similar results in her study of the Detention Home. Anne Burnet, "Study of Delinquent Girls," *Institution Quarterly* (June 30, 1912), cited in Bronner, *A Comparative Study of the Intelligence of Delinquent Girls*, 72, 73.

71. "Juvenile Crimes Not by Morons," *Chicago Daily Tribune* (August 1, 1916): 18.

72. In 1913, the Illinois State Charities Commission (ISCC) asserted that although the argument that one out of every 250 to 300 residents of Illinois was "feebleminded" may have been correct, it was "unsafe to accept that figure as final." The commission based their conclusion on the fact that so much depended upon the way in which one defined feeblemindedness, and the "standard of mentality" that one used for comparative purposes. According to the ISCC, contemporary studies were insufficient. They had not produced enough "positive, undoubted and unquestioned information to justify definite conclusions and recommendations." The commission went on to argue that the "Moron type," with whom experts were most concerned, presented "perplexing problems when we begin

to discuss segregation and forced celibacy." Illinois State Charities Commission, Fourth Annual Report (1913): 7–9.

73. Ibid.

74. Anna Dwyer, "The Morals Court of Chicago," *Institution Quarterly* 7 (September 1916): 40–41. The age of release for juvenile offenders was twenty-one.

75. Clara E. Hayes, "The State Training School for Girls," *Institution Quarterly* 9 (December 1918): 167–73.

76. "Women Who Are Making Good in Public Office," *Current Opinion* 55 (August 1913): 95. Like other professional maternalists, Bartelme went to college and upon the completion of her degree, used her knowledge and experience to work with women and girls. Born in Chicago on July 24, 1865, Bartelme was raised, along with her two sisters and her brother, on the family farm on north Halsted Street. She attended West Division public grade and high schools. After high school, Bartelme earned a bachelor of law degree from Northwestern University and immediately set up a practice. In 1897, Bartelme was appointed public guardian of Cook County by Governor Tanner and remained at that position until 1913, when she was made an assistant to the judge of the Juvenile Court. She was in charge of the "girls' division" of the court, which was the first of its kind in the country. Bartelme continued with her appointment as the assistant to the judge of the Juvenile Court until 1923, when she was elected the first woman judge of the Circuit Court and assigned to the Juvenile Court. She was reelected in 1927 and served there until her retirement in 1933. Like most maternalists, Judge Bartelme's civic-mindedness extended well beyond her official capacities. She was a member of the Chicago Woman's Club, the Woman's City Club, the Every Day Club, the Cordon Club, and the League of Women Voters, as well as the Illinois Bar Association and the Chicago Bar Association. She also served as the vice president of the National Probation Association. Bartelme's biographer described her as a woman who took a "keen interest in the work of organizations formed to bring about world peace and harmony, and in all work pertaining to the welfare of children." Although Bartelme was, in many respects, a New Woman, the media characterized her as traditional and conservative, someone who approached her duties with a matronly air, much like the traditional maternalists. *Current Opinion* described Bartelme as a woman with a "keenly intellectual face, sensitive, sympathetic and serious." The *New York Times* added that, although Bartelme was comparatively young for a judge, she was a "trifle old-fashioned in appearance," and was "certainly old-fashioned in her ideals and her outlook on life." "Mary M. Bartelme," Who's Who in Illinois. Bartelme Papers, box 92-15, folder 3-59, UIC Special Collections. "Collections Abstracts: Brief Biographical Statement," Bartelme Papers, UIC Special Collections.

77. "Women Who Are Making Good in Public Office," *Current Opinion* 55 (August 1913): 95. "Woman Judge Blames Parents for Juvenile Delinquency," (no title, no date) Bartelme Papers, box 92-15, folder 5-107, UIC Special Collections.

78. "Women Who Are Making Good in Public Office," 95.

79. "Speeches, Memorandum, Problems, No.8," Bartelme Papers, box 92-15, folder 3-50, UIC Special Collections.

Chapter 3. "The Relation Between Morality and Intellect"

Epigraph. Marion E. Kenworthy, "The Mental Hygiene Aspects of Illegitimacy," *Mental Hygiene* 5 (July 1921): 499–508. For a brief biography of Kenworthy, see Bernard, "Marion E. Kenworthy."

1. Chassell had begun her research as a graduate student at Columbia University in 1916, when her mentor, Edward L. Thorndike, suggested the topic. She completed her graduate work in 1920, but continued to study feeblemindedness and delinquency for the next fifteen years. In addition to working as the school psychologist at the Horace Mann School and as an instructor at Columbia's Teachers College, Chassell found time to amass an expansive array of evidence for her project. She examined nearly three hundred studies conducted in several countries and also made her own investigations. In the end, Chassell had gathered statistical data for well more than eleven thousand "feebleminded" persons, three hundred thousand delinquents, and twelve thousand "non-feebleminded" persons. She referred to her study as "one of the most extensive collections of data that have ever been brought together in the social sciences for a single purpose," and argued that it would be of "considerable usefulness" as a reference work for researchers in psychology, criminology, sociology, and education, as well as school and clinical psychologists and social workers. Chassell argued that her study would prove "exceedingly important" both theoretically and practically, because it would make possible "a more enlightened public opinion" concerning, among other things, "the isolation of the feeble-minded" and the "improvement of society through training and eugenics." The scope of Chassell's study and her statistical findings make her work a valuable entry point into the study of popular views concerning feeblemindedness, delinquency, and eugenic commitment during the 1920s and 1930s. Chassell, *The Relation Between Morality and Intellect,* preface and 5.

2. More-complex theories of causation began to make their way into the study of juvenile delinquency in 1915, largely through the work of Bronner and Healy. With his publication of *The Individual Delinquent* (1915), Healy became one of the most influential experts on juvenile delinquency in the country. Nearly a decade after its publication, a professor of sociology at the University of Chicago characterized Healy's book as an "epochmaking volume" that had "wrought a revolution in criminology." E. W. Burgess quoted in Reeves, *Training Schools for Delinquent Girls,* 245. Healy's *The Individual Delinquent* has almost been as influential on late-twentieth century scholars as it was on its contemporaries. Therefore, I do not wish to engage in a lengthy discussion of Healy's text. For an interesting analysis of Healy and *The Individual Delinquent,* see Haller, *Eugenics;* Lunbeck, *Psychiatric Persuasion;* Rafter, *Creating Born Criminals;* Schneider, *In the Web of Class;* Willrich, *City of Courts.* Healy himself noted in 1921 that "new values" and "new standards" had been established within the study of juvenile delinquency and that modern practitioners and researchers were "digging away at the facts as they may be unearthed, the real facts of child life, with the directly consequent development of an altogether better understanding of the causes of the special problems that we [psychiatrists, psychologists, criminologists, social workers] have to meet." William Healy, "In Terms of a Better Understanding of Personality

and Conduct Problems," in Proceedings of the National Conference of Social Work (1921): 82–85. Bronner and Healy collaborated on several studies during the 1920s and 1930s that greatly influenced the ways in which both reformers and professionals approached the question of causation and the possible treatments of juvenile delinquency. Healy and Bronner, *Delinquents and Criminals;* Healy and Bronner, *New Light on Delinquency and its Treatment;* Healy and Bronner, *Treatment and What Happened Afterward.*

3. Chassell, *The Relation Between Morality and Intellect,* 448, 449, 470.

4. Ibid., 488, 489. Chassell found a correlation of .50 between feeblemindedness and delinquency.

5. Cited in Chassell, *The Relation Between Morality and Intellect,* 491, 492.

6. See the unprocessed collection of school records for Geneva for the 1930s and Juvenile Court records. See also Lincoln and Dixon records.

7. See Chase, *The Legacy of Malthus;* Haller, *Eugenics;* Kevles, *In the Name of Eugenics;* Kline, *Building a Better Race;* Larson, *Sex, Race and Science;* Paul, *Controlling Human Heredity;* Rafter, *Creating Born Criminals;* and Reilly, *The Surgical Solution.*

8. Grace Abbott, for example, argued that it was clear that "fundamental changes" were necessary in the treatment of antisocial children if the state was going to reduce delinquency and crime. Grace Abbott, "Five Hundred Delinquent Women," a review submitted to the Harvard Law Review (12/4/35): 3. Grace and Edith Abbott Papers, box 25, folder 11 (University of Chicago). See also Caldwell at Lincoln, Lincoln State School and Colony, Department of Public Welfare, 4th Annual Report (1919/1920): 175–80.

9. Judge Hoffman of the Juvenile Court estimated that 10 percent of cases required compulsory commitment. In Grace Abbott, "The Juvenile Courts," *The Survey* 72 (May 1936): 132, and Grace and Edith Abbott Papers, box 25, folder 10 (University of Chicago). Records from the 1930s from Geneva indicate that compulsory commitments comprised approximately 5 percent of the total inmate population during that decade.

10. Clara E. Hayes, "Our Work as Seen from Geneva," *Institution Quarterly* 10 (December 1919): 116–20. Hayes did not waver in her conviction that Illinois' commitment law and the bill to establish an institution for "adult female offenders" represented "important steps toward solving the problems of deficiency and delinquency." See also George L. Wallace, "The Type of Feeble-Minded who can be Cared for in the Community," *Institution Quarterly* 10 (March 1919): 14–17.

11. Clara E. Hayes, "Our Work as Seen from Geneva." Hayes served as the managing officer at Geneva in 1919.

12. Charles L. Chute, secretary, "Juvenile Delinquency a Community Problem," in *Proceedings of the National Conference of Social Work* (1920): 122–23.

13. Calvin Derrick, "Planks in the 1920 Platform for Community Care of Delinquent Children (Report of Sub-Committee on Delinquent Children)," in *Proceedings of the National Conference of Social Work* (1920): 123–29. See also James S. Plant, "Community Responsibility for Delinquency," in *Proceedings of the National Conference of Social Work* (1934): 335–38.

14. Maude E. Miner, secretary, "A Community Program for Protective Work," in *Proceedings of the National Conference of Social Work* (1920): 140–48.

15. Elizabeth Dutcher, "Possibilities of Home Supervision of Moron Women," in *Proceedings of the National Conference of Social Work* (1921): 272–76. See also Carrie Weaver Smith, "The Elimination of the Reformatory," in *Proceedings of the National Conference of Social Work* (1921): 127–32.

16. Lenroot, "Social Responsibility for the Care of the Delinquent Girl and the Unmarried Mother," *Journal of Social Hygiene* 10 (February 1924): 74–80.

17. This was the original mission of Amigh and other reformers at Geneva. Reeves argues that the "fundamental purpose of a training school is to readjust and re-educate."(245). For Reeves's discussion of paradigmatic shift and shift of emphasis in treatment see Reeves, *Training Schools for Delinquent Girls,* 246–57.

18. Early-twentieth-century reformers often viewed domestic service as a morally protected environment. See Deutsch, *Women and the City;* Schneider, *In the Web of Class.*

19. Lincoln State School and Colony, Department of Public Welfare, 4th Annual Report (1919/1920): 175–80.

20. "Bundesen Asks Special School to Cure Morons," *Chicago Daily Tribune* (September 10, 1923): 19.

21. The service council would be a countywide (Cook County) organization and have no divisions. The case committee, which was one of twelve committees formed, would decide to accept or reject a case and, under the leadership of the director of social service, discuss the problems of girls under the care of the agency. The service council quickly gained momentum and a rapidly increasing caseload. It relied upon monetary contributions from women's clubs and individuals, and became a member of the Big Brother and Big Sister Federation in January 1927. "The Service Council for Girls," United Charities of Chicago, box 16, folder 4 (CHS).

22. "The Service Council for Girls," United Charities of Chicago, box 16, folder 4 (CHS): "The Training of the Big Sister," United Charities of Chicago, box 16, folder 4 (CHS). See also "Woman Judge Blames Parents for Juvenile Delinquency," newspaper article (no date, no page), Bartelme Papers, box 92-15, folder s-107, UIC Special Collections.

23. Sam Ryerson, "The Big Brothers and Sisters Association of Illinois," Department of Public Welfare, 19th Annual Report (1935/36): 522–27.

24. Division for Delinquency Prevention, Department of Public Welfare, 21st Annual Report (1937/1938): 282–92; Division for Delinquency Prevention, Department of Public Welfare, 22nd Annual Report (1938/1939): 227–40.

25. "The Chicago Area Project" and "Delinquents and Delinquency Areas" in The Chicago Area Project, box 78, folder 1 (CHS); "Area Projects," Criminologist and Institute for Juvenile Research, Department of Public Welfare, 19th Annual Report (1935/1936): 422–25. See also Shaw, *Delinquency Areas;* Shaw, *The Jack-Roller;* Shaw and Moore, *The Natural History of a Delinquent Career;* Shaw, et al., *Brothers in Crime;* Shaw and McKay, *Juvenile Delinquency and Urban Areas.*

26. Committee on Methods of Psychological Examining of Recruits; Brown, *The Definition of a Profession,* 111. On army tests, see Chapman, *Schools as Sorters,* 65–82; Chase, *The Legacy of Malthus,* 226–301; Gould, *The Mismeasure of Man,* 192–233; Kevles, *In the Name of Eugenics,* 80–84.

27. Gould, *The Mismeasure of Man*, 194.

28. Ibid., 197.

29. J. E. W. Wallin, "The Concept of the Feeble-Minded, Especially the Moron," *The Training School Bulletin* (May 1920): 47–48. For an analysis of immigration restriction, see Haller, *Eugenics*; Kevles, *In the Name of Eugenics*; Paul, *Controlling Human Heredity*; Tucker, "The Science and Politics of Racial Research." For an excellent analysis of the army tests, see Chase, *The Legacy of Malthus*, 226–301; Gould, *The Mismeasure of Man*, 192–233; Kevles, 80–84.

30. Herman M. Adler, "Mental Hygiene as a Problem of Public Health," *Institution Quarterly* 15 (June 1924): 59; Division of the Criminologist, Department of Public Welfare, 7th Annual Report (1923/1924): 52.

31. A short biography of Adler in Department of Public Welfare, 19th Annual Report (1935/1936): 430–32.

32. Division of Criminology, Department of Public Welfare, 10th Annual Report (1926/1927): 16.

33. William Healy, "Application of Mental Tests in Family Case Work," in *Proceedings of the National Conference of Social Work* (1921): 268–72.

34. Elizabeth Dutcher, "Possibilities of Home Supervision of Moron Women," in *Proceedings of the National Conference of Social Work* (1921): 272–76.

35. V. V. Anderson, "Mental Hygiene Problems of Subnormal Children: In Institutions," in *Proceedings of the National Conference of Social Work* (1921): 367–71.

36. Dutcher, "Possibilities of Home Supervision of Moron Women," 272–76.

37. "Moral Codes and Personality" and Edith R. Spaulding, "Imbalance in the Development of the Personality," in *Proceedings* 4 (1919): 25–45. See also "The Reduction of Feeble-Mindedness (A Few Reflections Concerning a Weighty Subject)," *Institution Quarterly* 15 (June 1924): 73–75. Charles F. Read, M.D., was the alienist in Illinois in 1924, but this article is anonymous.

38. George L. Wallace, "The Type of Feeble-Minded who can be Cared for in the Community," *Institution Quarterly* 10 (March 1919): 14–17. Quote on page 17.

39. For an excellent analysis of treating, see Peiss, *Cheap Amusements*.

40. Rachel S. Yarros, "The Prostitute as a Health and Social Problem," in *Proceedings of the National Conference of Social Work* (1919): 220–24. Between 30 and 50 percent was very common; See also Anderson, "Mental Hygiene Problems of Subnormal Children: In Institutions"; Chassell, *The Relation Between Morality and Intellect*; Emma Lundberg of the Federal Children's Bureau made a similar argument in her study of 320 women under the age of eighteen who had become mothers. Emma O. Lundberg, "The Child-Mother as a Delinquency Problem," in *Proceedings of the National Conference of Social Work* (1920): 167–68.

41. See also Kline, *Building a Better Race*, (chapter 2).

42. By the mid-1920s, Americans were deep in the midst of what one social observer called an "outbreak of psychology." As one historian has argued, Americans had clearly gained a "psychological perspective" by the 1920s. Craighead and Nemeroff, eds., *The*

Concise Corsini Encyclopedia of Psychology and Behavioral Science; Jansz and van Drunen, eds. *A Social History of Psychology*; Kazdin, ed. *Encyclopedia of Psychology*.

43. D'Emilio and Freedman, *Intimate Matters*, 223–34. See also "Sex O'Clock in America" *Current Opinion* 55 (August 1913): 113–14.

44. Bailey, *From Front Porch to Back Seat*.

45. George Jean Nathan, "The New View of Sex," *American Mercury* 7 (April 1926): 492.

46. On Freud, see Hale, *Freud and the Americans*. For the effects of the "new psychology" on experts, see *Proceedings of the International Conference of Women Physicians* (1919); Leonard Blumgart, "The Sexual Life of the Child," in *Proceedings* 3 (1919); "The Health of the Child" and "Moral Codes and Personality" in *Proceedings* 4 (1919): 24–45; Eleanor Bertine, "Health and Morality in the Light of the New Psychology" (5–14): *Social Hygiene* 5 (January, 1919): 1; *Institution Quarterly* (June 1919): 32–38. See also Healy and Bronner, *Delinquents and Criminals*, 102. See also Curtis, *Eugenic Reformers*. See also "Moral Codes and Personality" *Proceedings* 4 (1919); Edith R. Spaulding, "Imbalance in the Development of the Personality," in *Proceedings* 4 (1919): 25–45.

47. Jane Deeter Rippin, "Social Hygiene and the War Work with Women and Girls," *Journal of Social Hygiene* 5 (January 1919): 125–27. See also Brandt, *No Magic Bullet*.

48. Ibid.

49. Jane Deeter Rippin. "Social Hygiene and the War Work with Women and Girls," 125–36. See also: Kline, *Building a Better Race*, 44–48. For more on female sexuality, World War I, venereal disease, and prostitution, see Brandt, *No Magic Bullet*; Connelly, *The Response to Prostitution in the Progressive Era*; D'Emilio and Freedman, *Intimate Matters*; Hobson, *Uneasy Virtue*; Rosen, *The Lost Sisterhood*.

50. Purcell-Guild, "Study of One Hundred and Thirty-one Delinquent Girls Held at the Juvenile Detention Home in Chicago, 1917."

51. Marion E. Kenworthy, "The Mental Hygiene Aspects of Illegitimacy," *Mental Hygiene* 5 (July 1921): 499–508. For a brief biography of Kenworthy, see Bernard, "Marion E. Kenworthy."

52. Rachel S. Yarros, "The Prostitute as a Health and Social Problem," in *Proceedings of the National Conference of Social Work* (1919): 220–24.

53. Lundberg, "The Child-Mother as a Delinquency Problem."

54. Carrie Weaver Smith, "The Elimination of the Reformatory," in *Proceedings of the National Conference of Social Work* (1921): 127–32.

55. Elizabeth Dutcher, "Possibilities of Home Supervision of Moron Women," in *Proceedings of the National Conference of Social Work* (1921): 272–76.

56. Frances N. Maxfield, "The Relation of the School Program for Feeble-minded Children to Institutional Care and to Equipment for Community Life," in *Proceedings of the National Conference of Social Work* (1923): 404–8.

57. Olson was born in Chicago and graduated from Union College of Law in 1891. He worked as a state's attorney and was elected chief justice of Chicago's Municipal Court when it was founded in 1906; he remained its head for twenty-four years. Olson retired

from the bench in 1930 and went into private practice. He died shortly thereafter, on August 1, 1935, one week before his seventy-eighth birthday. "Harry Olson Dies; Chicago Ex-Jurist," *New York Times* (August 2, 1935): 17.

58. "Harry Olson Dies; Chicago Ex-Jurist," *New York Times* (August 2, 1935): 17; "Asserts Eugenics Can Stop Crime," *New York Times* (June 17, 1923): 9; "Scientists See Eugenics Aid in Doing Away with Crime," *New York Times* (July 29, 1923): X3.

59. "Harry Olson Dies; Chicago Ex-Jurist," *New York Times* (August 2, 1935): 17; "Asserts Eugenics Can Stop Crime," *New York Times* (June 17, 1923): 9; "Scientists See Eugenics Aid in Doing Away with Crime," *New York Times* (July 29, 1923): X3.

60. Hickson was born in New York and attended the University of Pittsburgh. He earned the degree of doctor of medicine from the University of Pennsylvania and conducted extensive studies in psychiatry during a two-and-a-half year stay in Europe. When he returned to the United States, Hickson became the director of medical research at the Vineland Training School for the Feebleminded in Vineland, New Jersey, where he remained until he moved to Chicago in 1914. Accompanying Hickson to Chicago was his wife and assistant, Marie Kittner Hickson. "Aided Chicago Court Work," *New York Times* (October 5, 1935): 15; H. Douglas Singer, "The Deranged or Defective Delinquent," in *The Illinois Crime Survey* (Illinois Association for Criminal Justice, 1929; reprint, Montclair, N.J.: Patterson Smith, 1968): 737–810; Worthington and Topping, *Specialized Courts Dealing with Sex Delinquency*, 3–82; Sharp, ed., *A Dynamic Era of Court Psychiatry, 1914–1944* (Chicago: The Psychiatric Institute of the Municipal Court of Chicago, [no date]); Willrich, *City of Courts*, 241–77.

61. Worthington and Topping, *Specialized Courts*, 31–36.

62. "Aided Chicago Court Work," *New York Times* (October 5, 1935): 15.

63. "William J. Hickson, Director, Psychopathic Laboratory, Municipal Court, Chicago," *Journal of Social Hygiene* 14 (April 1928): 242–44.

64. "Intelligence Test for Voters Urged," *New York Times* (January 6, 1928): 11.

65. "Mind-Cards," *Chicago Daily Tribune* (February 17, 1917): 13.

66. "Judge Denounces Hanging as Cure for Criminals," *Atlanta Constitution* (June 8, 1926): 9.

67. "Indict 2 Women in Poison Cases; Below Normal," *Chicago Daily Tribune* (November 21, 1922): 1; Haller, *Eugenics*, 102.

68. Victor V. Anderson, "A Classification of Borderline Mental Cases Amongst Offenders," *Journal of Criminal Law and Criminology* 6 (January 1916): 689–95. See also Lunbeck, *The Psychiatric Persuasion*; Rafter, *Creating Born Criminals*.

69. In her examination of 430 cases admitted and 455 cases readmitted to Geneva between March 1914 and March 1916, Dr. Stone found that 22 percent of the women whom she examined were "distinctly feeble minded"; 18 percent were "border-line cases, probably feeble"; and 60 percent were supposedly "normal." Although she acknowledged the inadequacies of conducting arbitrary mental and psychological examinations, Stone relied upon their results, as well as her own observations and investigation of each inmate's family history, to support her conclusions. Stone, "A Plea for Early Commitment to Correctional

Institutions of Delinquent Children, and an Endorsement of Industrial and Vocational Training in these Institutions," *Institution Quarterly* 9 (March 1918): 60-66.

70. Esther H. Stone. "A Plea for Early Commitment," 60-66. For more on psychopathology and delinquency in Illinois, see Herman M. Adler, "A Psychiatric Contribution to the Study of Delinquency," *Journal of Criminal Law Criminology* 8 (May 1917): 45-68.

71. Jane Addams, "Introduction," in *The Child, the Clinic, and the Court*, 1-2.

72. Willrich, *City of Courts*, 272-73.

73. Bronner, "The Contribution of Science to a Program for Treatment of Juvenile Delinquency," in *The Child, the Clinic, and the Court*, 87.

74. Healy, "The Psychology of the Situation: A Fundamental for Understanding and Treatment of Delinquency and Crime," in *The Child, the Clinic, and the Court*, 45-46.

75. Adler, "Our Responsibility for the Future," in *The Child, the Clinic, and the Court*, 67.

76. Bronner, "The Contribution of Science to a Program for Treatment of Juvenile Delinquency," 80-81.

77. "State Faces Big Crisis in Care of Feebleminded," *Chicago Daily Tribune* (February 4, 1919): 10; "Thorne Gives Figures to Show Illinois Needs in Care of the Mentally Defective," *Chicago Daily Tribune* (February 5, 1919): 6.

78. Cassius Poust (director, DPW), "A Five Year Summary," in 30th Annual Report of the Department of Public Welfare Springfield: State of Illinois (June 30, 1947): 1-27.

79. A. L. Bowen "Seven Years: 1933-1940," in 23rd Annual Report of the Department of Public Welfare, Springfield: State of Illinois (June 30, 1940): 21-37.

80. Ibid.

81. Cassius Poust (director, DPW), "A Five Year Summary," in 30th Annual Report of the Department of Public Welfare Springfield: State of Illinois (June 30, 1947): 1-27.

82. Willrich, *City of Courts*, 244-45.

83. Hickson quoted in *The Illinois Crime Survey*, 795.

84. Cassius Poust (director, DPW), "A Five Year Summary," in 30th Annual Report of the Department of Public Welfare, Springfield: State of Illinois (June 30, 1947): 1-27.

85. Healy and Bronner, *Delinquents and Criminals*, 24, 73.

86. Paul L. Schroeder, "Division of the Criminologist Including the Institute for Juvenile Research," in 23rd Annual Report of the Department of Public Welfare Springfield: State of Illinois (June 30, 1940): 801.

87. Unprocessed Geneva Collection. Mary W. Pickerill, "State Training School for Girls," in 23rd Annual Report of the Department of Public Welfare Springfield: State of Illinois (June 30, 1940): 681-89; Elizabeth H. Lewis, "State Training School for Girls," in 24th Annual Report of the Department of Public Welfare Springfield: State of Illinois (June 30, 1941): 34-41; Elizabeth H. Lewis, "State Training School for Girls," in 25th Annual Report of the Department of Public Welfare Springfield: State of Illinois (June 30, 1941): 38-49; Elizabeth H. Lewis, "State Training School for Girls," in 30th Annual Report of the Department of Public Welfare Springfield: State of Illinois (June 30, 1947): 178-81. The report covers the years 1942/43-1946/47—annual reports were not published for 1943-46

because of the war. Elizabeth H. Lewis, "State Training School for Girls," in 31st Annual Report of the Department of Public Welfare Springfield: State of Illinois (June 30, 1948): 137–39; Elizabeth H. Lewis, "State Training School for Girls," in 32nd Annual Report of the Department of Public Welfare, Springfield: State of Illinois (June 30, 1949): 209–12.

Chapter 4. "I Ain't Had Much Schooling"

First Epigraph. Healy, "Criminalism and Mental Defects," *Institution Quarterly* 6 (March 1915): 184.

1. Della Bolinsky case file. Unprocessed Collection Geneva Case Files.

2. Ibid.

3. Unprocessed Collection, Geneva Case Files. See also Elizabeth H. Lewis, "State Training School for Girls," in 24th Annual Report of the Department of Public Welfare Springfield: State of Illinois (June 30, 1941): 34–41; Elizabeth H. Lewis, "State Training School for Girls," in 25th Annual Report of the Department of Public Welfare Springfield: State of Illinois (June 30, 1941): 38–49; Elizabeth H. Lewis, "State Training School for Girls," in 30th Annual Report of the Department of Public Welfare Springfield: State of Illinois (June 30, 1947): 178–81. The report covers the years 1942/43–1946/47—annual reports were not published for 1943–46 because of the war. Elizabeth H. Lewis, "State Training School for Girls," in 31st Annual Report of the Department of Public Welfare Springfield: State of Illinois (June 30, 1948): 137–39; Elizabeth H. Lewis, "State Training School for Girls," in 32nd Annual Report of the Department of Public Welfare Springfield: State of Illinois (June 30, 1949): 209–12; Mary W. Pickerill, "State Training School for Girls," in 23rd Annual Report of the Department of Public Welfare Springfield: State of Illinois (June 30, 1940): 681–89.

4. Terry and Urla eds., *Deviant Bodies,* introduction. Natalist discourse in all parts of the world has been rooted in culturally constructed notions of race and citizenship. Gender, class, and ethnicity, moreover, have played a critical role in mediating power relations between individuals and groups, and have greatly influenced both natalist discourse and dominant understandings of race and citizenship. See Bock, "Equality and Difference in National Socialist Racism"; Cahn, "Spirited Youth or Fiends Incarnate"; Gilman, "Black Bodies, White Bodies"; Klaus, "Depopulation and Race Suicide"; Larson, *Sex, Race, and Science;* Nash, "Pronatalism and Motherhood in Franco's Spain"; Saraceno, "Redefining Maternity and Paternity."

5. Terry and Urla, *Deviant Bodies,* 2.

6. Sokal argues that phrenology was "the most serious nineteenth-century approach to the study of individual mental ability." Sokal, ed., *Psychological Testing and American Society, 1890–1930,* 10–13; Sokal, "James McKeen Cattell and Mental Anthropometry"; Zenderland, "The Debate over Diagnosis." Zenderland uses the term "measuring minds." Zenderland, *Measuring Minds.*

7. Sokal ed., *Psychological Testing and American Society, 1890–1930,* 10–13; Sokal, "James McKeen Cattell and Mental Anthropometry," 21–45; Zenderland. "The Debate over Diagnosis," 46–74.

8. Danziger, *Constructing the Subject*; Davis, *Bending Over Backwards*; Davis, *Enforcing Normalcy*; Rapley, *The Social Construction of Intellectual Disability*; Rose, "Power and Subjectivity."

9. Rose, "Power and Subjectivity."

10. See, for example, Lombroso and Ferrero, *The Female Offender*.

11. Sokal, ed., *Psychological Testing and American Society, 1890–1930*, 10–13; Sokal, "James McKeen Cattell and Mental Anthropometry," 21–45; Zenderland, "The Debate over Diagnosis," 46–74.

12. Ibid.

13. Ibid.

14. Town, "Mental Types of Juvenile Delinquents, Considered in Relation to Treatment," *Journal of Criminal Law and Criminology* 4 (May 1913): 89.

15. Walter Clarke, "Prostitution and Mental Deficiency," *Journal of Social Hygiene* 1 (June 1915): 369.

16. Danziger, *Constructing the Subject*; Rafter, *Creating Born Criminals*.

17. Tucker, *The Science and Politics of Racial Research*, 72.

18. Danziger, *Constructing the Subject*, 4, 8, 107–13.

19. Huey, *Backward and Feeble-Minded Children*, 9–10. There were many revisions of the Binet test made during the Progressive Era. In The *Mismeasure of Man*, Stephen J. Gould asserts, however, that the Binet test introduced in the United States in 1908 remained the basic means for assessing intelligence throughout the twentieth century.

20. Elizabeth S. Kite, "Method and Aim of Field Work at the Vineland Training School," *The Training School Bulletin* 9 (October 1912): 84. According to Christine Rosen, Kite was fluent in French and translated the Binet tests for Goddard. Rosen, *Preaching Eugenics*, 78.

21. Huey, *Backward and Feeble-Minded Children*, 6.

22. See Danziger, *Constructing the Subject*; Sokal, ed., *Psychological Testing and American Society, 1890–1930*; Zenderland, *Measuring Minds*.

23. Harrison L. Harley, "Observations on the Operation of the Illinois Commitment Law for the Feeble-Minded," *Institution Quarterly* 8 (December 1917): 102.

24. Danziger, *Constructing the Subject*, 112–13.

25. Foucault, *Discipline and Punish*, 184–94.

26. Ibid.

27. Helen Beardsley case file; Unprocessed Geneva Case Files.

28. See school newspapers *Training School Chat* and *Campus Gazette*. See also Herman M. Adler, "Report of the Criminologist," Third Administrative Report of the Directors of Departments, Third Annual Report of the Department of Public Welfare (1920): 346.

29. Unprocessed Geneva Case Files.

30. Ibid.

31. Ibid.

32. Ibid.

33. Several scholars have made compelling arguments for the social construction of mental "illness" and mental "defect." See Danziger, *Constructing the Subject*; Horwitz,

Creating Mental Illness; Rapley, *The Social Construction of Intellectual Disability;* Rose, "Power and Subjectivity."

34. Goddard and Hill, "Delinquent Girls Tested by the Binet Scale," *Training School Bulletin* 8 (June 1911): 51.

35. Unprocessed Geneva Case Files.

36. On sexuality and feeblemindedness, see also Hobson, *Uneasy Virtue;* Kline, *Building a Better Race;* Pernick, *The Black Stork;* Rafter, *Creating Born Criminals.*

37. Unprocessed Geneva Case Files.

38. Unprocessed Geneva Case Files. Ruth was sixteen when she was admitted and her "mental age" was twelve.

39. Unprocessed Geneva Case Files.

40. Ibid.

41. Ibid.

42. Superintendent's Additional Report, Illinois State Training School for Girls, Biennial Report (1902): 14, 15.

43. Teachers' Report, Illinois State Training School for Girls, Biennial Report (1906): 29.

44. Teachers' Report, Illinois State Training School for Girls, Biennial Report (1910): 15.

45. Unprocessed Geneva Case Files.

46. Huey, *Backward and Feeble-Minded Children,* 58–59.

47. See Huey for an example of the type of examinations employed by experts. Huey, *Backward and Feeble-Minded Children,* 173–202.

48. Unprocessed Geneva Case Files.

49. Superintendent's Additional Report, Illinois State Training School for Girls, Biennial Report (1902): 14–15.

50. Teachers' Report, Illinois State Training School for Girls, Biennial Report (1906): 29.

51. Teachers' Report, Illinois State Training School for Girls, Biennial Report (1910): 15.

52. School Report, Illinois State Training School for Girls, Biennial Report (1912): 8.

53. Knupfer, *Reform and Resistance,* 145.

54. School Report, Illinois State Training School for Girls, Biennial Report (1916): 7–8.

55. Department of Public Welfare, 19th Annual Report (1935/1936): 348.

Chapter 5. "How a Girl of the Road Wins Rides and Influences Motorists"

First Epigraph. Esther H. Stone, "A Plea for Early Commitment to Correctional Institutions of Delinquent Children, and an Endorsement of Industrial and Vocational Training in these Institutions," *Institution Quarterly* 9 (March 1918): 60–66.

Second Epigraph. Hauser, "Motion Pictures in Penal and Correctional Institutions," master's thesis (University of Chicago, 1933): 51.

1. Monahan, *Women in Crime,* 128–29.

2. Schneider, *In the Web of Class,* 76–77.

3. Superintendent's Report, State Home for Juvenile Female Offenders, Annual Report (1894): 8.

4. Superintendent's Report, Illinois State Training School for Girls, Biennial Report (1902): 6–8.

5. Superintendent's Report, Illinois State Training School for Girls, Biennial Report (1898): 7. In her study of Geneva, Knupfer argues that Amigh "reportedly ruled Geneva with an iron fist until politics forced her out." Knupfer, *Reform and Resistance*, 154.

6. Superintendent's Report, Illinois State Training School for Girls, Biennial Report (1902): 6–8.

7. Knupfer, *Reform and Resistance*, 144–46.

8. Superintendent's Report, Illinois State Training School for Girls, Biennial Report (1894): 9. Monahan, *Women in Crime*, 122.

9. The *Training School Chat* was published during the 1910s and the *Campus Gazette* was published during the 1930s. See also Monahan, *Women in Crime*, chapter 7; 110–24; and the Illinois State Training School for Girls, Annual Report and Biennial Report (1894–1940).

10. Monahan, *Women in Crime*, Chapter 7, 110–24.

11. See Knupfer, *Reform and Resistance*, on Geneva. See also Alexander, *The "Girl Problem"*; Clapp, *Mothers of All Children*; Curry, *Modern Mothers in the Heartland*; Kunzel, *Fallen Women, Problem Girls*; Mink, *The Wages of Motherhood*; Odem, *Delinquent Daughters*; Schneider, *In the Web of Class*; Solinger, *Wake up Little Susie*; and Stadum, *Poor Women and their Families*.

12. For more on race and sexuality, see Kunzel, *Fallen Women, Problem Girls*; Solinger, *Wake Up Little Susie*.

13. Knupfer, *Reform and Resistance*, 144–46; Monahan, *Women in Crime*, 123.

14. Ella Erlewine, "Presentation of Class," *Training School Chat* 2 (July/August 1916): 6.

15. "Always Be Polite," *Training School Chat* 1 (December 1914): 5; "Keep Sweet," *Training School Chat* 1 (April 1915): 15; "The Emancipation of Woman," *Training School Chat* 2 (July/August 1916): 20; "Debate," *Training School Chat* 2 (July/August 1916): 12; "Femininity," *Training School Chat* 1 (November 1914): 22; "Femininity," *Training School Chat* 1 (June 1915): 3.

16. "Address Given By Mrs. Frederick A. Dow President Federation Committee, Visitation of State Institutions, Chicago, Illinois, Who Presented Diplomas to 1916 Graduating Class," *Training School Chat* 2 (July/August 1916): 7.

17. Unprocessed Geneva Case Files.

18. Ibid.

19. For more on youth culture and institutional life, see Alexander, *The "Girl Problem"*; Fass, *The Damned and the Beautiful*; Inness, ed., *Delinquents and Debutantes*; Odem, *Delinquent Daughters*; Peiss, *Cheap Amusements*; Schrum, *Some Wore Bobby Sox*; Zeits, *Flapper*.

20. Ibid.

21. Stone, "A Plea for Early Commitment," 60–66.

22. Unprocessed Geneva Case Files.

23. Stone, "A Plea for Early Commitment," 60–66.
24. Ibid.
25. Ibid.
26. Ibid. See also manuscript collection for the Illinois State Training School for Girls, located at the Geneva History Center (Geneva, Illinois).
27. Unprocessed Geneva Case Files.
28. Ibid.
29. See letters from Geneva History Center; Illinois State Training School for Girls, school newspapers; Illinois State Training School for Girls, Annual Report and Biennial Report (1894–1940).
30. *Training School Chat* 1 (January, 1915): 6.
31. Unprocessed Geneva Case Files.
32. Knupfer, *Reform and Resistance*, 156.
33. See also Knupfer, *Reform and Resistance*, chapter 8.
34. Klein, "Success and Failure on Parole," 66–68.
35. Knupfer, *Reform and Resistance*, 157.
36. Klein, "Success and Failure on Parole," 66–68.
37. Stone, "A Plea for Early Commitment," 60–66.
38. Klein, "Success and Failure on Parole," 66–68.
39. Stone, "A Plea for Early Commitment," 60–66. See also Knupfer, *Reform and Resistance*, 156–58.
40. Klein, "Success and Failure on Parole." See also Knupfer, *Reform and Resistance*, 157.
41. Hauser, "Motion Pictures in Penal and Correctional Institutions," 36–41, 51, 59–61, 76.
42. Klein, "Success and Failure on Parole."
43. For a discussion of the "honey girl" phenomena, see Hauser, "Motion Pictures in Penal and Correctional Institutions," and Klein, "Success and Failure on Parole." See also the letters in State Training School for Girls Annual/Biennial Reports and in the school newspapers.
44. Hauser, "Motion Pictures in Penal and Correctional Institutions," 36–41, 51, 59–61, 76.
45. See also Kunzel, *Fallen Women, Problem Girls*; Solinger, *Wake Up Little Susie*.
46. Ibid.
47. Stone, "A Plea for Early Commitment," 60–66.
48. Anne Burnet, "A Study of Delinquent Girls," *Institution Quarterly* 3 (June 1912): 47–53.
49. Knupfer, *Reform and Resistance*, chapter 8.
50. Division of the Criminologist, Department of Public Welfare, 7th Annual Report (1923/1924): 53.
51. Burnet, "A Study of Delinquent Girls," 47–53.
52. Unprocessed Geneva Case Files.
53. Stone, "A Plea for Early Commitment," 60–66.

54. Ibid.
55. Levenkron, *Cutting*, 111.
56. Levenkron, *Cutting*.
57. See Stone "A Plea for Early Commitment," and Morrow and Bridgman, "Delinquent Girls Tested by the Binet Scale"; *Training School Bulletin* 9 (May 1912): 33–36.
58. Knupfer, *Reform and Resistance*; Stone, "A Plea for Early Commitment."
59. Illinois State Training School for Girls, Annual Report and Biennial Report (1894–1940). See also Knupfer, *Reform and Resistance*, chapter 8.
60. Monahan, *Women in Crime*, 128.
61. "Women who are making good in public office," *Current Opinion* 55 (August 1913): 95.
62. State Training School for Girls, Department of Public Welfare, 7th Annual Report (1923/1924): 251–53.
63. Unprocessed Geneva Case Files.
64. Hauser, "Motion Pictures in Penal and Correctional Institutions," 36–41, 51, 59–61, 76.
65. Monahan, *Women in Crime*, 129–30.
66. A. L. Bowen, "The Study of Four Girls at Geneva," *Institution Quarterly* 3 (December 1912): 63–67; "The Story of Four Girls," *Institution Quarterly* 3 (December 1912): 28–29.
67. Division of the Criminologist, Department of Public Welfare, 7th Annual Report (1923/1924): 52–53.
68. Unprocessed Geneva Case Files.
69. Unprocessed Geneva Case Files (spelling B, reading B, writing B, arithmetic B, needlework B, music B, and deportment A).
70. Morrow and Bridgman, "Delinquent Girls Tested by the Binet Scale," 33.
71. A. L. Bowen, "The Study of Four Girls at Geneva," *Institution Quarterly* 3 (December 1912): 63–67. "The Story of Four Girls," *Institution Quarterly* 3 (December 1912): 28–29.
72. Monahan, *Women in Crime*, 130. The term "psychopathic personality" came into widespread acceptance in the United States during the interwar years, and was used primarily to describe individuals who scored within the "normal" or "above-normal" range on intelligence tests but still engaged in "deviant" behavior. Much like the concept of feeblemindedness or mental defect, psychopathology was both gendered and malleable. Experts used psychopathology to explain a wide range of "deviant" actions, and they tended to classify young women as "sexual psychopaths" much more frequently than they did young men. See also Knupfer, *Reform and Resistance*, chapter 8; Lunbeck, *The Psychiatric Persuasion*; Rafter, *Creating Born Criminals*.
73. Monahan, *Women in Crime*, 131.
74. Ibid., 130.
75. Alexander, *The "Girl Problem"*; Freedman, *Their Sisters' Keepers*; Gordon, *Heroes of Their Own Lives*; Lunbeck, *The Psychiatric Persuasion*; Odem, *Delinquent Daughters*; Peiss, *Cheap Amusements*.
76. Quoted in "Letters Received from Girls," Illinois State Training School for Girls, Biennial Report (1902): 9–12. See also Illinois State Home for Juvenile Female Offend-

ers, Annual Report (1896): 12–13; Illinois State Training School for Girls, Biennial Report (1904): 11–17; Illinois State Training School for Girls, Biennial Report (1906): 14–26; Illinois State Training School for Girls, Biennial Report (1908): 15–29; Illinois State Training School for Girls, Biennial Report (1910): 22–34; *Training School Chat; Campus Gazette.*

77. Letters from Relatives of Girls, Illinois State Training School for Girls, Biennial Report (1910): 32.

78. Breckinridge and Abbott, *The Delinquent Child and the Home,* 70–89, 314–32.

79. Harrison L. Harley, "Observations on the Operation of the Illinois Commitment Law for the Feeble-Minded," *Institution Quarterly* 8 (December 1917): 101.

80. Harry G. Hardt's paper, entitled "The State Care of Feeble-Minded Women," was quoted in "Care of Feeble-Minded Women," *Institution Quarterly* 3 (March 1912): 179–85.

81. Ibid.

82. For an excellent analysis of the ways in which poor and working-class individuals influenced state policy and procedure and used the state to meet their own needs, see Gordon, *Heroes of Their Own Lives,* and Odem, *Delinquent Daughters.*

83. John Edward Ransom, "A Study of Mentally Defective Children in Chicago," *Institution Quarterly* 6 (June 1915): 48.

84. Manuscript collection from the state training school for girls, Geneva Historical Society.

85. Recent scholarship tends to adopt a concept of resistance that is overly capacious and romanticized, especially Knupfer in *Reform and Resistance.* See also Alexander, *The "Girl Problem"*; Odem, *Delinquent Daughters;* Peiss, *Cheap Amusements.*

86. See Levenkron, *Cutting.*

87. For more on the psychological motivations of cutters, see Levenkron, *Cutting.*

Chapter 6. "Little Savages" and "Psychopathic Deviates"

Epigraph. Richard C. Clendenen, "Neighborhoods of the Nation." Twenty-Third Annual Governor's Conference on Youth and Community Service (Illinois Youth Commission, 1954): 40–45.

1. The information on Geraldine's case was taken from the Unprocessed Geneva Case Files. For more on the transition from feeblemindedness theory to personality theory, see Rafter, *Creating Born Criminals,* 167–87.

2. Kline argues that eugenicists abandoned institutionalization for the supposedly cheaper and more effective method of sterilization. Yet sterilization, which figures so prominently in Kline's study—California performed more sterilizations than any other state—was never accepted in Illinois. Reformers introduced a model sterilization law (Appendix B) to the Illinois Legislature, but the plan was rejected. Kline, *Building a Better Race.*

3. Lunden, *War and Delinquency,* 67–85.

4. For more on the growth of the child guidance movement during the interwar period, see Smuts, *Science in the Service of Children, 1893–1935.*

5. The FBI started to develop a uniform system of crime reporting in 1930, which it issued semiannually in Uniform Crime Reports of the United States. The FBI did not report

juvenile offenses, but it did report police arrests of youths under eighteen years of age for whom fingerprint arrest records had been filed. The Federal Children's Bureau began gathering delinquency data on a voluntary basis in 1923. In 1927 the Children's Bureau standardized its data collection, which it organized by local juvenile court jurisdictions. Through 1945, the Children's Bureau published its data in Social Statistics, a supplement included in its bulletin, The Child. In 1946, the Children's Bureau began gathering data that included dependency, neglect, and delinquency from centralized state agencies rather than the individual courts; it published this data in Juvenile Court Statistics. Despite a proliferation of agencies and reports, delinquency data remained incomplete. In 1954, Juvenile Court Statistics contained information from only 586 courts in twenty-nine states, or 29 percent of the child population. Bloch and Flynn. *Delinquency*, 21–26, 29.

6. Kvaraceus, *The Community and the Delinquent*.

7. "Although the population of our children under seventeen increased only 5 percent between 1948 and 1951," Kluczynski said, "delinquency cases increased 17 percent." "We thought at first," Kluczynski added, "that this was true only in the congested communities, but the statistics tell us that the less populated areas had a greater increase in delinquency. Some of the cities under 100,000 experienced a 29 percent increase in that period, and in rural areas, smaller towns and hamlets, there were increases of 50 percent." Kluczynski's research showed that the number of children brought before the nation's juvenile courts "jumped up again" in 1952 to 385,000." "The Dilemma of Youthful Crime." Twenty-Third Annual Governor's Conference on Youth and Community Service (Illinois Youth Commission, 1954): 5. For more on the contemporary perceptions of the rise in delinquency rates, see Bloch and Flynn, *Delinquency,* 26–33.

8. "Underclass" is a term used to describe urban poor, especially African Americans. See, for example, Katz, *The "Underclass" Debate*.

9. See also Rachel Devlin, "Female Juvenile Delinquency and the Problem of Sexual Authority in America, 1945–1965."

10. Bloch and Flynn, *Delinquency*, 11. The study was, Herbert Aaron Bloch, *Disorganization, Personal and Social*.

11. Bloch and Flynn, *Delinquency*, 11–14.

12. Ernest W. Burgess, professor emeritus of sociology at the University of Chicago, found that, "A high proportion of [college] men admitted felonies including robbery, burglary, assault, and attempted rape. Yet these young men were not delinquents or criminals. At least, they did not so consider themselves and were not so thought of by others." He concluded that, "We are forced, then, to define 'delinquent' or 'criminal' not as having committed a delinquent or criminal act but as having the stigma of being a delinquent or criminal placed upon the individual by conventional society and by the person accepting this role and identifying himself as a delinquent or criminal." Ernest W. Burgess, "Can Potential Delinquents Be Identified Scientifically?" Twenty-Fourth Annual Governor's Conference on Youth and Community Service (Illinois Youth Commission, 1955): 33. In their book, *Delinquency: The Juvenile Offender in America Today,* Bloch and Flynn argued that, "if we are to analyze the causes of delinquency, we must look for motivations that cause children to become chronically maladjusted to conventional situations in the home, the streets, play-groups, and the school—situations in which we may reasonably expect

them to conform to generally accepted standards of behavior. Thus, in approaching the causes of delinquency, we must always reckon with the factors of motivation, environment, opportunity, and community attitude. Of these, environment, opportunity, and community attitude are—in the words of the research scientist—the dependent variables. Motivation is the independent variable, the primary focus from which a variety of human behaviors may come. In acknowledging that motivation is the basic problem, we must recognize that the motivation underlying the wide variety of youthful misbehavior encompassed by delinquency will include a gamut of children's disorders, ranging from the situation-caused protests of normal children (the 'situational delinquents') to the deeply disturbed pathological cases." Bloch and Flynn, *Delinquency,* 16, 17.

13. Frank H. Woods, "Why the Midcentury White House Conference on Children and Youth." Nineteenth Annual Conference on Youth and Community Service (Illinois: Department of Public Welfare, 1950): 80–84.

14. Quote in Smuts, *Science in the Service of Children,* 265. The conference was indicative of the changing times in at least one other way. Howard C. Smith, the youth delegate from Illinois, reported that, "the conference was entirely interracial, which was a new experience for many of the delegates. The sad part about holding our conference in Washington is that Washington D.C., is almost completely segregated. Those young people who were in on the planning for youth from the beginning knew of this fact and were determined that for once in the history of this country, youth were going to take their stand. They wanted to prove to the nation, to the world, and to adults that the part in the constitution [sic] which states that "all men are created equal with certain inalienable rights" is not just a hypothetical term but a real, living conviction in the hearts of the youth of today. And so, in spite of the discouragement given them by many of the adults, these youth secured two barracks at Fort Meyer, Virginia, just across the line from Washington D.C., and there the young people stayed, riding back and forth on buses every morning and night. No one was barred. Regardless of race, color, or religion you were entitled the same rights and privileges as the next fellow. In a very real sense these youth were exemplifying the very thing that the conference had set out to discover ways of instilling in youth: the awareness of the dignity and worth of every individual." Twentieth Annual Conference on Youth and Community Service (Illinois: Department of Public Welfare, 1951): 48. Smuts found that in its 1954 *Brown* decision, the Supreme Court cited the White House conference fact-finding report on the harmful effects of segregation on children. Smuts, *Science in the Service of Children,* 265.

15. Frank H. Woods, "Why the Midcentury White House Conference on Children and Youth," 80–84.

16. *New Directions in Delinquency Prevention, 1947–1957* (New York City Youth Board): 7.

17. *New Directions in Delinquency Prevention, 1947–1957,* 5.

18. The Division for Delinquency Prevention was founded in 1938 largely through the efforts of the Big Brothers and Sisters Association and was the first state-sponsored program of its type in the country. "Youth Services in Illinois—A Midcentury Inventory." Nineteenth Annual Conference on Youth and Community Service (Illinois: Department of Public Welfare, 1950): ix.

19. "Youth Services in Illinois—A Midcentury Inventory." Nineteenth Annual Conference on Youth and Community Service (Illinois: Department of Public Welfare, 1950): ix.

20. "Youth Services in Illinois—A Midcentury Inventory," x.

21. "Local Neighborhood Committees for Youth." Nineteenth Annual Conference on Youth and Community Service (Illinois: Department of Public Welfare, 1950): 68–78.

22. "From the Inside Out; Self Help in Social Welfare." Nineteenth Annual Conference on Youth and Community Service (Illinois: Department of Public Welfare, 1950): 64–71.

23. "Local Neighborhood Committees for Youth," 68–78; "From the Inside Out; Self Help in Social Welfare." Twentieth Annual Conference on Youth and Community Service (Illinois: Department of Public Welfare, 1950): 64–71.

24. John P. Meyer, "Report on a Study of Youth Correctional Services Conducted by the Illinois Legislative Commission on Youth." Twenty-Second Annual Governor's Conference on Youth and Community Service (Illinois: Department of Public Welfare, 1953): 41; "Forging the Links for Cooperative Action." Twenty-Third Annual Governor's Conference on Youth and Community Service (Illinois Youth Commission, 1954): 18–20.

25. Mead, "Coming of Age in 1952."

26. Ibid.

27. Richard C. Clendenen, "Neighborhoods of the Nation." Twenty-Third Annual Governor's Conference on Youth and Community Service (Illinois Youth Commission, 1954): 40–45.

28. Bloch and Flynn, *Delinquency*, 100–105.

29. Witmer and Kotinsky, eds., *Personality in the Making*, ix–xiv.

30. It is no coincidence that the first edition of the *Diagnostic and Statistical Manual of Mental Disorders* was also published in 1952. For an excellent analysis of the DSM, see Horwitz, *Creating Mental Illness*.

31. Witmer and Kotinsky, eds., *Personality in the Making*, 3.

32. Ibid., 3, 4.

33. Ibid., 6.

34. For more on the expansion of dynamic psychiatry and the transition to diagnostic psychiatry during the twentieth century, see Horwitz, *Creating Mental Illness*.

35. Witmer and Kotinsky, eds., *Personality in the Making*, 6, 7.

36. Healy quoted in Jones, *Taming the Troublesome Child*, 72.

37. Definitions quoted in Stagner, *Psychology of Personality*, 4, 5. In 1961, *Psychology of Personality* was in its third edition. It had been previously published in 1937 and 1948.

38. Valentine, *The Psychology of Personality*, vii.

39. Edmund Conklin quoted in Jones, *Taming the Troublesome Child*, 73.

40. Bruno Bettelheim, "Interpersonal Relationships in Behavior Control." Twentieth Annual Conference on Youth and Community Service (Illinois: Department of Public Welfare, 1951): 100.

41. Bloch and Flynn, *Delinquency*. Quote on 84. See 83–114.

42. Twenty-First Annual Conference on Youth and Community Service (Illinois: Department of Public Welfare, 1952).

43. Bloch and Flynn offer the following explanation of motivation: "Thus, in approaching the causes of delinquency, we must always reckon with the factors of motivation, environment, opportunity, and community attitude. Of these, environment, opportunity, and community attitude are—in the words of the research scientist—the dependent variables. Motivation is the independent variable, the primary focus from which a variety of human behaviors may come. In acknowledging that motivation is the basic problem, we must recognize that the motivation underlying the wide variety of youthful misbehavior encompassed by delinquency will include a gamut of children's disorders, ranging from the situation-caused protests of normal children (the 'situational delinquents') to the deeply disturbed pathological cases." Bloch and Flynn, *Delinquency*, 17.

44. Bloch and Flynn, *Delinquency*, 28.

45. Stagner, *Psychology of Personality*, 308. Although there existed a serious and well-developed critique of Freud, especially in the United States, Stagner argued that, "These comments [of the critics of Freud] do not indicate that Freud's view on motivation is rejected by American psychologists. On the contrary, a survey by Myerson (1939) showed the typical attitude to be 'favorable but somewhat skeptical.' Not more than 25 per cent of those responding could be counted as wholeheartedly endorsing Freud's views; on the other hand, less than 10 per cent completely rejected this approach to personality and motivation. The psychoanalytic doctrine, with all its shortcomings, has been a tremendous factor in the growth of a psychology of personality." (325).

46. Stephens, *Lawless Youth*, 31.

47. Friedlander, *The Psycho-Analytical Approach to Juvenile Delinquency*, 5–8, 13, 27.

48. Stephens, *Lawless Youth*, 31.

49. Friedlander, *The Psycho-Analytical Approach to Juvenile Delinquency*, 5–8, 13, 27.

50. Friedlander, *The Psycho-Analytical Approach to Juvenile Delinquency*, 13, 27, 50; Stagner, *Psychology of Personality*, 314–16.

51. Stephens, *Lawless Youth*, 15.

52. Ibid., 43.

53. Bloch and Flynn, *Delinquency*, 151–238.

54. Ibid., 158–75.

55. Ibid., 164.

56. Ibid., 164–71.

57. Witmer and Kotinsky, eds., *Personality in the Making*, 93–94.

58. Ibid., 94.

59. Ibid.

60. For more on gender, family, sexuality, and disability in the post–World War II United States, see D'Emilio, and Freedman, *Intimate Matters*; May, *Homeward Bound*; Meyerowitz, ed., *Not June Cleaver*; Serlin, *Replaceable You*.

61. See, for example, Wylie, *Generation of Vipers*. Wylie's book was reprinted in 1946 and 1955.

62. Stephens, *Lawless Youth*, chapter 3.

63. Friedlander, *The Psycho-Analytical Approach to Juvenile Delinquency*, 114.

64. Bloch and Flynn, *Delinquency*, 38.

65. Monachesi quoted in Bloch and Flynn, *Delinquency*, 38.

66. Dora F. Capwell, "Personality Patterns of Adolescent Girls: Delinquents and Nondelinquents," reprinted in Hathaway and Monachesi, eds., *Analyzing and Predicting Juvenile Delinquency with the MMPI,* 29–37.

67. Hathaway and Monachesi, eds., *Analyzing and Predicting Juvenile Delinquency with the MMPI,* 17–18.

68. Unprocessed Geneva Case Files.

69. One significant change was the marked increase of the percentage of African Americans at Geneva, which more than doubled to 24 percent. Although whites still outnumbered blacks about three to one at Geneva, data from other studies showed that in some cases, African Americans were being incarcerated at rates that actually exceeded those of whites. In their survey of the literature on delinquency, Bloch and Flynn found that, "Negro children figure about five times more often in the juvenile courts in New York City than white children, despite the marked disparity in obverse direction of their respective numbers in the total population of the city. In Los Angeles County, 4.2 percent of the juvenile population under eighteen was classified as Negro, according to a 1946 census, whereas 10.3 percent of all delinquent court cases involved Negro children." Bloch and Flynn, *Delinquency,* 46. In his study of "Negro and White Institutionalized Delinquents," Sidney Axelrad found that African American children were consistently committed to correctional institutions at earlier ages than whites and for less serious offenses than whites. Sidney Axelrod, "Negro and White Institutionalized Delinquents," *American Journal of Sociology* 57 (1952): 569–74.

70. Unprocessed Geneva Case Files.

71. Bloch and Flynn, *Delinquency,* 34–44.

72. Ibid., 115–22.

73. Unprocessed Geneva Case Files.

74. See above note 29.

75. For more on the growth of the child guidance movement during the interwar period, see Jones, *Taming the Troublesome Child;* Smuts, *Science in the Service of Children, 1893–1935.*

76. For more on mother blaming, see Jones, *Taming the Troublesome Child,* chapter 7, "The Critique of Motherhood."

77. See, for example, Horwitz, *Creating Mental Illness.*

Epilogue

1. Schaffner, *Girls in Trouble with the Law.*

2. Chesney-Lind and Sheldon, *Girls Delinquency, and Juvenile Justice;* Schaffner, *Girls in Trouble with the Law;* Zahn, ed., *The Delinquent Girl.*

3. Darrell Steffensmeier and Jennifer Schwartz, "Trends in Girls' Delinquency and the Gender Gap," in Zahn, ed., *The Delinquent Girl,* 50–83.

4. Barry C. Feld, "Girls in the Juvenile Justice System," in Zahn, ed., *The Delinquent Girl,* 225–64

5. Feld, "Girls in the Juvenile Justice System"; Steffensmeier and Schwartz, "Trends in Girls' Delinquency and the Gender Gap."

6. Feld, "Girls in the Juvenile Justice System."

7. Ibid.
8. Chesney-Lind and Sheldon, *Girls Delinquency, and Juvenile Justice*, 6.
9. See, for example, Horwitz.
10. Diana Fishbein, Shari Miller, Donna Marie Winn, and Gayle Dakof, "Biopsychological Factors, Gender, and Delinquency," in Zahn, ed., *The Delinquent Girl*, 84–106.
11. Horwitz, *Creating Mental Illness*, 213.
12. Feld, "Girls in the Juvenile Justice System"; Fishbein, Miller, Winn, and Dakof, "Biopsychological Factors, Gender, and Delinquency."
13. Feld, "Girls in the Juvenile Justice System," 261.

Appendix A. Illinois' Involuntary Commitment Law

Reprinted in "Illinois' Law for the Commitment of the Feeble-Minded," *Institution Quarterly* 6 (September 1915): 8–16.

Appendix B. Illinois' Model Sterilization Law

Reprinted in "Courts—Laws," *Journal of Criminal Law and Criminology* 7 (November 1916): 611–14.

Selected Bibliography

Manuscript and Archival Collections

ARCHIVES, AMERICAN PHILOSOPHICAL SOCIETY LIBRARY, PHILADELPHIA

Papers of the American Eugenics Society

CHICAGO HISTORICAL SOCIETY

Chicago Area Project Records, 1920–1972
Chicago Council of Social Agencies, 1928–1935
Chicago Municipal Court Papers
Chicago Women's Club Meeting Records, 1898–1902
United Charities of Chicago Records, 1867–1971
Service Council for Girls (restricted)
Welfare Council of Metropolitan Chicago Records

COOK COUNTY CIRCUIT COURT ARCHIVES, DALEY CENTER, CHICAGO

Juvenile Court Case Files, 1899–1926 (restricted)
Proceedings in Feeblemindedness, 1915–1936 (restricted)

GENEVA HISTORICAL SOCIETY

State Training School for Girls Papers

HAROLD WASHINGTON PUBLIC LIBRARY, MUNICIPAL REFERENCE COLLECTION, CHICAGO

Chicago Municipal Court Annual Report, 1906–1935
Cook County Juvenile Court Annual Report, 1901–1926
Cook County Juvenile Court Investigation, 1911
Cook County Municipal Court Annual Report, 1907–1917

ILLINOIS STATE ARCHIVES, SPRINGFIELD

Board of Administration Records, 1909–1917
Department of Public Welfare Records, 1917–1940
Lincoln Developmental Center (formerly Lincoln State School and Colony for the Feebleminded) Records, 1865–1930
Case Histories (restricted)
Institute for Juvenile Research Administrative Records, 1925–1940

ILLINOIS STATE LIBRARY, SPRINGFIELD

Campus Gazette (State Training School for Girls school newspaper), 1930s
Illinois State Charities Commission Annual Report, 1911–1913 and 1915
Illinois State Home for Juvenile Female Offenders Annual Report, 1894 and 1896
Illinois State Home for Juvenile Female Offenders Biennial Report, 1898
Illinois State Training School for Girls (formerly the State Home for Juvenile Female Offenders) Biennial Report, 1902–1916
Training School Chat (State Training School for Girls school newspaper), 1911–1917

NORTHWESTERN UNIVERSITY ARCHIVES

Harry Olson Papers

ST. CHARLES ILLINOIS YOUTH CENTER (FORMERLY THE ILLINOIS STATE TRAINING SCHOOL FOR BOYS, ST. CHARLES)

Unprocessed Collection of School Records for the Illinois State Training School for Girls, 1893–1973 (incomplete)

UNIVERSITY OF ARIZONA, SCIENCE LIBRARY, TUCSON

Proceedings of the International Conference of Women Physicians, 1919

UNIVERSITY OF ARIZONA, MAIN LIBRARY, TUCSON

Annual Conference on Youth and Community Service: Annual Conference on Delinquency Prevention, Sponsored by the Division for Delinquency Prevention, in Cooperation with the Big Brothers and Big Sisters Association of Illinois and the Department of Public Welfare, 1933–1953

UNIVERSITY OF CHICAGO, SPECIAL COLLECTIONS

Chicago Committee of Fifteen Papers
Chicago School of Civics and Philanthropy Collection
Papers of Edith and Grace Abbott
Papers of Sophonisba B. Breckinridge

UNIVERSITY OF CHICAGO, REGENSTEIN LIBRARY

Chicago Home for Girls Annual Report, 1916–1930
Chicago Refuge for Girls Annual Report, 1907–1915
Erring Women's Refuge of Chicago Annual Report, 1896–1906

UNIVERSITY OF ILLINOIS AT CHICAGO, SPECIAL COLLECTIONS

Hull House Bulletin
Hull House Association Records
Illinois Children's Home and Aid Society Papers
Juvenile Protective Association Papers
Case Studies (restricted)
Papers of Mary Bartelme
Jane Addams Papers

UNIVERSITY OF ILLINOIS, URBANA-CHAMPAIGN

Conference on Youth and Community Service (Session Summaries) 1934–1962
Department of Public Welfare Annual Report, 1917–1959

Journals and Newspapers

American Historical Review
American Journal of Sociology
American Mercury
American Youth
Atlanta Constitution
California History
Charities and Commons
Chicago Daily Tribune
Current History
Current Opinion
Eugenical News / Eugenics Quarterly
Eugenics
Good Housekeeping
Harper's
History and Philosophy of the Life Sciences
Illinois Federation of Women's Clubs Bulletin
Institution Quarterly
Journal of Abnormal and Social Psychology
Journal of American History
Journal of Criminal Law and Criminology
Journal of Educational Administration and History
Journal of Heredity
Journal of Historical Sociology
Journal of the History of Sexuality
Journal of Home Economics
Journal of Juvenile Research / Journal of Delinquency
Journal of Sexuality
Journal of Social History
Journal of Social Hygiene

Journal of Women's History
Ladies' Home Journal
McClure's Magazine
New Left Review
New Republic
New York Times
Newsweek
Psychological Bulletin
Psychological Review
Race & Class
Review of Reviews
School and Society
Science
Scientific American
Scientific Monthly
Social Forces
Social Politics
Social Service Review
Social Studies of Science
Sociological Inquiry
Survey
Teachers College Record
Time
Training School Bulletin
Welfare Bulletin (formerly *Institution Quarterly*)
World's Work

Unpublished Sources

Borodkin, Mildred Esther. "Healy's Contributions to the Study of the Causal Factors of Juvenile Delinquency." PhD diss., University of Arizona, 1950.

Corman, Bertha. "Study of 446 Delinquent Girls with Institutional Experience." Master's thesis, University of Chicago, 1923.

Curtis, Patrick A. "Eugenic Reformers, Cultural Perceptions of Dependent Populations, and the Care of the Feebleminded in Illinois." PhD diss., University of Illinois, Chicago, 1983.

Elks, Martin A. "Visual Rhetoric: Photographs of the Feeble-Minded During the Eugenics Era, 1900–1930." PhD diss., Syracuse University, 1992.

Hauser, Philip Morris. "Motion Pictures in Penal and Correctional Institutions: A Study of the Reactions of Prisoners to Movies." Master's thesis, University of Chicago, 1933.

Kavounas, Margaret J. "Feeblemindedness and Prostitution: The Laboratory of Social Hygiene's Influence on Progressive Era Prostitution Reform." Master's thesis, Saint Lawrence College, 1992.

Klein, Charlotte Ruth. "Success and Failure on Parole: A Study of 160 Girls Paroled from the State Training School at Geneva, Illinois." Master's thesis, University of Chicago, 1935.
Linehan, Mary. "Vicious Circle: Prostitution, Reform and Public Policy in Chicago, 1830–1930." PhD diss., University of Notre Dame, 1991.
Mehler, Barry Alan. "A History of the American Eugenics Society, 1921–1940." PhD diss., University of Illinois, Urbana-Champaign, 1988.

Published Sources

Abrams, Laura S. "Guardians of Virtue: The Social Reformers and the 'Girl Problem,' 1890–1920." *Social Service Review* 74 (September 2000): 436–52.
Addams, Jane. *The Child, the Clinic and the Court.* New York: New Republic, 1927.
———. *The Spirit of Youth and the City Streets.* New York: Macmillan, 1909.
Alexander, Ruth M. *The "Girl Problem": Female Sexual Delinquency in New York, 1900–1930.* Ithaca, N.Y.: Cornell University Press, 1995.
Axelrod, Sidney. "Negro and White Institutionalized Delinquents." *American Journal of Sociology* 57 (1952): 569–74.
Bailey, Beth L. *From Front Porch to Back Seat: Courtship in Twentieth Century America.* Baltimore: Johns Hopkins University Press, 1988.
Baker, Paula. "The Domestication of Politics: Women and American Political Society, 1780–1920." In *Women, the State, and Welfare,* edited by Linda Gordon, 55–91. Madison: University of Wisconsin Press, 1990.
Barkan, Elazar. *The Retreat of Scientific Racism: Changing Concepts of Race in Britain and the United States Between the World Wars.* Cambridge, U.K.: Cambridge University Press, 1992.
Beard, Belle Boone. *Juvenile Probation: An Analysis of the Case Records of Five Hundred Children Studied at the Judge Baker Guidance Clinic and Placed on Probation in the Juvenile Court of Boston.* New York: American, 1934.
Becker, Peter, and Richard F. Wetzell, eds. *Criminals and Their Scientists: the History of Criminology in International Perspective.* New York: Cambridge University Press, 2006.
Bederman, Gail. *Manliness and Civilization: A Cultural History of Gender and Race in the United States, 1880–1917.* Chicago: University of Chicago Press, 1995.
Benson, Susan P. *Counter Cultures: Saleswomen, Managers, and Customers in American Department Stores, 1890–1940.* Urbana: University of Illinois Press, 1988.
Bernard, "Marion E. Kenworthy: Trailblazer for Psychiatric Social Work." In *Women Physicians in Leadership Roles,* edited by Leah J. Dickstein and Carol C. Nadelson, 79–85. Washington, D.C.: American Psychiatric Press, 1986.
Bix, Amy Sue. "Experience and Voices of Eugenics Field-Workers: 'Women's Work' in Biology." *Social Studies of Science* 27 (1997): 625–68.
Black, Edwin. *War Against the Weak: Eugenics and America's Campaign to Create a Master Race.* New York: Four Walls Eight Windows, 2003.

Blair, Karen J. *The Clubwoman as Feminist: True Womanhood Redefined, 1868–1914.* New York: Holmes & Meier, Publishers, 1980.

Bland, Lucy, and Laura Doan, eds. *Sexology in Culture: Labeling Bodies and Desires.* Chicago: University of Chicago Press, 1998.

Bloch, Herbert Aaron, and Frank T. Flynn. *Delinquency: The Juvenile Offender in America Today.* New York: Random House, 1956.

Bock, Gisela. "Racism and Sexism in Nazi Germany." In *When Biology Became Destiny: Women in Weimar and Nazi Germany,* edited by Renate Bridenthal et al. New York: Monthly Review Press, 1984.

———. "Equality and Difference in National Socialist Racism." In *Feminism and History,* edited by Linda Gordon, 267–90. New York: Oxford University Press, 1996.

Bott, Helen McMurchie. *Adult Attitudes to Children's Misdemeanours.* Toronto: University of Toronto Press, 1937.

Bowman, Paul Hoover, et al. *Mobilizing Community Resources for Youth: Identification and Treatment of Maladjusted, Delinquent, and Gifted Children.* Chicago: University of Chicago Press, 1956.

Brandt, Allan M. *No Magic Bullet: A Social History of Venereal Disease in the United States Since 1880.* New York: Oxford University Press, 1985.

Breckinridge, Sophonisba P. *Family Welfare Work in a Metropolitan Community: Selected Case Records.* Chicago: University of Chicago Press, 1924.

Breckinridge, Sophonisba P., and Edith Abbott. *The Delinquent Child and the Home: A Study of the Delinquent Wards of the Juvenile Court of Chicago.* New York: Survey Associates, 1916.

Brigham, Carl C. *A Study of American Intelligence.* Princeton, N.J.: Princeton University Press, 1923. Repr. Millwood, N.Y.: Kraus Reprint Co., 1975.

Brill, Jeanette Goodman, and E. George Payne. *The Adolescent Court and Crime Prevention.* New York: Pitman, 1938.

Broberg, Gunnar, and Nils Roll-Hansen. *Eugenics and the Welfare State: Sterilization Policy in Denmark, Sweden, Norway, and Finland.* East Lansing: Michigan State University Press, 1996.

Bronner, Augusta F. *A Comparative Study of the Intelligence of Delinquent Girls.* New York: Teachers College, Columbia University, 1914.

Brown, JoAnne. *The Definition of a Profession: The Authority of Metaphor in the History of Intelligence Testing, 1890–1930.* Princeton, N.J.: Princeton University Press, 1992.

Brownworth, V. A., and S. Raffo, eds. *Restricted Access: Lesbians on Disability.* Seattle: Seal Press, 1999.

Bruinius, Harry. *Better for All the World: The Secret History of Forced Sterilization and America's Quest for Racial Purity.* New York: Alfred A. Knopf, 2006.

Bucur, Maria. *Eugenics and Modernization in Interwar Romania.* Pittsburgh: University of Pittsburgh Press, 2002.

Burt, Cyril Lodowic. *The Subnormal Mind.* London: Oxford University Press, 1955.

Cahn, Susan. "Spirited Youth or Fiends Incarnate: The Samarcand Arson Case and Female Adolescence in the American South." *Journal of Women's History* 9 (December 1998): 152–80.

Capshew, James H. *Psychologists on the March: Science, Practice, and Professional Identity in America, 1929–1969*. Cambridge, U.K.: Cambridge University Press, 1999.

Carlson, Elof Axel. *The Unfit: A History of a Bad Idea*. Cold Spring Harbor, N.Y.: Cold Spring Harbor Laboratory Press, 2001.

Carr, Lowell Julliard. *Delinquency Control*. New York: Harper and Brothers, 1941.

Castles, Katherne. "Quiet Eugenics: Sterilization in North Carolina's Institutions for the Mentally Retarded, 1945–1965." *Journal of Southern History* 68 (November 2002): 849–78.

Caudill, Edward. *Darwinian Myths: The Legends and Misuses of a Theory*. Knoxville: University of Tennessee Press, 1997.

Cavan, Ruth S., and Katherine H. Ranck. *The Family and the Depression: A Study of One Hundred Chicago Families*. Chicago: University of Chicago Press, 1938.

Chase, Allan. *The Legacy of Malthus: The Social Costs of the New Scientific Racism*. New York: Knopf, Random House, 1976.

Chassell, Clara Frances. *The relation between morality and intellect; a compendium of evidence contributed by psychology, criminology, and sociology*. New York: Teachers College, Columbia University, 1935.

Chesney-Lind, Meda, and Randall G. Shelden. *Girls Delinquency, and Juvenile Justice*. 2nd ed. Belmont, Calif.: West/Wadsworth, 1998.

Chung, Yuehtsen Juliette. *Struggle for National Survival: Eugenics in Sino-Japanese Contexts, 1896–1945*. New York: Routledge, 2002.

Clapp, Elizabeth J. *Mothers of All Children: Women Reformers and the Rise of Juvenile Courts in Progressive Era America*. University Park: Pennsylvania State University Press, 1998.

Clark, Robert Emmet. *Children and the Courts in New Mexico*. Albuquerque: University of New Mexico Press, 1953.

Cobble, Dorothy S. *Dishing It Out: Waitresses and Their Unions in the Twentieth Century*. Urbana: University of Illinois Press, 1991.

Cohen, Frank J. *Children in Trouble, An Experiment in Institutional Child Care*. New York: Norton, 1952.

Collins, Alan F. "The Enduring Appeal of Physiognomy: Physical Appearance as a Sign of Temperament, Character, and Intelligence." *History of Psychology* 2 (November 1999): 251–76.

Connelly, Mark. *The Response to Prostitution in the Progressive Era*. Chapel Hill: University of North Carolina Press, 1980.

Costin, Lela B. *Two Sisters for Social Justice: A Biography of Grace and Edith Abbott*. Urbana: University of Illinois Press, 1983.

Costin, Lela B., Howard Jacob Karger, and David Stoesz. *The Politics of Child Abuse in America*. New York: Oxford University Press, 1996.

Craighead, W. Edward, and Charles B. Nemeroff, eds. *The Concise Corsini Encyclopedia of Psychology and Behavioral Science*. 3rd ed. Hoboken, N.J.: John Wiley & Sons, 2004.

Cressey, Paul G. *The Taxi-Dance Hall: A Sociological Study in Commercial Recreation and City Life*. Chicago: University of Chicago Press, 1932.

Crow, Lester Donald, and Alice Crow. *Our Teen-age Boys and Girls: Suggestions for Parents, Teachers, and other Youth Leaders.* New York: McGraw-Hill, 1945.
Curry, Lynne. *Modern Mothers in the Heartland: Gender, Health, and Progress in Illinois, 1900–1930.* Columbus: Ohio State University Press, 1999.
Daley, Mary Wood. "Delinquents and Sex-Education." *Journal of Social Hygiene* 10 (May 1924): 278–83.
D'Antonio, Michael, *The State Boys Rebellion.* New York: Simon & Schuster Paperbacks, 2004.
Danziger, Kurt. *Constructing the Subject: Historical Origins of Psychological Research.* Cambridge, U.K.: Cambridge University Press, 1990.
Darwin, Leonard. *What is Eugenics?* London: Watts, 1928.
Davis, Lennard J. *Bending Over Backwards: Disability, Dismodernism, and Other Difficult Positions.* New York: New York University Press, 2002.
———. *Enforcing Normalcy: Disability, Deafness, and the Body.* New York: Verso, 1995.
De Francis, Vincent. *Child Protective Service in the United States, Reporting a Nationwide Survey.* Denver: American Humane Association, 1956.
Degler, Carl V. *In Search of Human Nature: The Decline and Revival of Darwinism in American Social Thought.* New York: Oxford University Press, 1991.
D'Emilio, John, and Estelle B. Freedman. *Intimate Matters: A History of Sexuality in America.* 2nd ed. Chicago: University of Chicago Press, 1997.
Deutsch, Nathaniel. *Inventing America's "Worst" Family: Eugenics, Islam, and the Fall and Rise of the Tribe of Ishmael.* Berkeley: University of California Press, 2009.
Deutsch, Sarah. *Women and the City: Gender, Space, and Power in Boston, 1870–1940.* Oxford: Oxford University Press, 2000.
Devlin, Rachel. "Female Juvenile Delinquency and the Problem of Sexual Authority in America, 1945–1965." In *Delinquents and Debutantes: Twentieth-Century American Girls' Cultures,* edited by Sherrie A. Inness, 83–105. New York: New York University Press, 1998.
Diamond, Solomon. "Francis Galton and American Psychology." In *Psychology: Theoretical-Historical Perspectives,* edited by Robert W. Rieber and Kurt D. Salzinger, 45–55. Washington, D.C.: American Psychological Association, 1998.
Dikotter, Frank. "Race Culture: Recent Perspectives on the History of Eugenics." *American Historical Review* 103 (June 1998): 467–78.
Dodge, L. Mara. *"Whores and Thieves of the Worst Kind": A Study of Women, Crime, and Prisons, 1835–2000.* Dekalb: Northern Illinois University Press, 2002.
Donovan, Frances. *The Woman Who Waits.* Boston: Gorham Press, 1920.
Dorr, Gregory Michael. *Segregation's Science: Eugenics and Society in Virginia.* Charlottesville and London: University of Virginia Press, 2008.
Dowbiggin, Ian R. *The Sterilization Movement and Global Fertility in the Twentieth Century: The Sterilization Movement in the Cold War Era.* Oxford: Oxford University Press, 2008.
———. *Keeping America Sane: Psychiatry and Eugenics in the United States and Canada, 1880–1940.* Ithaca, N.Y.: Cornell University Press, 1997.
Duis, Perry R. *The Saloon: Public Drinking in Chicago and Boston, 1880–1920.* Urbana: University of Illinois Press, 1983.

———. *Challenging Chicago: Coping with Everyday Life, 1837–1920.* Urbana: University of Illinois Press, 1998.
Ellis, Havelock. *Essays in War-Time: Further Studies in the Task of Social Hygiene.* Boston: Houghton Mifflin, 1917.
Emens, Elizabeth F. "Shape Stops Story." *Narrative* 15 (January 2007): 124–32.
Epstein, Henry. *Perspectives on Delinquency Prevention.* New York: Office of the Mayor, 1955.
Evans, Elizabeth G., and Mary W. Dewson. "Feeble-Mindedness and Juvenile Delinquency: A Study from Experience." *Charities and the Commons* 20 (May 2, 1908): 183–91.
Evans, Sara M. *Born for Liberty: A History of Women in America.* New York: Free Press Paperbacks, 1997.
Faris, Robert E. L., and H. Warren Dunham. *Mental Disorders in Urban Areas: An Ecological Study of Schizophrenia and Other Psychoses.* Chicago: University of Chicago Press, 1939.
Fass, Paula S. "Cultural History/Social History: Some Reflections on a Continuing Dialogue." *Journal of Social History* 37 (Fall 2003): 39–46.
———. *The Damned and the Beautiful: American Youth in the 1920s.* New York: Oxford University Press, 1977.
Fernald, Mary R., Mary Holmes Stevens Hayes, and Almena Dawley. *A Study of Women Delinquents in New York State.* New York: Century, 1920.
Filene, Peter G. *Him/Her/Self: Gender Identities in Modern America.* 3rd ed. Baltimore: Johns Hopkins University Press, 1998.
Finzsch, Norbert, and Robert Jutte, eds. *Institutions of Confinement: Hospitals, Asylums, and Prisons in Western Europe and North America, 1500–1950.* New York: Cambridge University Press, 1996.
Fitzpatrick, Ellen. *Endless Crusade: Women Social Scientists and Progressive Reform.* New York: Oxford University Press, 1990.
Flanagan, Maureen A. *Seeing with Their Hearts: Chicago Women and the Vision of the Good City, 1871–1933.* Princeton, N.J.: Princeton University Press, 2002.
Foucault, Michel. *Discipline and Punish: The Birth of the Prison.* New York: Vintage Books, 1995.
———. *The Birth of the Clinic: An Archeology of Medical Perception.* New York: Vintage Books, 1994.
———. *The History of Sexuality: Volume I: An Introduction.* Translated by Robert Hurley. New York: Vintage Books, 1990.
Francis, Richard C. *Why Men Don't Ask for Directions: The Seductions of Sociobiology.* Princeton, N.J.: Princeton University Press, 2004.
Franks, Angela. *Margaret Sanger's Eugenic Legacy: The Control of Female Fertility.* Jefferson, N.C.: McFarland, 2005.
Freedman, Estelle B. *Their Sisters' Keepers: Women's Prison Reform in America, 1830–1930.* Ann Arbor: University of Michigan Press, 1981.
———. *Maternal Justice: Miriam Van Waters and the Female Reform Tradition.* Chicago: University of Chicago Press, 1996.
Friedlander, Kate. *The Psycho-Analytical Approach to Juvenile Delinquency: Theory, Case-Studies, Treatment.* New York: International Universities Press, 1947.

Gabaccia, Donna. *From the Other Side: Women, Gender, and Immigrant Life in the U.S., 1820–1990*. Bloomington: Indiana University Press, 1994.

Gallagher, Nancy L. *Breeding Better Vermonters: The Eugenics Project in the Green Mountain State*. Hanover, N.H.: University Press of New England, 1999.

Galloway, T. W. *Sex and Social Health: A Manual for the Study of Social Hygiene*. New York: American Social Hygiene Association, 1924.

Garrison, Karl C. *The Psychology of Adolescence*. 6th ed. Englewood Cliffs, N.J.: Prentice-Hall, 1965.

Gelb, Steven A. "'Not Simply Bad and Incorrigible': Science, Morality, and Intellectual Deficiency." *History of Education Quarterly* 29 (Autumn 1989): 359–79.

Gillette, Aaron. *Eugenics and the Nature-Nurture Debate in the Twentieth Century*. New York: Palgrave Macmillan, 2007.

Gillham, Nicholas Wright. *A Life of Sir Francis Galton: From African Exploration to the Birth of Eugenics*. Oxford: Oxford University Press, 2001.

Gittens, Joan. *Poor Relations: The Children of the State in Illinois, 1818–1990*. Urbana: University of Illinois Press, 1994.

Glueck, Sheldon, and Eleanor Glueck. *Delinquents in the Making: Paths to Prevention*. New York: Harper, 1952.

———. *Five Hundred Delinquent Women*. New York: Alfred A. Knopf, 1934. Repr. New York: Kraus Reprint Corporation, 1965.

Goddard, Henry H. *The Kallikak Family: A Study in the Heredity of Feeble-mindedness*. New York: Macmillan, 1912.

Goldberg, Harriet L. *Child Offenders: A Study in Diagnosis and Treatment*. New York: Grune & Stratton, 1948.

Goldberg, Jacob A., and Rosamond A. Goldberg. *Girls on City Streets: A Study of 1400 Cases of Rape*. New York: Foundation Books, 1940.

Goodheart, Lawrence B. *Mad Yankees: The Hartford Retreat for the Insane and Nineteenth-Century Psychiatry*. Amherst: University of Massachusetts Press, 2003.

Goodwin, Joanne L. *Gender and the Politics of Welfare Reform: Mother's Pensions in Chicago, 1911–1929*. Chicago: University of Chicago Press, 1997.

Gordon, Linda. *Heroes of Their Own Lives: The Politics and History of Family Violence*. New York: Penguin Books, 1989.

———. *Woman's Body, Woman's Right: Birth Control in America*. New York: Penguin Books, 1990.

———. *Pitied But Not Entitled: Single Mothers and the History of Welfare, 1890–1935*. New York: Free Press, 1994.

Gould, Stephen Jay. *The Mismeasure of Man*. New York: W.W. Norton, 1981.

Graumann, Carl F., and Kenneth J. Gergen, eds. *Historical Dimensions of Psychological Discourse*. New York: Cambridge University Press, 1996.

Grob, Gerald N. *The Mad Among Us: A History of the Care of America's Mentally Ill*. New York: Free Press, 1994.

———. *From Asylum to Community: Mental Health Policy in Modern America*. Princeton, N.J.: Princeton University Press, 1991.

---. *The Inner World of American Psychiatry, 1890–1940: Selected Correspondence.* New Brunswick, N.J.: Rutgers University Press, 1985.
---. *Mental Illness and American Society, 1875–1940.* Princeton, N.J.: Princeton University Press, 1983.
---. *Mental Institutions in America: Social Policy to 1875.* New York: Free Press, 1972.
---. *The State and the Mentally Ill: A History of Worcester State Hospital in Massachusetts, 1830–1920.* Chapel Hill: University of North Carolina Press, 1966.
Groves, Ernest R. *Preparation for Marriage.* New York: Greenberg, 1936.
Gurney, Peter. "'Intersex' and 'Dirty Girls': Mass-Observation and Working-Class Sexuality in England in the 1930s." *Journal of the History of Sexuality* 8 (June 1997): 256–90.
Hale, Nathan G. *Freud and the Americans: The Beginnings of Psychoanalysis in the United States, 1876–1917.* New York: Oxford University Press, 1971.
Haller, Mark H. *Eugenics: Hereditarian Attitudes in American Thought.* New Brunswick, N.J.: Rutgers University Press, 1963.
Hasian, Marouf Arif, Jr. *The Rhetoric of Eugenics in Anglo-American Thought.* Athens: University of Georgia Press, 1996.
Hathaway, Starke R., and Elio D. Monachesi, eds. *Analyzing and Predicting Juvenile Delinquency with the MMPI.* Minneapolis: University of Minnesota Press, 1953.
Hawkins, Mike. *Social Darwinism in European and American Thought, 1860–1945: Nature as Model and Nature as Threat.* New York: Cambridge University Press, 1997.
Healy, William. *The Individual Delinquent: A Text Book of Diagnosis and Prognosis for All Concerned in Understanding Offenders.* Boston: Little, Brown, 1929.
Healy, William, and Augusta F. Bronner. *Delinquents and Criminals, Their Making and Unmaking: Studies in Two American Cities.* New York: Macmillan, 1926.
---. *New Light on Delinquency and its Treatment: Results of a Research Conducted for the Institute of Human Relations Yale University.* New Haven, Conn.: Yale University Press, 1936.
---. *Treatment and What Happened Afterword: A Study from the Judge Baker Guidance Center.* Boston: Judge Baker Guidance Center, 1939.
Henderson, Charles R. *Preventive Agencies and Methods.* Philadelphia: Wm. F. Fell, 1910.
Hoag, E. B., and E. H. Williams. *Crime, Abnormal Minds, and the Law.* Indianapolis: Bobbs-Merrill, 1923.
Hobson, Barbara M. *Uneasy Virtue: The Politics of Prostitution and the American Reform Tradition.* New York: Basic Books, 1987.
Holmes, Samuel J. *The Eugenic Predicament.* New York: Harcourt, Brace, 1933.
Horn, David G. "This Norm Which is Not One: Reading the Female Body in Lombroso's Anthropology." In *Deviant Bodies: Critical Perspectives on Difference in Science and Popular Culture,* edited by Jennifer Terry and Jacqueline Urla, 109–25. Bloomington: Indiana University Press, 1995.
Horwitz, Allan V. *Creating Mental Illness.* Chicago: University of Chicago Press, 2002.
Huey, Edmund B. *Backward and Feeble-Minded Children: Clinical Studies in the Psychology of Defectives, with a Syllabus for the Clinical Examination and Testing of Children.* Baltimore: Warwick and York, 1912.

Hughes, Bill. "What Can a Foucauldian Analysis Contribute to Disability Theory?" in *Foucault and the Government of Disability,* edited by Shelly Tremain, 78–92. Ann Arbor: University of Michigan Press, 2005.

Ingstad, B., and S. R. Whyte, eds. *Disability and Culture.* Berkeley: University of California Press, 1995.

Irving, Katrina. *Immigrant Mothers: Narratives of Race and Maternity, 1890–1925.* Urbana: University of Illinois Press, 2000.

Jansz, Jeroen, and Peter van Drunen, eds. *A Social History of Psychology.* Malden, Mass.: Blackwell, 2004.

Joint Committee on Methods of Preventing Delinquency. *Three Problem Children: Narratives from the Case Records of a Child Guidance Clinic.* New York: Joint Committee on Methods of Preventing Delinquency, 1926.

Jones, Kathleen W. *Taming the Troublesome Child: American Families Child Guidance, and the Limits of Psychiatric Authority.* Cambridge, Mass.: Harvard University Press, 1999.

Katz, Michael B., ed. *The Underclass Debate: Views from History.* Princeton, N.J.: Princeton University Press, 1993.

Kazdin, Alan E. *Encyclopedia of Psychology: 8-Volume Set.* New York: Oxford University Press, 2000.

Kazdin, Alan E., ed. *Encyclopedia of Psychology.* Washington, D.C.: American Psychological Association; New York: Oxford University Press, 2000.

Kevles, Daniel J. *In the Name of Eugenics: Genetics and the Uses of Human Heredity.* New York: Alfred A. Knopf, 1985.

Kline, Wendy. *Building a Better Race: Gender, Sexuality, and Eugenics from the Turn of the Century to the Baby Boom.* Berkeley: University of California Press, 2001.

Kluchin, Rebecca M. *Fit to be Tied: Sterilization and Reproductive Rights in America, 1950–1980.* Rutgers, N.J.: Rutgers University Press, 2009.

Knupfer, Anne Meis. *Reform and Resistance: Gender, Delinquency, and America's First Juvenile Court.* New York: Routledge, 2001.

———. "'To Become Good Self-Supporting Women' : The State Industrial School for Delinquent Girls in Geneva, Illinois, 1900 to 1935." *Journal of the History of Sexuality* 9 (October 2000): 420–46.

Koven, Seth, and Sonya Michel, eds. *Mothers of a New World: Maternalist Politics and the Origins of the Welfare State.* New York: Routledge, 1993.

Kunzel, Regina G. *Fallen Women, Problem Girls: Unmarried Mothers and the Professionalization of Social Work, 1890–1945.* New Haven, Conn.: Yale University Press, 1993.

Kvaraceus, William Clement. *Juvenile Delinquency and the School.* Yonkers-on-Hudson, N.Y.: World Book, 1945.

———. *The Community and the Delinquent: Co-operative Approaches to Preventing and Controlling Delinquency.* Yonkers-on-Hudson, N.Y.: World Book, 1954.

Kvaraceus, William Clement, et al. *Delinquent Behavior: Principles and Practices.* Washington, D.C.: National Education Association of the United States, 1959.

Ladd-Taylor, Molly. "Eugenics, Sterilization, and Modern Marriage in the USA: The Strange Career of Paul Popenoe." *Gender & History* 13 (August 2001): 298–327.

———. "Saving Babies and Sterilizing Mothers: Eugenics and Welfare Politics in the Interwar United States." *Social Politics* (Spring 1997): 136–53.

———. *Mother-Work: Women, Child Welfare, and the State, 1890–1930.* Urbana: University of Illinois Press, 1994.

Largent, Mark A. *Breeding Contempt: The History of Coerced Sterilization in the United States.* Rutgers, N.J.: Rutgers University Press, 2007.

Larson, Edward J. *Sex, Race, and Science: Eugenics in the Deep South.* Baltimore: Johns Hopkins University Press, 1995.

———. "'In the Finest, Most Womanly Way': Women in the Southern Eugenics Movement." *American Journal of Legal History* 39 (1995): 119–47.

———. "Belated Progress: The Enactment of Eugenic Legislation in Georgia." *Journal of the History of Medicine and Allied Sciences* 46 (March 1991): 44–64.

Laslett, Barbara, Sally Gregory Kohlstedt, Helen Longino, and Evelynn Hammonds, eds. *Gender and Scientific Authority.* Chicago: University of Chicago Press, 1996.

Lears, Jackson T. J. *No Place of Grace: Antimodernism and the Transformation of American Culture, 1880–1920.* New York: Pantheon Books, 1981.

Lee, Sharon M. "Racial Classification in the U.S. Census: 1890–1990." *Ethnic and Racial Studies* 16 (March 1993): 75–94.

Levenkron, Steven. *Cutting: Understanding and Overcoming Self-Mutilation.* New York: W.W. Norton, 1998.

Lombroso, Caesar, and William Ferrero. *The Female Offender.* New York: Philosophical Library, 1895.

Louisiana Youth Commission. *Juvenile Delinquency and Juvenile Courts.* Baton Rouge: Louisiana Youth Commission, 1952.

Love, Rosaleen. "'Alice in Eugenics-Land': Feminism and Eugenics in the Scientific Careers of Alice Lee and Ethel Elderton." *Annals of Science* 36 (1979): 145–58.

Lunbeck, Elizabeth. *The Psychiatric Persuasion: Knowledge, Gender, and Power in Modern America.* Princeton, N.J.: Princeton University Press, 1994.

Lunden, Walter A. *War and Delinquency: An Analysis of Juvenile Delinquency in Thirteen Nations in World War I and World War II.* Ames, Iowa: Art Press, 1963.

Lynd, Robert S. *Middletown: A Study in Contemporary American Culture.* New York: Harcourt, Brace, 1929.

Martin, Victoria Claflin Woodhull. *The Rapid Multiplication of the Unfit.* Women's Anthropological Society of America, 1891.

Massachusetts Child Council. *Juvenile Delinquency in Massachusetts as a Public Responsibility: An Examination into the Present Methods of Dealing with Child Behavior, its legal background and the indicated steps for greater adequacy.* Boston: Massachusetts Child Council, 1939.

May, Elaine Tyler. *Homeward Bound: American Families in the Cold War Era.* New York: Basic Books, 1988.

Mazumdar, Pauline M. H. *Eugenics, Human Genetics and Human Failings: The Eugenics Society, Its Sources and Its Critics in Britain.* New York: Routledge, 1992.

McCann, Carole. *Birth Control Politics in the United States, 1916–1945.* Ithaca, N.Y.: Cornell University Press, 1994.

McDonagh, Patrick. *Idiocy: A Cultural History.* Liverpool, U.K.: Liverpool University Press, 2008.

McGerr, Michael. *A Fierce Discontent: The Rise and Fall of the Progressive Movement in America, 1870–1920.* New York: Oxford University Press, 2005.

McKinnon, Susan. *Neo-Liberal Genetics: The Myths and Moral Tales of Evolutionary Psychology.* Chicago: Prickly Paradigm Press, 2005.

McLaren, Angus. *The Trials of Masculinity: Policing Sexual Boundaries, 1870–1930.* Chicago: University of Chicago Press, 1997.

———. *Our Own Master Race: Eugenics in Canada, 1885–1945.* Toronto: McClelland & Stewart, 1990.

McRuer, R. "We Were Never Identified." *Radical History Review* 94 (Winter 2006): 148–54.

Mead, Margaret. "Coming of Age in 1952." *Twenty-First Annual Conference on Youth and Community Service.* Illinois: Department of Public Welfare (1952): 39–57.

Meyerowitz, Joanne J., ed. *Not June Cleaver: Women and Gender in Postwar America, 1945–1960.* Philadelphia: Temple University Press, 1994.

———. *Women Adrift: Independent Wage Earners in Chicago, 1880–1930.* Chicago: University of Chicago Press, 1988.

Miles, Robert. *Racism and Migrant Labour.* London: Routledge & Kegan Paul, 1982.

Mink, Gwendolyn. *The Wages of Motherhood: Inequality in the Welfare State, 1917–1920.* Ithaca, N.Y.: Cornell University Press, 1995.

Minton, Henry L. *Lewis M. Terman: Pioneer in Psychological Testing.* New York: New York University Press, 1988.

Miringoff, Marque-Luisa. "The Impact of Population Policy upon Social Welfare." *Social Service Review* 54 (September 1980): 301–16.

Moldow, Gloria. *Women Doctors in Gilded-Age Washington: Race, Gender, and Professionalization.* Urbana: University of Illinois Press, 1987.

Monahan, Florence. *Women in Crime.* New York: Ives Washburn, 1941.

Monroe, Day. *Chicago Families: A Study of Unpublished Census Data.* Chicago: University of Chicago Press, 1932.

Moran, Jeffrey P. "'Modernism Gone Mad': Sex Education Comes to Chicago, 1913." *Journal of American History* 83 (June 1996): 481–513.

———. *Teaching Sex: The Shaping of Adolescence in the 20th Century.* Cambridge, Mass.: Harvard University Press, 2000.

More, Ellen. *Restoring the Balance: Women Physicians and the Profession of Medicine, 1850–1995.* Cambridge, Mass.: Harvard University Press, 1999.

Muir, Donald E. "Race: The Mythic Root of Racism." *Sociological Inquiry* 63 (September 1993): 339–50.

Mumford, Kevin J. *Interzones: Black/White Sex Districts in Chicago and New York in the Early Twentieth Century.* New York: Columbia University Press, 1997.
Muncy, Robyn. *Creating a Female Dominion in American Reform, 1890-1935.* Oxford: Oxford University Press, 1991.
Murchison, Carl. *Criminal Intelligence.* Spencer, Mass.: Heffernan Press, 1926.
Murdock, Catherine G. *Domesticating Drink: Women, Men, and Alcohol in America, 1870-1940.* Baltimore: Johns Hopkins University Press, 1998.
Murolo, Priscilla. *The Common Ground of Womanhood: Class, Gender, and Working Class Girls' Clubs, 1884-1928.* Urbana: University of Illinois Press, 1997.
Myerson, Abraham. *The Inheritance of Mental Diseases.* Baltimore: Williams & Wilkins, 1925.
Napoli, Donald S. *Architects of Adjustment: The History of the Psychological Profession in the United States.* London: Kennikat Press, 1981.
Nash, Mary. "Pronatalism and Motherhood in Franco's Spain." In *Maternity and Gender Policies: Women and the Rise of the European Welfare States, 1880s-1950s,* edited by Gisela Bock and Pat Thane, 160-77. London: Routledge, 1994.
New York City Youth Board. *New Directions in Delinquency Prevention, 1947-1957.* New York: The Board, 1957.
New York City Youth Board. *Pattern for Prevention.* New York: The Board, 1953.
Newman, Louise M. *White Women's Rights: The Racial Origins of Feminism in the United States.* Oxford: Oxford University Press, 1999.
Noll, Steven. *Feeble-Minded in Our Midst: Institutions for the Mentally Retarded in the South, 1900-1940.* Chapel Hill: University of North Carolina Press, 1995.
Odem, Mary E. *Delinquent Daughters: Protecting and Policing Adolescent Female Sexuality in the United States, 1885-1920.* Chapel Hill: University of North Carolina Press, 1995.
Ordover, Nancy. *American Eugenics: Race, Queer Anatomy, and the Science of Nationalism.* Minneapolis: University of Minnesota Press, 2003.
Osborn, Frederick. *Preface to Eugenics.* Rev.ed. New York: Harper & Brothers, 1951.
Paul, Diane B. "On Drawing Lessons from the History of Eugenics." In *Reprogenetics: Law, Policy, and Ethical Issues,* edited by Lori P. Knowles and Gregory E. Kaebnick, 3-19. Baltimore: Johns Hopkins University Press, 2007.
———. *Controlling Human Heredity, 1865 to the Present.* Atlantic Highlands, N.J.: Humanities Press, 1995.
———. *The Politics of Heredity: Essays on Eugenics, Biomedicine, and the Nature-Nurture Debate.* Albany: State University of New York Press, 1998.
Pavalko, Ronald M. "Racism and the New Immigration: A Reinterpretation of the Assimilation of White Ethnics in American Society." *Sociology and Social Research* 65 (March 1980): 56-77.
Peck, Harris B., and John J. Horowitz. *A New Pattern for Mental Health Services in a Children's Court.* Springfield, Ill.: Thomas, 1958.
Peiss, Kathy. *Cheap Amusements: Working Women and Leisure in Turn-of-the-Century New York.* Philadelphia: Temple University Press, 1986.

Pernick, Martin S. *The Black Stork: Eugenics and the Death of "Defective" Babies in American Medicine and Motion Pictures Since 1915.* Oxford: Oxford University Press, 1996.
Petrina, Stephen. "The 'Never-to-Be-Forgotten Investigation': Luella W. Cole, Sidney L. Pressey, and Mental Surveying in Indiana, 1917–1921." *History of Psychology* 4 (August 2001): 245–71.
Philpott, Thomas Lee. *The Slum and the Ghetto: Immigrants, Blacks, and Reformers in Chicago, 1880–1930.* Belmont, Calif.: Wadsworth Publishing, 1991.
Pickens, Donald K. *Eugenics and the Progressives.* Nashville: Vanderbilt University Press, 1968.
Popenoe, Paul, and Roswell Hill Johnson. *Applied Eugenics.* 3rd ed. New York: Macmillan, 1933.
Popplestone, John A., and Marion W. McPherson. "Pioneer Psychology Laboratories in Clinical Settings." In *Explorations in the History of Psychology in the United States,* edited by Joseph Brozek. London: Associated University Presses, 1984.
Proctor, Robert N. "The Destruction of 'Lives Not Worth Living.'" In *Deviant Bodies: Critical Perspectives on Difference in Science and Popular Culture,* edited by Jennifer Terry and Jacqueline Urla, 170–96. Bloomington: Indiana University Press, 1995.
———. *Racial Hygiene: Medicine Under the Nazis.* Cambridge, Mass.: Harvard University Press, 1988.
Rafter, Nicole H. "The Criminalization of Mental Retardation." In *Mental Retardation in America: A Historical Reader,* edited by Steven Noll and James Trent Jr., 232–57. New York: New York University Press, 2004.
———. *Creating Born Criminals.* Urbana: University of Illinois Press, 1997.
———. "Claims Making and Socio-Cultural Context in the First U.S. Eugenics Campaign." *Social Problems* 39 (March 1992): 17–34.
———. "White Trash: Eugenics as Social Ideology." *Society* 26 (March 1988): 43–49.
Rapley, Mark. *The Social Construction of Intellectual Disability.* New York: Cambridge University Press, 2004.
Recchiuti, John Louis. *Civic Engagement: Social Science and Progressive-Era Reform in New York City.* Philadelphia: University of Pennsylvania Press, 2007.
Reckless, Walter Cade, and Mapheus Smith. *Juvenile Delinquency.* New York: McGraw-Hill, 1932.
Reeves, Margaret. *Training Schools for Delinquent Girls.* Philadelphia: Wm. F. Fell, 1929.
Regal, Brian. *Henry Fairfield Osborn: Race, and the Search for the Origins of Man.* Burlington, Vt.: Ashgate Publishing, 2002.
Reilly, Philip R. *The Surgical Solution: A History of Involuntary Sterilization in the United States.* Baltimore: Johns Hopkins University Press, 1991.
Reith, David. "U.S. Census Data: Ethnicity and the American Census." *Ethnic Forum* 10 (March–June 1990): 98–105.
Robb, George. "The Way of All Flesh: Degeneration, Eugenics, and the Gospel of Free Love." *Journal of the History of Sexuality* 6 (December 1996): 589–603.

Robinson, Paul A. *The Modernization of Sex: Havelock Ellis, Alfred Kinsey, William Masters, and Virginia Johnson.* New York: Harper & Row, 1976.
Rose, Hilary, and Steven Rose, eds. *Alas, Poor Darwin: Arguments Against Evolutionary Psychology.* New York: Harmony Books.
Rose, Nikolas. "Power and Subjectivity: Critical History and Psychology." In *Historical Dimensions of Psychological Discourse,* edited by Carl F. Graumann and Kenneth J. Gergen, 103–24. New York: Cambridge University Press, 1996.
Rose, Steven, and Hilary Rose. "Less than Human Nature: Biology and the New Right." *Race & Class* 27 (Winter 1986): 47–66.
Rosen, Christine. *Preaching Eugenics: Religious Leaders and the American Eugenics Movement.* Oxford: Oxford University Press, 2004.
Rosen, Ruth. *The Lost Sisterhood: Prostitution in America, 1900–1918.* Baltimore: Johns Hopkins University Press, 1982.
Rosenberg, Charles E. *No Other Gods: On Science and American Social Thought.* Baltimore: Johns Hopkins University Press, 1997.
Rossiter, Margaret W. *Women Scientists in America: Struggles and Strategies to 1940.* Baltimore: Johns Hopkins University Press, 1982.
Rubin, Herman H. *Eugenics and Sex Harmony.* New York: Pioneer Publications, 1936.
Russett, Cynthia E. *Sexual Science: The Victorian Construction of Womanhood.* Cambridge, Mass.: Harvard University Press, 1989.
Ryan, Patrick J. "Unnatural Selection: Intelligence Testing, Eugenics, and American Political Cultures." *Journal of Social History* 30 (Spring 1997): 669–85.
Saleeby, C. W. *Woman and Womanhood: A Search for Principles.* New York: Mitchell Kennerley, 1911.
Sangster, Joan. *Girl Trouble: Female Delinquency in English Canada.* Toronto: Between the Lines, 2002.
———. "Incarcerating 'Bad Girls': The Regulation of Sexuality through the Female Refuges Act in Ontario, 1920–1945." *Journal of Sexuality* 7 (June 1996): 239–75.
Saraceno, Chiara. "Redefining Maternity and Paternity: Gender Pronatalism and Social Policies in Fascist Italy." In *Maternity and Gender Policies: Women and the Rise of the European Welfare States, 1880s–1950s,* edited by Gisela Bock and Pat Thane, 196–212. London: Routledge, 1994.
Scarborough, Elizabeth, and Laurel Furumoto. *Untold Lives: The First Generation of American Women Psychologists.* New York: Columbia University Press, 1987.
Schaffner, Laurie. *Girls in Trouble with the Law.* New Brunswick, N.J.: Rutgers University Press, 2006.
Scharleib, Mary. *Womanhood and Race-Regeneration.* New York: Moffat, Yard, 1912.
Schlossman, Steven. *Love and the American Delinquent: The Theory and Practice of "Progressive" Juvenile Justice, 1825–1920.* Chicago: University of Chicago Press, 1977.
Schlossman, Steven, and Stephanie Wallach. "The Crime of Precocious Sexuality: Female Juvenile Delinquency in the Progressive Era." *Harvard Educational Review* 48 (February 1978): 65–94.

Schneider, Eric C. *In the Web of Class: Delinquents and Reformers in Boston, 1810s-1930s.* New York: New York University Press, 1992.

Schneider, William H. *Quality and Quantity: The Quest for Biological Regeneration in Twentieth-Century France.* Cambridge, U.K.: Cambridge University Press, 1990.

Schoen, Johanna. *Choice & Coercion: Birth Control, Sterilization, and Abortion in Public Health and Welfare.* Chapel Hill: University of North Carolina Press, 2005.

Schrum, Kelly. *Some Wore Bobby Sox: The Emergence of Teenage Girls Culture, 1920–1945.* New York: Palgrave Macmillan, 2004.

Schultz, Rima Lunin, and Adele Hast, eds. *Women Building Chicago, 1790–1990: A Biographical Dictionary.* Bloomington: Indiana University Press, 2001.

Schweik, Susan M. *The Ugly Laws: Disability in Public.* New York: New York University Press, 2009.

Scott, Anne Firor. *Natural Allies: Women's Associations in American History.* Urbana: University of Illinois Press, 1992.

Selden, Steven. *Inheriting Shame: The Story of Eugenics and Racism in America.* New York: Teachers College Press, 1999.

———. 1988. "Resistance in School and Society: Public and Pedagogical Debates About Eugenics, 1900–1947." *Teachers College Record* 90 (March 1988): 61–84.

———. "Educational Policy and Biological Science: Genetics, Eugenics, and the College Textbook, c. 1908–1931." *Teachers College Record* 87 (Fall 1985): 35–51.

Serlin, David. *Replaceable You: Engineering the Body in Postwar America.* Chicago: University of Chicago Press, 2004.

Shaw, Clifford R. *Delinquency Areas: A Study of the Geographic Distribution of School Truants, Juvenile Delinquents, and Adult Offenders in Chicago.* Chicago: University of Chicago Press, 1929.

Shaw, Clifford Robe, and Maurice E. Moore. *The Natural History of a Delinquent Career.* Chicago: University of Chicago Press, 1931.

Silverberg, Helene, ed. *Gender and American Social Science: The Formative Years.* Princeton, N.J.: Princeton University Press, 1998.

Slavson, S. R. *Re-educating the Delinquent through Group and Community Participation.* New York: Harper, 1954.

Smith, B. G., and B. Hutchison, eds. *Gendering Disability.* New Brunswick, N.J.: Rutgers University Press, 2004.

Smith, Carl S. *Chicago and the American Literary Imagination, 1880–1920.* Chicago: University of Chicago Press, 1984.

Smith, David, J. *The Eugenic Assault on America: Scenes in Red, White, and Black.* Farfax, Va.: George Mason University Press, 1993.

———. "The Eugenic Assault on America: Scenes in Red, White, and Black." *Journal of Southern History* 60 (September 1994): 613–14.

Smith, Sawn M. *American Archives: Gender, Race, and Class in Visual Culture.* Princeton, N.J.: Princeton University Press, 1999.

Smith-Rosenberg, Carroll. *Disorderly Conduct: Visions of Gender in Victorian America.* Oxford: Oxford University Press, 1985.

Smuts, Alice Boardman. *Science in the Service of Children, 1893–1935.* New Haven, Conn.: Yale University Press, 2006.
Snyder, Sharon L., and David T. Mitchell. *Cultural Locations of Disability.* Chicago: University of Chicago Press, 2006.
Sokal, Michael M., edr. *Psychological Testing and American Society, 1890–1930.* New Brunswick, N.J.: Rutgers University Press, 1987.
———. "James McKeen Cattell and Mental Anthropometry: Nineteenth-Century Science and Reform and the Origins of Psychological Testing." In *Psychological Testing and American Society, 1890–1930,* edited by Michael M. Sokal, 21–45. New Brunswick, N.J.: Rutgers University Press, 1987.
Sokal, Michael M., and Patrice A. Rafail. *A Guide to Manuscript Collections in the History of Psychology and Related Areas.* Millwood, N.Y.: Kraus International Publications, 1982.
Solinger, Rickie. *Wake up Little Susie: Single Pregnancy and Race before Roe v. Wade.* New York: Routledge, 1992.
Solomon, Ben. *Juvenile Delinquency, Practical Prevention.* Peekskill, N.Y.: Youth Service, 1947.
Soloway, Richard A. *Demography and Degeneration: Eugenics and the Declining Birthrate in Twentieth-Century Britain.* Chapel Hill: University of North Carolina Press, 1990.
Somerville, Siobhan. "Scientific Racism and the Emergence of the Homosexual Body." *Journal of the History of Sexuality* 5 (June 1994): 243–66.
Spaulding, Edith R. *An Experimental Study of Psychopathic Delinquent Women.* New York: Rand McNally, 1923.
Stadum, Beverly A. *Poor Women and their Families: Hard Working Charity Cases, 1900–1930.* Albany: State University of New York Press, 1992.
Stagner, Ross. *Psychology of Personality.* New York: McGraw-Hill, 1961.
Stansell, Christine. *American Moderns: Bohemian New York and the Creation of a New Century.* New York: Metropolitan Books, Henry Holt, 2000.
———. *City of Women: Sex and Class in New York, 1789–1860.* Urbana: University of Illinois Press, 1987.
Stebner, Eleanor J. *The Women of Hull House: A Study in Spirituality, Vocation, and Friendship.* Albany: State University of New York Press, 1997.
Stepan, Nancy L. *The Hour of Eugenics: Race, Gender, and Nation in Latin America.* Ithaca, N.Y.: Cornell University Press, 1991.
Stephens, Ellis Arthur. *Lawless Youth: A Psychiatric Study of the Causes and Prevention of Adolescent Crime.* New York: Pageant Press, 1953.
Sterelny, Kim. *Dawkins vs. Gould: Survival of the Fittest.* Duxford, Cambridge, U.K.: Icon Books, 2001.
Stern, Alexandra Minna. *Eugenic Nation: Faults and Frontiers of Better Breeding in Modern America.* Berkeley: University of California Press, 2005.
Tappan, Paul W. *Juvenile Delinquency.* New York: McGraw-Hill, 1949.
Taylor, Graham. *Pioneering on Social Frontiers.* Chicago: University of Chicago Press, 1930.

Terman, Lewis M. *The Measurement of Intelligence: An Explanation of and a Complete Guide for the use of the Stanford Revision and Extension of the Binet-Simon Intelligence Scale.* Boston: Houghton Mifflin, 1916.

Terry, Jennifer, and Jacqueline Urla, eds. *Deviant Bodies: Critical Perspectives on Difference in Science and Popular Culture.* Bloomington: Indiana University Press, 1995.

Thomas, William I. *The Unadjusted Girl with Cases and Standpoint for Behavior Analysis.* New York: Little, Brown, 1923. Repr. Montclair, N.J.: Patterson Smith, 1969.

Thomson, Mathew. *The Problem of Mental Deficiency: Eugenics, Democracy, and Social Policy in Britain c.1870–1959.* Oxford: Clarendon Press, 1998.

Thurston, Henry W. *Concerning Juvenile Delinquency: Progressive Changes in Our Perspectives.* New York: Columbia Press, 1945.

Tice, Karen W. *Tales of Wayward Girls and Immoral Women: Case Records and the Professionalization of Social Work.* Urbana: University of Illinois Press, 1998.

Trattner, Walter I., ed. *Biographical Dictionary of Social Welfare in America.* New York: Greenwood Press, 1986.

Tremain, Shelley. "On the Government of Disability: Foucault, Power, and the Subject of Impairment." In *The Disability Studies Reader,* edited by Lennard J. Davis, 185–96. 2nd ed. London: Routledge, 2006.

Tremain, S., ed., *Foucault and the Government of Disability.* Ann Arbor: University of Michigan Press, 2005.

Trent, James W. "To Cut and Control: Institutional Preservation and the Sterilization of Mentally Retarded People in the United States, 1892–1947." *Journal of Historical Sociology* 6 (March 1993): 56–73.

———. *Inventing the Feeble Mind: A History of Mental Retardation in the United States.* Berkeley: University of California Press, 1994.

Tucker, William H. *The Funding of Scientific Racism: Wickliffe Draper and the Pioneer Fund.* Urbana: University of Illinois Press, 2002.

———. *The Science and Politics of Racial Research.* Urbana: University of Illinois Press, 1994.

Tylor, Peter. "Denied the Power to Choose the Good: Sexuality and Mental Defect in American Medical Practice 1850–1920." *Journal of Social History* 10 (June 1977): 472–89.

Ullman, Sharon R. *Sex Seen: The Emergence of Modern Sexuality in America.* Berkeley: University of California Press, 1997.

Valentine, P. F., *The Psychology of Personality.* New York: D. Appleton, 1931.

Van Waters, Miriam. *Youth in Conflict.* New York: Republic Publishing, 1925.

Vigue, Charles L. "Eugenics and the Education of Women in the United States." *Journal of Educational Administration and History* 19 (June 1987): 51–55.

Walkowitz, Judith R. *Prostitution and Victorian Society: Women, Class, and the State.* Cambridge, U.K.: Cambridge University Press, 1995.

Wasserman, D., and R. Wachbroit, eds. *Genetics and Criminal Behavior.* Cambridge, U.K.: Cambridge University Press, 2001.

Weidensall, Jean. *The Mentality of the Criminal Woman: A Comparative Study of The Criminal Woman, The Working Girl, and The Efficient Working Woman in a Series of Mental and Physical Tests*. Baltimore: Warwick & York, 1916.

Weiner, Lynn Y. *From Working Girl to Working Mother: The Female Labor Force in the United States, 1820–1980*. Chapel Hill: University of North Carolina Press, 1985.

White House Conference on Child Health and Protection. New York: Century, 1930.

Willemse, W. A. *Constitution-types in Delinquency: Practical Applications and Bio-Physiological Foundations of Kretschmer's Types*. New York: Harcourt, 1932.

Willrich, Michael. *City of Courts: Socializing Justice in Progressive Era Chicago*. Cambridge, U.K.: Cambridge University Press, 2003.

———. "The Two Percent Solution: Eugenic Jurisprudence and the Socialization of American Law, 1900–1930." *Law and History Review* 16 (Spring 1998): 63–111.

Wilson, Samuel Paynter. *Chicago and its Cess-pools of Infamy*. Repr. General Books, 2010.

Winfield, Ann Gibson. *Eugenics and Education in America: Institutionalized Racism and the Implications of History, Ideology, and Memory*. New York: Peter Lang, 2007.

Wirt, Robert D., and Peter F. Briggs. *Personality and Environmental Factors in the Development of Delinquency*. Washington, D.C.: American Psychological Association, 1959.

Witmer, Helen Leland, and Ruth Kotinsky, eds. *Personality in the Making: The Fact-Finding Report of the Midcentury White House Conference on Children and Youth*. New York: Harper & Brothers, 1952.

Wood, Mary E. *The Writing on the Wall: Women's Autobiography and the Asylum*. Urbana: University of Illinois Press, 1994.

Worthington, George E. and Ruth Topping. *Specialized Courts Dealing with Sex Delinquency: A Study of the Procedure in Chicago, Boston, Philadelphia, and New York*. New York: American Social Hygiene Association, 1925.

Wylie, Philip Gordon. *Generation of Vipers*. New York: Holt, Rinehart and Winston, 1955.

Zahn, Margaret A., ed., *The Delinquent Girl*. Philadelphia: Temple University Press, 2009.

Zeits, Joshua. *Flapper: A Madcap Story of Sex, Style, Celebrity, and the Women Who Made America Modern*. New York: Three Rivers Press, 2007.

Zenderland, Leila. "The Parable of The Kallikak Family." In *Mental Retardation in America: A Historical Reader*, edited by Steven Noll and James Trent Jr., 165–85. New York: New York University Press, 2004.

———. *Measuring Minds: Henry Herbert Goddard and the Origins of American Intelligence Testing*. Cambridge, U.K.: Cambridge University Press, 1998.

———. "The Debate over Diagnosis: Henry Herbert Goddard and the Medical Acceptance of Intelligence." In *Psychological Testing and American Society, 1890–1930*, edited by Michael M. Sokal, 46–74. New Brunswick, N.J.: Rutgers University Press, 1987.

Index

Abbott, Edith, 20, 36, 38, 40, 41
Abbott, Grace, 68, 180n8
Addams, George, 43
Addams, Jane, 68
Adler, Herman M., 34, 60, 69, 106, 110
African American inmates: average mental age of, 59; incarcerated at IJR, 4; interracial relationships, 104–5
Amigh, Ophelia L., 21, 89; on custodial care of "feebleminded" women, 24, 42; superintendent of State Training School for Girls, 91, 96–97
anthropometric mental testing, 75
antisocial behavior: and environmental factors, relationship between, 20; eugenicists views on, 67; importance of heredity in, 21–22, 76; of male and female delinquent, 136; motivation problem and, 132; of neurotic delinquent, 135; origin of, 132; pathological causes of, 65, 67, 112; of young people, 133, 134
antisocial impulse control, 132
anxiety pattern, children, 133
army mental tests: effects of, 60; limitations of, 59–60; results, 59

Ball, Lucy, 108
Bartelme, Mary Margaret, 33–34, 43, 51, 57, 108, 178n76
Big Brothers (community based program), 57
Big Brothers Association, 57
Big Sister program, 57
Binet intelligence tests, 42; administered to young girls, 42, 49, 52, 77; factors influencing scores of, 49
Bloch, Herbert, 126, 137, 195–96n43
Bott, George, 116
Bowen, A. L., 44, 108–9
Breckinridge, Sophonisba, 20, 36, 38, 40, 41
Bridgman, Olga, 112
Bronner, Augusta, 41–42, 49, 69, 71, 177n70
Burgess, Ernest W., 193–94n12
Burnet, Anne, 106, 172n10, 177n70
Butler, Amos, 44
Butler, Walter, 125

Caldwell, C. B., 29, 56
Cattell, James McKeen, 75
charity girl. *See* "khaki mad girl"
Chassell, Clara, 53, 179–80n2, 179n1
Chicago Area Project, 58
Chicago Daily Tribune: article on enactment of commitment law, 29; articles on eugenics, 17; description of commitment law, 22–23
child development, 126; antisocial impulse control, 132, 133; arrested emotional, 134; heredity influence on, 126–27; interrelated stages of, 129; personality, 127–28; role of mother in, 133
child guidance movement, 122, 142
Clarke, Walter, 75
Clendenen, Richard C., 126

222 · INDEX

Committee on Protective Work for Girls, 62–63
The Commons (settlement), 24, 25
community care: community-based programs for, 56–58; importance of, 54–55; parole to inmates, 56; vocational training, 56. *See also* parole
Conference on Youth and Community Service (Illinois), 124–25, 131
correctional institutions. *See* custodial institutions
criminal traits, inheritance of, 21. *See also* heredity
"cultural deviants," 134
custodial care, "feebleminded" women, 24
custodial institutions: for "feebleminded" women, 29–30, 44; number of Illinois residents admitted to, 69–71. *See also* Lincoln State School and Colony; State Training School for Girls, Geneva

Danziger, Kurt, 76–77
Dean, Maria, 30–31
Delinquency: The Juvenile Offender in America Today (Bloch and Frank), 126
Dewson, Mary W., 45–46, 176n59
Diagnostic and Statistical Manual of Mental Disorders (DSM), 145, 146
disability and impairment, 4, 164n8
Division for Delinquency Prevention, 58, 124, 194n14
Draft of Sterilization Law for Illinois, 158–61
Dutcher, Elizabeth, 55, 60, 65
Dwyer, Anna, 14, 50–51, 177n72, 178n72
Dye, Charlott, 89

early employment impact on young women, 35, 36
egocentric waywardness, 134, 135
ego development, 133
embodied deviance, 74, 186n4
emotional outbursts, 101, 107
Erikson, Erik, 128
Erlewine, Ella, 97
eugenic commitment campaign: gendered nature of, 45–46, 139–40, 176–77n60; women's active role in, 15, 45, 164n8. *See also* maternalist reformers
eugenic commitment law. *See* involuntary commitment law
eugenic institutionalization, 3; of "feeble-minded" persons, 23, 28, 45, 64; Illinois residents between 1920 and 1947, 69–70; inmates and their families response to, 115–16, 118; ISCC support for, 50; of "mentally defective" women, 46–47, 54, 59; practical challenges associated with, 29; rationalization of, 26–27; voluntary, 24
eugenicists: on involuntary commitment law, 2–3; and "Progressives," divide between, 21
eugenic marriage law, 18
eugenics: acceptance among Americans, 17; coursework on, 19; individuals and organizations promoting, 18; and *psy* discourses, 8–11; as theory of human development, 16–17; women's involvement in, 14, 16; works on, 164n14
Eugenics Education Society of Chicago, 18
eugenic segregation, 4, 13–14, 68; efficacy of, 26–27; *vs.* eugenic sterilization, 27; of "feebleminded" persons, 31, 48, 50, 59; of female sex delinquents, 65; during interwar period, 55, 121; of "mentally defective people," 46; of "mentally diseased" delinquents, 69
eugenics program, nationwide, 3
Eugenics Record Office (ERO), 3; official extension department, 19; trained field workers, 168–69n42
Evans, Elizabeth G., 45–46, 176n59
Evans, W. A., 167n16; articles on eugenics, 9–10, 17; on child development, 21; on Laughlin's plan, 3; reform efforts, 10

Fabian cottage, 109, 226
Federal Bureau of Investigation (FBI): studies of delinquency, 122, 192–93n5
"feebleminded" individuals, 5, 21; comparative study of intelligence of, 49; definition of, 23; "good" and "bad," divide between, 60–61; legal commitment of, 13, 149–57, 162n1; long-term incarceration of, 27, 51; overcrowding at correctional institutions, 30; permanent custodial care for, 15, 25, 44, 44nn52–53, 46; population of, 23n62, 78; rights of, 30–31; and slum perpetuation, 22; subcategories of, 23; threat to society and race, 29, 44
"feebleminded" male, 44; JPA on problems of, 47
feebleminded menace, 45; dangers of, 26; and maternalist reformers, 22–25. *See also* "khaki mad girl"
feeblemindedness, 63; and army mental tests,

59–61; as cause of juvenile crime, 49–50; challenges in application of, 48–51; classification scheme, 77–78; and delinquency, relationship between, 53, 59, 110, 179nn1–2; and immorality, correlation between, 43, 48–49; middle-class women and men concerns about, 28; prevalence of, 78. *See also* "feebleminded" individuals

female juvenile delinquency. *See* juvenile delinquency

female labor force in Chicago, 35

female professionals, eugenic discourse influence on, 16

female sex delinquents, 4; around military camps, 62–63; attempts to escape abusive situation, 37–38; average age of, 139; Binet intelligence test of, 42–43, 175n42, 175n44; case files of, 33–34, 36; comparative study of intelligence of, 49; environmental factors influencing, 63–64, 125; family history, 37; "feebleminded," 42–43; impact of early employment on, 35, 36; incarceration of, 37, 38, 65; inherited mental defect, 20–22; language and cultural barriers faced by, 38; and male delinquents, moral offenses committed by, 40–41, 174n33; manifestation of mental disorders in, 145–47; parents or relatives of, 37–38; participation in urban youth culture, 35; pathologized antisocial acts, 136; physical attractiveness and sexual overdevelopment, 61; popular perceptions of, 61; pregnancy of, 39; sexual lives of, 39; venereal disease among, 39, 173–74n25; violent crime referrals of, 143–44. *See also* eugenic institutionalization; statistical psychological studies

Flower, Lucy L., 176–77n60

Flynn, Frank, 126, 137, 195–96n43

Foucault, Michel, 78–79

Friedlander, Kate, 132, 137

Galton, Francis, 10, 17, 126

gender: and eugenic commitment, 44–48; role in eugenic reform, 45–46, 176–77n60

Geneva classroom, 223

Geneva's inmates, 39; actions outside exam room, 98–99, 111; African Americans, 4, 139, 197n69; benefits of institutional segregation of, 2; Binet tests of, 42–43, 175n42, 175n44; case files, 1, 119–20, 162n11, craving for attention, 101, 107; delinquency of, 1–2; education, training, and work experience, 96–98; engaging in physical activity, 224; escaped from institutions, 107–9; immorality committed by, 43; insight and encouragement to, 98; practice of feigning illness, 101; prenatal care to pregnant inmates, 39–40; psychological evaluation of, 73; with psychopathic personality, 191n72; racial and sexual transgressions, 103, 104–5; reaction to incarceration, 98; reading in classroom, 223; rebellious and deviant behavior of, 100; self-mutilating behavior of, 106–7; sense of being afflicted by imaginary maladies, 105–6; stolid and uncooperative behavior of, 100; Whites, 139, 197n69; working in industrial rooms, 224; "wrong doing" while on parole, 102, 103; youth-oriented peer culture, 99–100. *See also* inmate families; mental deviance, creation of; ritual of psychological examination

girls' delinquency: during and after World War II, 121; causes of, 112; class and race role in, 144–45; historical continuity in treatment of, 145; and mental disorders, connections between, 145–47; neo-liberal policy changes and, 144; "personality aberrations" associated with, 137. *See also* female sex delinquents

Goddard, Henry, 23, 75, 86

Haiselden, H. J., 28

Hammond, John Hays, 21

Hardt, Harry, 114–15

Harley, Harrison, 29, 30

Hayes, Clara E., 2, 51, 180n10; on commitment of "feebleminded" girls, 51; on community care, 54–55; on eugenic institutionalization, 26–27; on incarceration programs, 28

healthy personality development, 128–29

Healy, William, 44, 71

heredity: and antisocial behavior, link between, 21; influence on child development, 126–27

heterosexual relationships, 104–5

Hickson, William, 65, 184n60; eugenics program devised by, 66–67

Hill, Helen, 86

Hinrichsen, Annie, 24; call for reform in Wabash County, 25; family studies, 25; investigation of "Tin Town" and "The Commons," 24–25

Hoover, J. Edgar, 122
Horwitz, Allan, 146
Huey, Edmund, 89, 187n19
human testing: anthropometric mental testing, 75; intelligence testing, 75–76; phrenology, 74, 75, 186n6; physiognomy, 74, 75; *psy* discourses, 74
"hysteria" cases, 106

Illinois: annual Conference on Youth and Community Service, 124–25; local neighborhood committees for youth, 125; residents admitted to custodial institutions, 69–71; support for delinquency prevention, 125
Illinois' "defective" residents. *See* "feebleminded" individuals
Illinois Federation of Community Committees, 125
Illinois Federation of Women's Clubs (IFWC), 14; members of, 15; support to eugenic commitment law, 15–16, 20
Illinois State Charities Commission (ISCC), 31; support for eugenic commitment, 50, 177n72, 178n72
Illinois Youth Commission, 125
imaginary maladies, inmates sense of being afflicted by, 105–6
immorality: and feeblemindedness, correlation between, 43; professional maternalists on, 48–49
impairment and disability, 4, 164n8
incarceration, institutional: anxiety and stress involved with, 82; benefits of, 27; of "defective delinquents," 69; of "feebleminded" individuals, 30; inmate families challenges to, 113, 114–16, 118; of "psychopathic" individuals, 67; of young women, 39–41, 45–46, 61; young women resistance to, 98, 99
inmate families: appreciation for incarceration and parole system, 113–14; challenges to incarceration, 113, 114–16; role in shaping eugenic commitment, 117
Institute for Juvenile Research (IJR): community-based program, 58; on girls committed to custodial institutions, 71; interviewing room, 225; psychological examination of young women at, 79–81
Institution Quarterly, The, 13; on feeblemindedness and immorality, 48–51
intellect and conduct, correlation between, 53
intelligence testing, 75–76

intemperate progenitors, degeneracy inherited from, 21
interracial relationships, among inmates, 104
interwar period, eugenic commitment debate during: army mental tests, 59–61; child guidance movement, 122, 142; on eugenics crusade, 65–69; Illinois residents admitted to institutions, 69–71; on "khaki mad girl," 62–63. *See also* community care
involuntary commitment law: campaign to enact, 14; constitutionality issues, 30–31; as eugenic measure, 2, 64–69; influence on admissions to state institutions, 29; inmate families role in shaping, 116–17; legal commitment of "feebleminded" persons under, 13; and maternalist reformers, 14–20; practical challenges associated with, 29–30; support for, 3, 13–14. *See also* eugenic commitment campaign
irritating behavior problems, 112

Jathro, Edna, 22
juvenile court cases: in 1953 and 1960, 122, 193n7; violent crime referrals, 143–44; during World War I, 121
"Juvenile Crimes Not by Morons," 49
juvenile delinquency, 1–2; during and after World War II, 121–25; causes of, 34, 42–43, 121, 123, 124, 133, 137, 193–94n12; diagnosis and treatment of, 68–69; motivation problem in, 132, 195–96n43; New York state legislature moved to combat, 124; in rural areas, 122; "scientific" personality theory of, 129; social or community problem, 55; young women, 36. *See also* female sex delinquents
Juvenile Protective Association (JPA), 46; eugenic measures to "feeblemindedness," 46–48; study of "mentally defective" children, 46, 176–77nn60–61

Kenworthy, Marion, 64
"khaki mad girl," 62–63
Kite, Elizabeth S., 23, 86–87, 170n64, 187n20
Klein, Charlotte Ruth: on interracial relationships among inmates, 103, 104; on sterilization *vs.* institutionalization, 192n2
Kluczynski, Thomas, 122, 193n7
Kotinsky, Ruth, 127, 129

Laughlin, Harry, 3
Lenroot, Katharine, 55

Leonard, Thomas, 44
Lincoln State School and Colony: overcrowding at, 29; parole system at, 56
Lundberg, Emma, 65

Mae, Dora: behavior and attitude, 1–2; as "borderline defective," 1–2; cause of delinquencies of, 1
"maladjusted" personality, 136
male delinquents: average age of, 139; crimes committed by, 41; and female sex delinquents, moral offenses committed by, 40–41, 174n33; incarceration of, 40–41; sexual conduct of, 41
maternalist reformers: campaign to create commitment law, 15–16, 19–20, 45; and eugenic commitment law, 14–20; on "feebleminded" female offenders, 48; and feebleminded menace, 22–25; on heredity and antisocial behavior, 21; male experts and lawmakers views on, 20; middle-class white women, 5, 14, 35; portrait of "feebleminded menace," 45; "progressive," 21; rationalization of "negative" eugenic measure, 23; scientific expertise and commitment campaign, 19–20, 32; Walker, A. E., 14–16
maternal rejection, 136
Mead, Margaret, 126
Medical Review of Reviews, eugenic campaign of, 18
medico-scientific model, rise in status of, 20
Mendelian theories of inheritance and eugenics, 21
mental anthropometry, 75
"mental defectives": confined to institutions, 24; crisis study conducted by JPA, 46–48; incarceration programs for, 27–28; sexual agency of, 47; sexual victimization of, 46–47; as victims of sexual abuse, 87–88
mental deviance: "high grade mental defective," 111; markers of, 86–87; and social deviance, 109–13
mental deviance, creation of: "extreme suggestibility," 88; language difficulties, 88–89; "mentally defective," 86–87, 89–90
mental health professionals, 20
"mentally diseased" delinquents, 69
Meyer, John P., 195n24
Miner, Maude, 55
Minnesota Multiphasic Personality Inventory (MMPI), 137
Monahan, Florence, 94; on escape behavior of inmate, 107–8; on irritating behavior problems, 112; on "psychopathic personality," 191n72
morality and intellect, relationship between, 53, 58
"morons," social problem due to, 23
Morrow, Louise, 112
mother-child relationship: creating "quality," 135–36; and delinquency, 134–35, 138–39; role in child development, 133, 135
motivation problem, 132, 195–96n43; Freud's view on, 132, 196n45

national eugenics movement, 3
neo-Lamarckian eugenics, 21
neurotic delinquent, 134; attitude of mother of, 135
"new girl problem," 40, 143
New York City Youth Board, 124
New York state legislature, 124
"normal" delinquents: eugenic solutions for, 68; examination of, 67, 184–85n69

Ochsner, A. J.: on feebleminded menace, 22; on importance of health, 17
Olson, Harry, 183–84n57; eugenics program devised by, 66–67; on incarceration programs, 27, 28, 65; objections to provisions within commitment bill, 30
Ordahl, George, 42, 175n42
Ordahl, Louise, 42, 175n42
overcrowding at correctional institutions, 29–30

parental care and child development, 133–36
parole: to "feebleminded offenders," 55–56; to Geneva inmates, 72, 102; at Lincoln State School and Colony, 56; violation of, 72, 102, 107–8
personality: definition of, 127–28, 130; and environment, interaction between, 132–33
Personality in the Making (1952), 127
personality "states," delinquent, 133–34; and mothering types, relation between, 134–35
personality theory: of delinquency prevention, 129–31; importance of, 138
phrenology, 74, 186n6
physiognomy, 74
professional maternalists: on feeblemindedness and immorality, 48–49; female physicians, 16, 167n18; on "mentally deficient" delinquents, 20; role in creating custodian

institutions, 16; role in involuntary commitment campaign, 19–20
psychological examination, ritual of. *See* ritual of psychological examination
"psychopathic" individuals: incarceration of, 67; "psychopathic deviate," 137; psychopathic personality, 191n72
psy discourses: and eugenics, 8–11; works on, 164n14
public family-style institutions, 95–96
Purcell-Guild, June, 33–34, 63–64, 172n9, 173n22

race, human, 3; and class role in disposition of delinquent girls, 144–45; and human reproduction, 17
racial and sexual transgressions, 103, 104–5
"Rebuilding a Nation," 3–4
Reeves, Margaret, 28
Renz, Emile, 43, 175n44
Rippin, Jane Deeter, 62
ritual of psychological examination, 1–2, 95; anxiety and stress involved with, 82–86; case records of, 79–81; influence on lives of subjects, 79, 90–92; limitations of, 89–90; social and scientific factors influencing, 91; subjects attitude during, 82. *See also* mental deviance, creation of
Ryerson, Samuel R., 57, 58

self-mutilation, 106–7
Service Council for Girls, 57, 181n21
sexually delinquent young women. *See* female sex delinquents
sexual transgressions: definition of, 34; between white inmates, 104–5
Shaw, Clifford, 125
Singer, Frank, 125
Smith, Carrie Weaver, 65
Smith, Howard C., 194n14
social and environmental factors, delinquency, 21
social deviance: biologization of, 31–32; environmental causes of, 111–12; and mental deviance, 109–13
"socialized delinquent," 134, 136–37
Sokal, Michael M., 186n6
Spaulding, Edith, 60
Stagner, Ross, 196n45
State Home for Juvenile Female Offenders, 96

State Training School for Girls, Geneva, 1; bedroom at, 225; classroom at, 223; disciplinary regime, 95–96; educational and vocational programs, 96–97; Fabian Cottage, 226; industrial rooms, 224, 225; nurturing respectable citizens, 97–98. *See also* Geneva's inmates; youth-oriented peer culture
statistical psychological studies: Binet intelligence test, 77; feeblemindedness classification scheme, 77–78; importance of, 76; subject's perceived intellectual level, 77
status offenders, impact of deinstitutionalization of, 144
status offenses, impact of decriminalization of, 144
Stephens, E. A., 132
sterilization and eugenic segregation, 27, 165n19, 192n2
Stevens, Alzina P., 176–77n60
Stone, Esther H.: eugenic solutions recommended by, 68; on "goody-goody girls," 102; on misbehavior of inmates, 100–103, 107; on "normal" delinquents, 67, 184–85n69; psychological examination of young women, 184–85n69
"super baby" contest, 18

Terman, Lewis, 53
Terry, Jennifer, 74, 186n4
Tin Town (settlement), 24
Town, Clara Harrison: on custodial care of "feebleminded" individuals, 24, 27; definition of "feebleminded" persons, 23
Tucker, William, 76

unsocialized aggression, 133–34
Urla, Jacqueline, 74, 186n4

venereal disease (VD), 63; among delinquent girls, 39
violent crime referrals, 143–44

Wabash County: criminal records in, 25; need for reform in, 25
Walker, A. E., 14–16
Wallace, George, 61
Wallin, J. E. Wallace, 59
Washburne Social Adjustment Inventory, 137
White House Conference on Children and Youth, 123–24, 194n14

white inmates, sexual transgressions between, 104
Witmer, Helen, 127, 129
women professionals: proponents of eugenics, 19; and public policy, 19
Woods, Frank, 123
working-class girls: incarceration of, 40–41; surveillance of, 40

Yarros, Rachel, 61, 64–65
Yerkes, Robert, 59
young women: delinquency, 36, 43; vulnerability and their sexual victimization, 45. *See also* female sex delinquents
youth-oriented peer culture: impact on inmates, 99; rebellious and deviant, 100

MICHAEL A REMBIS is a visiting scholar in the Center for Disability Studies and the department of history at the University at Buffalo.

The University of Illinois Press
is a founding member of the
Association of American University Presses.

University of Illinois Press
1325 South Oak Street
Champaign, IL 61820-6903
www.press.uillinois.edu